# BARRY BRACEWELL-MILNES

# THE TAXATION OF INDUSTRY

## FISCAL BARRIERS
## TO THE CREATION OF WEALTH

PANOPTICUM PRESS LONDON, 1981

**OTHER BOOKS
PUBLISHED BY PANOPTICUM PRESS LONDON
INCLUDE**

In English:

POEMS by Tudor Arghezi (translated from Romanian by N.M. Goodchild
and C. Michael-Titus)

ROMANIA UNDER PRESSURE (political documentary) Report I, 1979; Report II
and III,1981; by C. Michael-Titus

EUROPE IN ROMANIA, 1980, by C. Michael-Titus
HUNGARIAN REALITIES IN ROMANIA, 1980, by N. M. Goodchild
BRITAIN LOOKS EASTWARDS (political documentary), 1980, by N. M. Goodchild
and C. Michael-Titus

In French:

Moires de Ciel (poems) 1981, by C. Michael-Titus

French and English comments and index:

Miroir de sagesse populaire européenne
Mirror of European popular wisdom

(Romanian proverbs and sayings translated into French and English and accompanied
by equivalents in Latin and eight European languages including French and English)
1981, compiled by N.M. Goodchild and C. Michael-Titus

In Romanian:

UNGHIUL DE LUMINĂ (poems) 1975, by Solo Herescu
TRĂIRI PESTE FURTUNI (short stories) 1975, by George Bar-On
POEME DE IERI ŞI DE AZI (poems) 1981, by C. Michael-Titus

\*      \*      \*      \*      \*      \*      \*      \*      \*      \*      \*      \*

Deadline for factual information Spring 1981
ISBN 0 907256 06 6
Copyright PANOPTICUM PRESS, LONDON
44 Howard Road, Upminster RM14 2UF
1981

TO ANN

Well may we afford
Our givers their own gifts, and large bestow
From large bestow'd, where Nature multiplies
Her fertile growth, and by disburd'ning grows
More fruitful; which instructs us not to spare.

*Paradise Lost* V 316

# THE TAXATION OF INDUSTRY
## FISCAL BARRIERS TO THE CREATION OF WEALTH

# PREFACE

This book analyses the damage done by taxation to the creation of wealth in Britain and elsewhere. Even after the tax cuts of 1979, the creation of wealth is still more heavily taxed in Britain than anywhere else in the Western world, and the relative impoverishment of Britain during the post-war period is not surprising.

The frustration of industry by taxes is harmful even to those whose interests it is intended to serve. Taxes on the creation of wealth yield little revenue, and total revenue might even be increased by their abolition. The obstacles to their abolition are not in objective realities but in confused thinking.

The traditional consensus on tax policy has been a recipe for poverty and discord. It has also been a farrago of inconsistency. As long as the traditional framework of thinking is maintained, only marginal improvements in the situation are to be expected. For radical improvements we require a different conceptual apparatus, which this book seeks to provide. The main conflicts of interest are not between citizen and citizen, as has traditionally been believed, but between the citizens and the government.

I am grateful to Professor J.E. Meade for the use of material. (Chapter VII, note 6). I should also like to thank my typist, Miss M.E. Robertson, for a number of valuable comments on the text.

Barry Bracewell-Milnes

May 1981

# SUMMARY

1. For the purposes for which they are used, the conventional figures of wealth distribution are a palpable statistical falsehood. (Page 25).

2. Both the traditional concepts of wealth have serious defects. An alternative concept is proposed in which wealth is a flow, not a stock, and is measured by the maximum level of spending per unit of time which it can support in perpetuity. (Page 65 and Appendix I).

3. There are four methods of wealth creation — by brute force, by private ownership, by investment in second-hand assets and by enterprise in ideas. The preference for the first of these four over the remaining three is superstitious and has no rational foundation. (Chapter II; page 41).

4. Socialist assets are valuable once, in use, whereas capitalist assets are valuable twice, in use and in ownership. Socialism can create wealth only by brute force; capitalism can also create wealth out of thin air through the institution of private ownership. This magic of capitalism has been ignored by conventional economics (Western as well as communist), which concentrates on output and misses the dimension of ownership, partially or even entirely. (Chapters II—IV).

5. Saving and taxation are alternative means of financing any given volume of productive investment. In this sense the taxable capacity of saving is negative: the more the taxation of saving, the more the need for other taxes to finance the investment. (Page 52).

6. In general, saving has no economic taxable capacity: the wealth destroyed by the taxation of saving is not less than the revenue from the taxes to which saving is subject. If the economic taxable capacity of saving is negative, the loss of wealth to the taxpaying community exceeds the loss to the taxpayer from the payment of tax. (Pages 52—53).

7. The attempt to tax the wealth created by ownership and investment in second-hand goods is an attempt to turn immaterial wealth into material and must necessarily fail. (Page 47).

8. The taxation of wealth from "non-productive" assets is more damaging than any form of socialism with compensation, per million pounds of revenue yield or asset value: socialism with compensation leaves some positive amount, however small, whereas taxation of ownership and investment in second-hand goods destroys more wealth than it yields tax revenue. (Page 74)

9. If there were a justifiable distinction between productive and non-productive assets, productive assets should be taxed more heavily, because they have a positive economic taxable capacity. But no such distinction can be sustained. (Page 63).

10. By libertarian criteria, the case for tax reductions is independent of arguments from incentives. (Page 75).

11. The environmentalist lobby has neglected the advantages to be had from clean and costless wealth creation through the institution of capitalism. (Page 82).

12. Prosperity and justice are allies rather than enemies. (Page 55).

13. All taxes on saving that diminish the amount of gross-of-tax saving or wealth in private hands are "regressive", not only on spending but in general; and this effect is intensified if the taxes are graduated instead of proportional. (Page 136).

14. Conflicts of interest between government and citizen are far and away more serious than any conflicts between one group of citizens and another. (Page 98).

15. Tax is always and necessarily damaging to the creation of wealth, since it represents an artificial barrier between the creator and his achievement. The damage done increases as the rate of tax rises. Both taxation and inflation can make the creation of wealth not merely difficult but impossible: even worse, they can make the destruction of wealth profitable. In 1981 fiscal prohibition of saving in the United Kingdom could be reached at the modest level of £100−200,000. (Page 76; "Fiscal prohibition of saving", Chapter IX and Appendix IV).

16. In 1981, the tax system continued to be more heavily biased against capital in the United Kingdom than in any other European country. (Page 148; Appendix IV, Tables 5 and 7).

17. The maximum-revenue rate of tax on earning and spending is of the order of 58 per cent, as compared with a maximum of some 65 per cent in the United Kingdom in 1981 on earning-for-spending or spending-out-of-earnings. (Pages 104, 146; Appendix V).

18. The maximum-revenue rate of tax on saving is much lower than the 58 per cent maximum-revenue rate for earning and spending; and it is the rate calculated from the combined burden of all taxes on investmen income and its parent capital. If any tax is retained on saving it should be levied on investment income at not more than the basic rate of income tax. There is no room for taxes on capital: capital transfer tax and capital gains tax should be abolished. If the maximum-revenue criterion is replaced by the more socially justifiable criterion of economic taxable capacity, the tax on investment income should be abolished as well. ( Pages 108—111 ).

CHAPTER I

# INTRODUCTION

The Camel's Back [1] analysed the tax revenues and tax rates of the United Kingdom and other OECD countries so as to show the quality as well as the weight of the tax burden here and abroad. It started with the simple and traditional measure of taxation as a proportion of national income and moved on to successively more subtle measures which indicated how a tax system with a lower total burden might nevertheless be more painful or destructive than another system with a higher total burden but a different distribution. As for the camel, so for the taxpaying community: a heavier burden can be borne if it is broadly distributed and not lopsided and if it does not press sharply in particular places. A broadly-based consumption tax at the same proportional rate on the different goods and services subject to charge is the tax that comes nearest to satisfying this specification [2].

The Taxation of Industry takes the story forward, not only in time (the figures are updated by some seven years), but also in theme. Its theme is the effect of taxation on the creation of wealth. Wealth must be created before it can be taxed; and the tax process is not neutral towards its creation. The tax system also causes the destruction of wealth, which is the obverse of wealth creation. Tax is a destroyer [3]; but even in its own interest it must leave enough for next year. The metaphors of the camel's back and the goose that lays the golden eggs are too dramatic in suggesting that the answer is all or nothing, that the damage is either fatal or no damage at all. Not so: the economy may be weakened by taxation even if it is not ruined. There is a maximum yield of tax over a period of years: if the yield goes beyond this level, the fisc itself is losing money by being too greedy. Both the fisc and the economy have a common interest in reducing taxes to the level of maximum yield. Below this level, the interests of the fisc and the economy diverge: the economy is weakened by taxation even though the fisc is enriched. The present book discusses the influence of taxation on the creation and destruction of wealth and considers which taxes are the least destructive and which are the most.

It has often been argued that there is a conflict between tax "equity" and tax "efficiency" [4]: that the most equitable taxes do the most harm economically, so that a balance must be struck between fairness and prosperity. But the terms "equity", "efficiency", "fairness", "prosperity" are susceptible of more than one interpretation. The present book argues that equity and efficiency are allies rather than enemies: the deepest and most valid meanings of these terms indicate that they are in harmony and not in conflict.

The essence of the argument is logical and *a priori*. It is not possible to prove statistically either that a tax is damaging or that it is not damaging [5]. But the figures nevertheless have two useful and relatedf unctions. The first is to indicate the degree or direction of probability: a tax of 75 per cent is more likely to be damaging than a tax of 60 per cent, and if Country A has a tax of 75 per cent, it is more likely to reduce damage by cutting the tax rate than if the tax rate is 60 per cent. The second is to show the relative standing of the various tax jurisdictions: if Country A has a tax rate of 75 per cent and Country B a tax rate of 60 per cent, the maintenance of existing rate structures is less likely to be doing damage in B than in A and a reduction in rates is more likely to do good in A than in B.

## CHAPTER II

# INDUSTRY AND WEALTH

## The conventional wisdom

Wealth is created by a partnership between labour and capital, runs the conventional wisdom. Workers need capital, and capital needs workers. Investment puts financial muscle power at the worker's elbow. Investment is in the worker's interest as well as his employer's. Profits reinvested are not a loss to the workforce, but a gain. Profits have recently been too low: investment has been too low and growth has been too low. Everyone has lost. The squeeze on profits has been excessive. An increase in profits is in the general interest, provided that it is used to increase investment — investment in real assets, of course, plant and machinery and industrial buildings. The argument does not apply to investment in paper assets, which create no additional wealth and merely enrich the investor at the expense of his fellows.

Something like this has been the prolefeed regularly purveyed in recent years by the British industrial establishment and its Parliamentary supporters, the "right wing" of the Labour Party and the "left wing" of the Conservative Party. It is the pure milk of Communist orthodoxy. There is nothing in it that would cause Stalin a moment's disquiet. It is not for this reason wrong: even Stalin was right from time to time. But there is a capitalist alternative to communism; and there are solid arguments, logically and empirically, for considering capitalism preferable. Empirically, the record speaks for itself in the comparison between the USSR and the USA, between socialist Britain and capitalist Hong Kong. It is a remarkable accomplishment of social engineering to achieve a chronic food shortage in the USSR, the world's largest country with what Tsarist experience indicates as being some of the world's most fertile land. But the logical arguments go deeper. They concern ends as well as means and meanings as well as mechanisms. They concern the meaning of wealth as well as its creation and the meaning of industry as well as its encouragement.

In its attitude to investment, as in its approach to economic management, the British industrial and political establishment has for most of the post-war period been obsessed by the importance of things and by the unimportance of money. The neglect of money has been a disaster in both areas. In economic management it has led to the combination of accelerating inflation and growing unemployment long predicted by Hayek and others [1]. In investment policy it has led to fiscal preference for real assets relatively to monetary assets even though investment in first-hand real assets like plant and machinery makes a real call on resources and imposes a real cost on society for which investment in monetary assets like stocks, shares and debentures provides no analogue.

The establishment's preference for making things over making money stands common sense on its head. The creation of wealth by heavy industry is the creation of wealth by brute force. It is in general a necessary evil. Large industrial establishments are not generally pleasant to look at or to work in. At the other extreme, the creation of wealth through monetary skill or artistic effort may be a joy in itself as well as a benefit to society. The promotion of investment in manufacturing and heavy industry at the expense of wealth creation through clean and enjoyable activities is as sensible as subsidising coal mines at the expense of cheaper fuels [2].

## Mutual advantage in voluntary exchange

Part of the trouble is the superstitious belief that the production of things creates additional wealth whereas financial activity merely redistributes an existing stock. This contrast is wrong on both counts. The production of things may destroy wealth instead of creating it, as when a nationalised or private industrial concern makes losses. And financial activity, like the production of things, creates wealth when it is profitable and destroys wealth when it makes losses.

Financial activity is no different from any other service [3]. Transport services, for example, do not produce things that can be touched or seen; but they create wealth when they are profitable (and destroy wealth when they are unprofitable). Profit is the criterion because it is the outward and visible sign of the mutual advantage in voluntary exchange. Voluntary exchange creates wealth for the most fundamental of all reasons: because it is voluntary. Both parties must volunteer. Voluntary trading is maintained only if it is profitable; if it yields a continuing loss it will cease.

This principle applies as much to manufacture as to commerce, as much to financial services as to other services. Profitable activities are financially self-supporting and wealth-creating; loss-making activities and state-financed non-commercial activities are financially dependent and wealth-destroying.

## Meaning of "industry"

If "industry" is construed today as meaning manufacturing or other mechanised activity and is interpreted in this sense as being synonymous with the creation of wealth, this is due to the growth of special pleading and the decline of economic understanding. There is no logical relationship between the creation of wealth and manufacturing or mechanisation (still less between the creation of wealth and the heavy end of industry). Investment in plant and machinery is simply a means by which wealth can be created or destroyed: created if the investment is profitable and destroyed if it is unprofitable. Adam Smith, for example, in "The Wealth of Nations", had much to say about the creation of wealth and little to say about industry in the sense of mechanisation: less than about corn or gold or trade or Scotland. The division of labour is logically independent of mechanisation.

The original meanings of "industry" were ingenuity, skill and industriousness. The earliest use of "industry" in its modern sense cited by the Oxford English Dictionary is indeed as early as 1566; but industrial activity was generally described until recently by such terms as arts and manufacturing. For our present purposes, the older meaning of "industry" is the more illuminating: the secret of economic progress is ingenuity and industriousness and not a mountain of plant and machinery. Plant and machinery (and industrial and commercial buildings) are economically useful only in so far as ingenuity and industriousness make them so. More plant and machinery and buildings indeed generally create more wealth, just as more labour input generally creates more wealth; but the inputs of capital impose a cost, just as the input of labour imposes a cost, and the question is whether the cost is worth the return. The best or even the only criteria for the resolution of this problem are, retrospectively, profit and, prospectively, the expectation of profit through voluntary economic exchange. Industry is not merely brute-force investment but also ingenuity (enterprise or entrepreneurship) and industriousness (hard work); the right mixture can only be decided by maximum profitability (self-interest under voluntary exchange).

Whether investment is active or passive by the criterion of day-to-day participation in management, its potential quality improves as its entrepreneurial component increases. Brute-force investment in material investments has its passive counterpart in such purchases of the portfolio investor as building society shares and National Savings certificates. After allowance for price rises, both active and passive brute-force investment may show a loss. So indeed may active or passive entrepreneurial investment; but here the potential rewards are greater. Where the investor gains, he shares his profit with the rest of the economy.

## Meaning of "wealth"

### Material and immaterial wealth

Wealth is the stock of assets that produce economic wellbeing or yield economic value. The meaning of wealth is as subtle as the meaning of value. Value, like beauty, is in the eye of the beholder. It is determined by the assessments of the individual consumers. It is variable and subject to the influence of fashion. Value can be created and destroyed by changes of opinion.

19

This capitalist concept of wealth, which makes the judgment of the consumer the determining criterion, overlaps with the socialist concept which measures wealth by the efforts of the producer. But where they differ the capitalist concept is superior: unwanted goods or unusable plant and machinery are worth only what they will fetch on the market, which may be zero or less however much they cost to produce. The consumer rules.

Real assets obtain their value from their application, material or immaterial. The oil was there under the ground before the means of using it were discovered; but it was not wealth. The same is true of immaterial use. The Lake District was not so different at Wordsworth's death from what it had been at the time of his birth. What changed was the way it was perceived. It was regarded as a place of beauty and no longer as a wasteland. Wordsworth created wealth with his pen, not just in the material sense of earning fees by writing, but because he changed opinion. Similarly, the Victorian churches were all there before Sir John Betjeman came along; but they are worth more now.

Similarly for assets that can be valued in money. Collectors' items owe their value solely to the willingness of collectors to buy them. They must be rare; but they need not be beautiful or otherwise notable artistically. The growth of collecting hobbies creates additional wealth. A fashion for Victorian paperweights or vintage cars makes the existing stock of assets more valuable. If the supply is fixed (Old Masters, first editions, stamps or coins of past periods), the process is immaterial and has nothing to do with production; but it can nevertheless be stable and continuing. The rise in value of Penny Blacks or Maria Theresa dollars, of "Breeches" Bibles or medieval silver, can in principle create wealth year by year for ever. It may or may not do so in practice; here, as elsewhere, the economic out-turn is neither smooth nor predictable.

Financial services also create wealth, though in a different sense. Whenever an investor rearranges his portfolio of assets he is exchanging assets he values less for assets he values more. But the market, his collective counterpart, is doing the same. Each side is gaining, or the transaction would not take place. Wealth is created.

The creation of wealth in the ways indicated is not costless. Wordsworth and Betjeman require paper for their writings and shoe-leather for their peregrinations. Stamp dealers and stockbrokers occupy offices and charge fees. These costs must be deducted. But there is still something left; and it is with this remainder that we are concerned, the wealth created by a change of opinion, a shift of attitudes, a pure victory of mind over matter.

The idea that wealth can be created immaterially is not universally accepted or even understood. Among socialists and even manufacturers there is sometimes an irrational reverence for the use of machinery and the production of things (perhaps including material services), a preference for investment over profitability and a mistrust of financial activity as chicanery and manipulation from which one party must lose whatever another gains. This distinction between material and immaterial economic activity is superstitious and has no rational basis. Both the production of things and financial activity can create wealth through the operation of voluntary exchange or destroy wealth through fraudulent dealings or government subsidies (nationalised industries, British Leyland); for example, the wealth from North Sea oil could be entirely destroyed if it were invested in loss-making manufacturing industries. The creation of wealth by immaterial processes is the invention of voluntary exchange in the market economy. Those who reject the painless prosperity of capitalism are not generally people working with their hands but academics, industrialists, journalists, MPs, trade union officials and others accustomed to interesting work and comfortable working conditions.

Parallel to the preference for material over immaterial wealth creation is the preference for "productive" over "non-productive" assets. "Productive" assets are often noisy, smelly eyesores, the sort of installation which gives pleasure to nobody and which can at best be accepted only with regret. Assets of this kind receive generous fiscal encouragement. "Non-productive" assets are most of the artefacts that make life beautiful: homes and gardens, parks and estates, pictures, jewellery, books. With some qualification for houses, the thrust of tax policy in recent years has been to make the acquisition and retention of "non-productive" assets in private hands more and more difficult.

Unless tax policy is totally ineffective, this discrimination must damage the appearance of the country, multiplying ugly factories and destroying beautiful gardens. But this damage, like much of the damage done by government, cannot be measured in money. What can be measured in money is the loss to wealth creation caused by fiscal discrimination in favour of "productive" assets at the expense of "non-productive". In a fiscally neutral environment the citizens will invest in "productive" or "non-productive" assets according to their personal proclivities or assessments of the future. A man who invests in a collection of old stamps may accept the loss of income by comparison with an investment in shares because he enjoys collecting stamps and is willing to spend money on his hobby. That is one motive. But he may also do so because he believes that the stamp collection will be the better investment. Both motives are entirely rational not only for the individual but also for the economy. If a man likes to spend income on a hobby like stamp collecting that he would otherwise have spent on current goods and services, that is his decision, and it is unhelpful both for him and for the economy if his decision is distorted by taxation. But the same principle holds good if the motive for stamp collecting is entirely investment, if the investor cares nothing for stamp collecting, if the stamps are held for him at the bank or elsewhere and he never sees them at all. The investor has a choice between investing in old stamps or investing in shares which will help to build a new factory. The distinction between "productive" and "non-productive" assets implies that the factory should be preferred to the stamps, that society has an interest in biasing the investor's decision in this direction. This is totally false. The investment in the factory may be judicious or injudicious; it may turn out well or ill. But so may the investment in old stamps. Either investment may be good or bad for the investor. The economy has no interest in biasing the decision away from stamps and in favour of factories.

The difference between factories and old stamps lies not so much in the assessment that many factories are ugly and many stamps beautiful as in the the fact that investment in new factories uses up real resources whereas investment in old stamps does not. Even if all new factories were beautiful, the argument would be the same. Investment in old stamps creates wealth out of thin air: the new demand increases the value of the existing stock. This is an argument for fiscal discrimination in favour of "non-productive" assets at the expense of "productive" assets, if any discrimination can be justified at all. The ugliness of "productive" assets is a possible argument for further discrimination in the same direction. Discrimination in favour of "non-productive" assets at the expense of "productive" is the opposite of what happens at present. A move towards neutrality would at least be a move in the right direction.

As for investment, so for wealth: wealth is the sum of past investment. The distinction between "productive" and "non-productive" is the same for assets as for investment. But investment is a flow, whereas wealth is a stock: and the meaning and measurement of the stock are more complex than those of the flow.

### Two concepts of wealth

There are traditionally two ways of defining and measuring wealth. In the first, wealth is the present value of future income [4]; it is determined solely by what the assets yield net of tax. In the second, wealth is the market value of assets; the yield of the assets is irrelevant to their valuation. The two methods are the same if all assets yield the same rate of return and all taxation is equiproportionate. The first method gives the higher value of wealth for higher-yielding assets at any given rate of discount: if one asset yields 5 per cent and the other 10 per cent, then the higher-yielding asset is twice as valuable at any common rate of discount (5 per cent or 10 per cent or any other), even though the two asset values are necessarily the same if the yield of the 5 per cent asset is discounted at 5 per cent and the yield of the 10 per cent asset is discounted at 10 per cent. The second method gives a higher valuation than the first for higher graduated tax rates at any given level of gross-of-tax yields: if the higher rate of tax is 75 per cent gross and the lower rate is 50 per cent, then the second method gives a valuation of wealth twice as high as the first method for the 75 per cent taxpayer by comparison with the 50 per cent tax-payer (because (100−50) is twice as large as (100−75)).

Each of these concepts has its uses and neither has a monopoly of the truth. The income concept is rich in significant implications: personal wealth may be held to include the present value of future earning power, the value of education received, claims to a future "national insurance" pension or other claims on the state, the value to the tenant of a rent-controlled tenancy or the occupation of a council house, monopoly privileges granted by law to dockers, and many other such items. All are valuable in the same sense in which a stamp collection is valuable: it is better to have them than not to have them, even if they do not generate an immediate or specifically identifiable flow of income. If a magnitude is positive and substantial but difficult to measure, it is unscientific to imply that its value is nil by neglecting it entirely; any honest estimate would be less inaccurate [5].

*Discount for unmarketability*

The market valuation of wealth is equivalent to the income valuation if taxes are equiproportionate, gross-of-tax and net-of-tax yields are identical, and all assets are fully marketable. Since in practice taxes are highly graduated and many assets are difficult or impossible to sell, the two methods would give widely differing results even if all yields were the same. The reconciliation of the two methods involves a discount for lack of marketability: the discount would be small for assets like a funded pension which the pensioner or prospective pensioner would not generally wish to sell and larger for assets like the enjoyment of a subsidised tenancy which the tenant might well wish to realise if he could. The discount must be assessed subjectively; but it is unscientific to put the discount at 100 per cent when the true discount is much less than this merely on the ground that the true figure cannot be known. The discount is smaller and may be zero when no element of state compulsion is involved because the non-marketability of the assets is an arrangement to which the parties have voluntarily consented; the discount is larger and may be 100 per cent when the non-marketability of the assets is due to state compulsion: for example, the true discount may be at or near 100 per cent for communally-owned real assets like roads. The discount is less than 100 per cent not only for real or financial assets but even for the present capitalised value of future earnings from labour: houses are often bought with a mortgage against future earnings, and this process is nothing other than realising the asset which this future income stream represents. Selling oneself or others into slavery is also a method of realising future earnings from labour. This wide range of variation in the true rate of discount shows how socialism and state intervention destroy wealth, not only by inefficiency (which is a separate question) but also more directly by increasing the rate of discount (for lack of marketability) by which the value of an asset falls below the present value of the income stream it generates, discounted at market rates of interest net of tax. Wealth is in the eye of the beholder; like Wordsworth and Betjeman, capitalism creates wealth out of thin air.

*Wealth gross and net of tax*

If gross-of-tax yields are identical, the gross-of-tax value of marketable assets is the present value of their income streams discounted at the common gross-of-tax yield. This value is diminished by taxation; it falls to the present discounted value of the income stream net of all tax on the income and its parent capital for ever [6]. Wealth, like income, can be measured gross of tax and net of tax. The gross-of-tax distribution of income or wealth is nominal and contains a systematic double counting: it attributes to the taxpayer funds which the government has extracted or will extract from him by force. The net-of-tax distribution represents the real situation because the tax charge, computed or estimated, is deducted from the taxpayer's income or wealth.

If marketable assets yield 10 per cent gross of tax and one taxpayer pays income tax at 50 per cent and another at zero, then by the income-stream method of measuring wealth £100 of assets gross of tax are worth only half as much net of tax to the 50 per cent taxpayer as to his colleague. This result is obtained by discounting both income streams at 10 per cent. The assets are worth £100 net of tax to both taxpayers only if a discount rate of 5 per cent is used for the 50 per cent taxpayer. But this is merely to restate the problem in another form. The income-stream method gives different measures of wealth net of tax for taxpayers paying tax at different rates: the rationale of the method requires that allowance be made for tax. It follows that in the income-stream method assets with identical yields both before and after tax show the same distribution of wealth as of income, both gross of tax and net; and the distributions of wealth and income are also the same if the gross yields are the same but the net yields vary as a result of graduation in the tax structure.

Thus, in the income-stream method of measuring wealth, assets are worth the present value of their net-of-tax income flow discounted at the gross-of-tax yield. Taxes other than income tax are all expressed in income equivalents, future liabilities to transfer taxation being calculated actuarially [7]. These magnitudes may not be known exactly; but, as we have noted in similar contexts elsewhere, that is not a good reason for neglecting them entirely or implying that they are zero when they are undeniably substantial. The combination of taxes on capital with taxes on income may take the total tax burden to more than 100 per cent of income; permanent saving is in this situation futile, and by the income-stream method the value of marginal assets falls to zero and below.

A particular problem of estimation under the income-stream method is the allowance to be made for avoidability. Taxes on investment income and its parent capital may be avoidable by spending, by capital export or by emigration; and they may also be avoided by gifts *inter vivos*, charitable donations and other means. The maximum tax liability is relatively easy to identify [8]; the minimum liability may be as little as zero, but if this involves spending millions of pounds within a short period it may not represent an attractive or practicable option. The two figures of significance are the maximum liability and the maximum adjusted for the possibilities of avoidance. These possibilities may be estimated in more than one way; but all ways may give much the same answer, and the use of any of them will be preferable to the use of none. If a man of ninety with gross assets of £100 m. is facing capital

24

transfer tax at 75 per cent, the real value of his assets (net of tax) may be £ 25 m. or £26 m. or £27 m.; but it will not be £100 m.

The use of gross-of-tax figures of wealth distribution in contexts requiring net-of-tax figures (that is, in practically all applications of any political significance) constitutes a large and systematic overestimation of the inequality in the distribution of wealth. For the purposes for which they are used, the conventional figures of wealth distribution are a palpable statistical falsehood.

For any one taxpayer at any one time, the income-stream method of measuring wealth gives the same result from discounting the gross-of-tax income at the rate of discount gross of tax as from discounting the net-of-tax income at the rate of discount net of tax, so long as net income (and thus the net discount rate) remains positive. But even if the discount rate is still positive, this identity is dangerously misleading. The income-stream method is about income, and the value of wealth computed by the income-stream method ought to fall if income falls because taxes on the income rise. The absurdity of the net method (net income discounted at net-of-tax rates of discount) becomes apparent when tax rates rise so as to absorb more than 100 per cent of income: under the net method, wealth is unimpaired so long as discount rates remain positive, however small; but it suddenly disappears when income and the discount rate fall through zero and turn negative. The same absurdity vitiates the gross method (gross income discounted at gross-of-tax rates of discount): even though the gross income and the gross discount rate remain positive, it makes no sense to value wealth from an income stream more than 100 per cent of which is absorbed in taxation. If marginal net income falls to zero and turns negative, the value of marginal wealth calculated by the income-stream method should fall to zero and turn negative likewise even though marginal gross income remains positive.

The valuation of wealth as net income discounted at gross rates avoids this meaningless quantum jump: as net income falls to zero, so does the value of wealth. The net-income-discounted-at-gross-rates version of the income-stream method underestimates the value of wealth when net income falls to zero (because wealth still has some positive value as spending power), just as the market-value-of-assets method overestimates it (because *individually* or at the *micro-economic* level no owner of substantial wealth can realise its value by spending it immediately and *in aggregate* or at the *macro-economic* level it would be impossible for all owners of substantial wealth to realise their assets simultaneously, since any attempt to do so would reduce the value of these assets to little more than zero). But the range from the market-value-of-assets method to the net-income-discounted-at-gross-rates version of the income-stream method of valuing wealth encompasses the objectively identifiable extremes and avoids the absurdities of applying to the valuation of assets the net-income-discounted-at-net-rates version of the income-stream method of investment appraisal.

The net-income-discounted-at-gross-rates version of the income-stream method correctly indicates that, as the combined burden on income of income and capital taxes rises to absorb more than 100 per cent of the income, the net-of-tax yield from assets falls to zero and below and the corresponding value of the assets disappears and turns negative. Any remaining value of the assets is represented by their potential purchasing power (which is positive, though it might be very small when account is taken of the effect on asset values of many proprietors attempting to realise their asset values simultaneously).

In his article *The Income Burden of Capital Taxes* (Review of Economic Studies, Summer 1942), Kaldor showed that the combined weight of income and capital taxes on investment income rendered saving "futile" above the point where taxation rose to more than 100 per cent of the marginal yield and (at a higher level) "impossible" above the point where taxation rose to more than 100 per cent of the total yield. (This happens whenever the yield net of income tax is inadequate to fund liabilities to taxes on capital: see Chapter IX below and Appendix IV, "Fiscal prohibition of saving"). But his analysis was flawed by the argument that even above the point of "futility" wealth has a positive value because it generates a positive income net of income tax but gross of capital taxes on death. This is a confusion of the income-stream method with the market-value-of-assets method of measuring wealth. The income-stream method measures wealth as permanent saving; and the marginal value of wealth for this purpose falls to zero at the point of "futility", where the yield net of the combined burden of income and capital taxes falls to zero [9].

Thus, by the income-stream method, an estate is a money-losing entity and so of negative marginal value above the point of "futility" where the combined effects of income tax, capital taxes and tax graduation absorb the whole of the permanent gross yield and reduce the permanent net yield to zero. The point of "futility" rises as the gross-of-tax yield rises and rises as the taxation of income or capital falls However high the taxation of income and capital, the gross rate of return can in principle be high enough to keep the permanent net return positive; but at high rates of tax the gross yield required for this purpose is totally unrealistic. (Chapter IX and Appendix IV, "Fiscal prohibition of saving"). However high the taxation of income and however low the gross yield, by contrast, the point of "futility" is never attained if the tax on capital is zero; and the point of "futility" is likewise never attained if the taxation of income and capital falls within the compass of the gross yield.

Above the point of "futility" the value of wealth by the income-stream method is negative. Its value by the market-value-of-assets method, however, remains positive. Proprietors retain assets for a number of different reasons none of which has anything to do with the height of discount rates, gross or net: the treatment of wealth as potential spending; commitment to particular assets [10]; intention to emigrate; expectation of a less unfavourable tax regime; or mere inertia or excessive optimism.

26

The conventional method of valuing wealth for purposes of taxation and statistics exaggerates the value by the criterion of both logical extremes, instantaneous spending and permanent saving. The value of wealth as instantaneous spending is exaggerated because it could not all be realised for spending simultaneously. Its value as permanent saving is exaggerated because it makes no allowance for the large element of tax liability. The taxation of wealth on the basis of market value systematically overestimates the tax base, because these values are not and could not be realised simultaneously; it is a fiscal attack on the capitalist process of creating wealth out of thin air. This process is due to the element of permanence in all saving: values are maintained and increased by the pressure of buyers over sellers. Chapter III below argues that permanent saving has no taxable capacity and that the attempt to tax it destroys more wealth than it yields revenue.

*Variations in the discount for time*

Under a neutral tax system, the proportion of income disbursed in saving rises as income rises; in technical language, saving is a "luxury". A neutral tax system for this purpose is one in which the saving of richer taxpayers is taxed no more heavily than the saving of poorer, such as a system with a strictly proportional income tax and no taxes on capital. In practice, the taxation of saving is generally graduated ("progressive"), but saving is still a "luxury" over much of the income range: tax neutrality is a sufficient but not a necessary condition for a rise in the proportion of income saved as income rises, and over much of the range the rise in the demand for saving as income rises outweighs the increasing burden of graduated taxation that this saving attracts (in technical terms, the income effect outweighs the price effect).

The reciprocal of the yield is the price of saving; for example, if the yield is 5 per cent, the price of saving is 20. As income rises, some items of expenditure that were formerly "luxuries" become "necessaries" and correspondingly less price-sensitive: for example, if the price of motoring rises for fiscal or other reasons, poorer taxpayers are more likely than richer taxpayers to give up their cars. Similarly, as income rises, a larger proportion is disbursed on items of expenditure that were formerly luxuries and thus sensitive to variations in price. An equiproportional rise in prices for all disbursements, whether for fiscal or other reasons, is equivalent to a reduction in income and reduces demand for "luxuries" (dining out, holidays abroad) more than for "necessaries" (food, fuel); and a tax reduction is correspondingly more favourable to "luxuries" than to "necessaries". Saving is a "luxury"; an equiproportional tax on all disbursements is thus disproportionately damaging to saving and the wealth it creates, and any form of graduated taxation of saving or discriminatory taxation of saving by comparison with spending is destructive of wealth.

An equiproportional tax on all disbursements (spending and saving) is disproportionately damaging to all "luxuries", of which saving is only one. A tax system that tried to minimise the distortion of activity in the monetary economy (and thus the destruction of monetary wealth) would tax "necessaries" more heavily than "luxuries", which is the opposite of what usually happens. The libertarian argument for taxing "necessaries" no more heavily than "luxuries" has nothing to do with subsidising the poor at the expense of the rich; it is simply that discriminatory taxation of "necessaries" is effectively a tax on leisure (just as the usual discrimination in favour of "necessaries" grants leisure an effective advantage) and that, by libertarian standards, decisions about what is a "necessary" and what is a "luxury" are too delicate to be entrusted to any government.

The monetary principle of minimising the damage done by taxation to the monetary economy and the libertarian principle of minimising the damage done to the whole economy, monetary and non-monetary, are thus both directly opposed to the principle of taxable capacity or ability to pay, which informs so much of tax policy at present, both in Britain and abroad. The monetary and libertarian principles indicate that taxation should do as little damage as possible to the process of wealth creation. The principle of taxable capacity, by contrast, indicates that the creation of wealth should be the principal target for attack by the fisc.

An equiproportional tax on all disbursements is disproportionately damaging to saving not only because saving is a "luxury" but also because taxes on spending fall also on saving. Saving is purchasing power or potential spending, and its value is diminished by taxes on spending. Although it is a logical extreme to argue that taxes on spending fall with equal weight on saving, it is also a logical extreme to argue that they do not fall on saving at all (which is the conventional assumption); and the truth is much nearer to the former extreme (with which it may even coincide) than it is to the latter [11].

It follows that the tax system that maximises neutrality and minimises the destruction of wealth taxes saving less than spending and may not tax it at all.

The conclusion that any tax on saving is destructive of wealth may be reached by another route. The subjective rate of discount is higher for government than for taxpayers both because elective governments have time-horizons limited by the date of the next Election and because most assets other than money-substitutes have personal associations which make them worth more in the hands of private persons than in the hands of the State: this is true not only of houses, family heirlooms and other personal possessions but also of land and other business assets, especially where there is a strong personal connection. The most palpable example is that of historic houses, which are more costly for the State than for the family to maintain: this is because they have a personal value for the family which is destroyed by their transfer to the State, and this personal value (or capitalised notional income) makes the families willing to look after the houses for less, often much less, than would be required by hired custodians. In other words, the subjective discount rate is higher for the State than for the families, and wealth is destroyed if such houses are transferred from the families to the State. But, although this argument

28

is most tangible in the example of historic houses, it is of general application: it even extends to the general advantages of "privatisation" over "nationalisation", though we are here concerned, not with an administrative, but with a fiscal shift of assets from government to the private economy by reducing or even annihilating the taxes on saving. The thrust of the arguments for "privatisation" supports the conclusion that the taxes on saving should be abolished.

The taxation of saving, whether graduated or proportional, similarly gets no support from the "marginal-utility" principle applied (or often misapplied) to the relative spending of richer and poorer. It is in some sense undeniable that an additional pound of spending is worth less to the very rich than to the very poor: some such principle has always underlain every private venture for the relief of poverty. But this principle is wholly inapplicable to the distribution of wealth: it would hold good for wealth only under the impossible conditions, first, that all income came from investments and none from earnings and, second, that there was no new saving.

Taxes on saving destroy wealth by shifting assets from holders with a lower discount rate (taxpayers) to holders with a higher discount rate (government) or more simply by turning taxpayers' assets into government spending. This principle also holds good for confiscatory taxes on existing savings. As the tax on savings rises to absorb the whole of the yield and more, the principal motive for retaining assets in this unfavourable situation instead of realising them is personal commitment to assets with personal associations [12]; here too the discount rate is lower and the value of the assets higher for the taxpayers than for the government.

Finally, the argument implies that a graduated tax on saving is more destructive of wealth than a proportional tax of equivalent yield and that the least destructive schedule of tax on saving would be *degressive* (the opposite of "progressive": in other words, the rate of tax would fall as the volume of saving rose). The subjective rate of interest or discount would seem to fall from poorer to richer: for example, the high net-of-tax rates of interest payable by hire purchasers fall predominantly on the poorer sections of the population, and the richer seldom either pay or receive interest at such high rates. The subjective gross-of-tax interest rate for the rich is thus below the gross-of-tax market rate [13]. A given gross-of-tax investment income is therefore worth more to a richer taxpayer than to a poorer: for example, £ 1,000 a year is worth £10,000 at 10 per cent but £20,000 at 5 per cent. A proportional income tax of 15 per cent destroys £1,500 of wealth if the subjective discount rate is 10 per cent but £3,000 of wealth if the subjective discount rate is 5 per cent.

If I do not press this argument, it is partly because the history of welfare economics shows the dangers of moving from market realities to their subjective and ghostly counterparts in the satisfaction of the individual. The argument is in any case subsidiary to the principle that the taxation of saving is destructive of wealth whether the tax is "progressive", proportional or even degressive. But it has the merit of presenting in the sharpest possible form the contrast between taxation based on capacity-to-pay and taxation based on minimum-destruction-of-wealth: capacity-to-pay appears to imply that the taxation of saving should be heavy and graduated, whereas minimum-destruction-of-wealth implies that saving should be taxed at worst degressively and at best not at all.

*Variations in the gross-of-tax yield*

We are left with differences in gross-of-tax yields. Since these differences are arge and persistent, how do they fit into our analytical scheme? The principal reasons for differences in asset yields are the following: (a) the yield may be taken in enjoyment rather than in money (a swimming pool in a private garden); (b) the yield may be considered risky and there may be a discount for risk; (c) the yield may be low now but expected to rise faster than average; (d) the asset may not be easily marketable; (e) fiscal or other misgovernment may so distort economic relationships that assets in category (a), such as owner-occupied houses, become better long-term investments than assets yielding an income (the cost of occupying house-room becomes negative); this shades into (f), where the possibility of gain from collecting or hoarding, which is inherent even in a well-run economic system though always balanced by the possibility of loss, is exaggerated by fiscal and other misgovernment and stamps, coins, books, paperweights, or almost any form of collection becomes a better investment than the investment of funds in income-yielding industry or commerce. Of these six, (b), (c) and (d) fit directly into the analytical framework and require no special consideration here.

Assets falling under (a) yield a non-monetary income: the best-known example is owner-occupied houses in circumstances where the house is owned for use and not for investment, but there are many other examples of notional (or non-monetary) income, each of which is derived from a source representing an asset or element of wealth. Economic activity can be non-monetary as well as monetary; and the usual analysis of a monetary economy remains valid, except that the absence of money makes some forms of measurement more difficult or less accurate. The boundary between monetary and non-monetary activity is important, and there are sound theoretical as well as practical arguments for leaving non-monetary activity untaxed and otherwise immune from government interference; but this does not imply that non-monetary income is not income or that ordinary economic analysis is inappropriate. On the contrary, assets yielding a non-monetary income are in principle valued, like other assets, at the discounted present worth of their stream of future income, even though this income is non-monetary and not precisely measurable. If the income is not taxed either directly or through a tax on the parent capital, the value of the asset is the same for rich as for poor and the same rate of discount is appropriate to both for the calculation of market prices.

Where assets yield no income-stream, the principal motive for ownership may be the pleasure or satisfaction of ownership as such [14]. The pleasure of personal ownership may also be a reason for accepting a relatively low yield on capital: a personal asset yielding less is preferred to an impersonal asset yielding more.

The remaining cases are (e) and (f) where non-income-yielding assets are held as investments either through economic misgovernment or through the operation of fashion and scarcity even in a well-run economy. Non-income-yielding assets held as investments are the only example of wealth without income. It is playing with words to say that they generate income if they appreciate in price because part of the principal can be sold each year and this may be regarded as an income: first, it is not an income, but part of the capital; and, second, income-yielding assets also can be sold little by little, but this has nothing to do with the distinction between assets that yield an income and assets that do not. The creation of wealth through the collection of scarce goods (including land) is a means of wealth creation different from its creation through the generation of additional income. Although it is all done by mirrors, it is equally real. The rise in the price of old stamps is not a measure of inflation, like the rise in the price of current goods and services. It does not affect the money stock, since the higher sum received by the seller exactly matches the higher sum paid by the purchaser. For the majority of collectors in any short period, the gain merely accrues; for some of them it may never be realised at all. Wealth is created out of thin air by a change of sentiment: but it is just as real as fixed assets or the capitalisation of income growth. A rise in stock-exchange prices due to false expectations of income growth contains the seeds of its own destruction; but a rise in the value of old stamps can (although it need not) go on for ever, because there is no income out-turn to disappoint the collector.

The rise in the value of old stamps or scarce land is real additional wealth, but it has no economic taxable capacity; in so far as it is taxed it is destroyed. (Chapter III, "The taxable capacity of saving"). It is real additonal wealth only in the hands of an individual taxpayer, not in the hands of the State. It cannot be transferred to collective ownership. If old stamps double in value and it is possible to tax the increment at 50 per cent, only the other 50 per cent (or less) remains. The money taxed away represented the pleasure of ownership. It was not part of national income nor of the stock of income-yielding assets. It cost nothing to produce; and its fiscal destruction leaves nothing in its place. This is true whether the collectors pay for the tax by realising their stamps or by the sale of other assets. The tax is not a zero-sum transfer from taxpayer to State: it involves the destruction of the amount transferred or more. If old stamps double in value there need be no increase in the money stock or in the price of current goods and services, and no cost in resources used. The increase in wealth is achieved solely by a change in sentiment. Fiscal interference in this process must damage sentiment and impede the creation of wealth. A tax on sentiment is not a tax that can be passed on. Stamp prices must fall. Suppose that the government raise a tax of 50 per cent on an increase of £100 m. in stamp prices, which collectors finance by selling government securities and which the government spend by redeeming public debt. £50 m. of government debt has been sold by stamp collectors and £50 m. has been bought from the gilt-edged market by the government. Prices of gilt-edged securities need not be affected; there has been a straight transfer on capital account from the public to the government. But what has happened to stamp prices meanwhile? Stamps are less valuable to collectors than they were, to new collectors as well as to old. If stamp-collecting were solely an investment and not a hobby, and the 50 per cent tax was believed to be permanent and unavoidable, the return on new investment would be halved; and if this loss were capitalised on the introduction of the tax, the 100 per cent gain would be totally destroyed by a halving in the price of the stamps. If the loss is not entirely capitalised at once, the destruction of wealth is spread out over time, though it is just as large in total. The destruction is diminished only in so far as stamp-collecting is a hobby rather than an investment: if stamp-collecting is pure investment, a wholly capitalised tax of 100 per cent on price rises reduces the value of existing collections to nil, although the reduction of value is less than total in so far as stamp-collecting is a hobby. If stamp-collecting is pure investment, a 50 per cent tax on capital appreciation destroys not merely 50 per cent of the capital appreciation for ever, but also 50 per cent of the existing capital value. It is only if stamp-collecting is a pure hobby that a tax on capital appreciation leaves the value of the existing capital stock unimpaired.

## A few conundrums

The last section explained that wealth can be created not only by brute force (through work and investment in new physical assets) but also immaterially (through changes in opinion or behaviour increasing the valuation of existing assets and skills). Since the latter concept is less familiar than the former it may be useful to test the rule with some difficult cases illustrating general principles. Capital values are more interesting philosophically than current values because they are less affected by current production and more susceptible to the influence of ideas.

The prices of goods in current production are determined by the supply of money and the velocity of its circulation. Relative prices may change; but rises and falls offset each other at a given volume of output if the supply of money and the velocity of its circulation are constant: the general price level remains the same. Existing assets are another story. Prices can and do change on sentiment alone. The stock market can move up or down with the news even when it is closed. There are no transactions, no money changes hands; but when it opens again, prices have altered. Thus prices of capital assets can move even without monetary impulsion; this is not possible (or is of negligible importance) for current goods unless monetary policy is so profligate as to confer the attributes of long-term assets on current stock-in-trade. But capital values can also be increased or reduced by a rise or fall in the money supply, although here again there is a distinction between capital values and current goods and services. If the money supply doubles, the price of current goods and services can be expected to double: money is working capital for the production process, and there is only a limited flexibility in this relationship (through changes in the velocity of circulation). But for existing capital assets, this is a consideration of minor importance. Working capital is indeed needed for the purchase and sale of existing capital assets; but changes in the money supply do not affect capital values primarily in this way. The main effect is through changes in sentiment which the change in the money supply causes. If the country is awash with money and investors are bidding up prices of existing assets, there must still be a seller for every buyer; additional money spent on the purchase of second-hand assets soon comes back into circulation again, unlike additional money spent on the purchase of current goods and services, where it is absorbed as working capital.

The distinction between goods in current production and existing assets is a matter not merely of common sense but also of degree. It is a distinction between goods which can be reproduced and goods which cannot; and this is a distinction with some shades of grey between the extremes of black and white. The individual citizen, not producers or the government, determines how far a new asset is a satisfactory substitute for an old.

*Pastiche.* This leads us to the first conundrum. How far can wealth be created by imitations of antiques, old jewellery, old paintings, old buildings? This is fairly straightforward. Wealth is created (though partially at the expense of the originals) as long as a profit is obtainable on current production. When current production can be expanded no further, the originals retain such a premium as is invulnerable to imitation.

*Forgery.* The forgery of Old Masters must be distinguished from the forgery of banknotes. The forger of banknotes destroys wealth. He is like a trader selling 9 carat gold as 18 carat, or a government debasing the coinage (whether through mixing base metals with precious metals or through overexpanding the supply of fiat money in the manner of British governments in the nineteen-seventies). The interesting question is not false trade descriptions or the abuse of State monopoly powers; it is the fraudulent imitation of originals whose value depends on their artistic quality.

What happens when Han van Meegeren imitates Vermeer or when Tom Keating imitates Palmer? Is wealth created or destroyed? Even when the fraud has been discovered, such pictures may have an artistic value as well as a curiosity value. The curiosity value is not of much interest; it is a criterion that might earn a place in a museum for anything associated with someone who had become famous for good or ill, for Dr. Crippen's slippers or Hitler's toothbrush. What is interesting is the comparison of the commercial value before and after the fraud is discovered (curiosity value being deducted from the latter).

The use of Vermeer's name is not much like the illicit use of a trademark. Pirating a trademark can succeed because purchasers are too busy (or know too little) to check the authenticity of everyday purchases. Someone who sets out to imitate Vermeer is not dealing with that type of customer. He is challenging the experts. If the experts are deceived for years on end and the value of the forgeries plummets when the forgeries are discovered, this suggests that the value of the originals is in substantial measure historical rather than artistic and resembles the value of old stamps rather than that of new paintings.

The creation of wealth through the creation of history (or at least through its improvement in rediscovery) is a process not unknown to tourist Ministries in a number of governments. If the tourists go home happier because they believe they have seen the tomb of the saint, when in fact they have not, it is hard to argue that no wealth has been created in any sense by a certain embellishment of the truth.

The key to these conundrums is the artificiality in values caused by experts or laymen making judgments beyond their competence. Both the Vermeer experts and the tourists vote with their money on matters they understand imperfectly. The same phenomenon can be found in the purchase of current goods and services. A wine or an electrical gadget or the service of a professional man may sell better if the price is increased, because the purchaser believes that he is buying something of better quality.

Unlike fraudulent trade descriptions, fraudulent utterances of banknotes and fraudulent election promises, successful artistic forgery creates wealth. It adds more wealth in total than it subtracts from the targets, if any, at which it is aimed. Likewise, the exposure of artistic forgery destroys wealth. This is not to say that artistic forgery is commendable or its exposure reprehensible. The pursuit of truth is a higher value than the creation of wealth. The pursuit of truth requires the demolition of falsehood. But it also requires a recognition that falsehood can itself create wealth until its falsity is demonstrated.

*Destruction.* Pliny tells the story of the Cumaean Sybil, who offered Tarquinius Superbus nine books of oracular utterances. When the king refused to pay what she asked, she burnt three and returned to offer the remainder at the price of the nine. When he refused again, she burnt three more and returned; the king then bought the last three at the original price [15].

This precedent has not been lost on modern artists. It is commonplace in certain lines for promoters to offer limited editions and to promise that the plates will be defaced or destroyed after a stated number of copies has been taken.

Can wealth be created by destruction? This is a hard doctrine to stomach; and yet it is so. The artist may correctly judge that there is a limited demand for his work. He may maximise his profit by producing 200 copies: 100 copies would be too little and 500 would flood the market. This is conventional monopoly theory with the difference that the artist decides whether to produce or not. At 200 copies the operation may be economic, whereas at 500 copies it might not compete with the attractions of leisure or other activities. Destruction of the plates after 200 copies are taken creates wealth: otherwise there might be no plates or copies at all.

This is the creation of wealth by the limitation of current production. Can wealth also be created by the destruction of existing assets? If I own all the Vermeers in the world, can I increase my wealth by burning some of them? Can the principle of the Sibylline books apply? Can an asset that cannot be reproduced be worth more to its owner in small quantities than large? This is clearly impossible in general; but is it possible at all?

Pliny's story of the Sibylline books is mysterious and magical. Its point is its irrationality. If the owner of existing assets faces a price-inelastic demand (so that he would make more by selling less), his best policy is to keep the surplus assets in his attic, not to destroy them: he may then be able to sell them later. Destruction is in the interest of an owner only if it is a prequisite for the sale of current production.

The creation of wealth through the use of existing assets requires their preservation, not their destruction.

*Metamorphosis.* Different considerations are in play if the value of a good or service is not exaggerated by the failure of lay or expert understanding to rise to a challenge (as under forgery) but transformed in the certainty that such expertise will never again be brought to bear. When a bottle of wine changes hands at a world record price of £8,300 (September 1977; previous year's record £7,800), it is not bought to grace a banquet where the food is served on gold plate; it is not bought to be drunk at all. "I don't think the purchaser wants to drink it," said his agent; "I think he just wants to own it." [16]

Such a purchase is not a wasteful extravagance, like serving guests at a banquet with a dish of nightingales' tongues. If it creates wealth at all, it consumes no resources and wastes nothing: any transaction costs it imposes are exceeded by the wealth it creates. In one sense, it is much the same as the purchase at a similar price of an old stamp with little artistic merit. But in another sense it is quite different. The stamp is of no use except to collectors, and its value is from the outset artificial, an illustration of the ability of capitalism to create wealth out of thin air. But a £10,000 bottle of wine adds another dimension to this achievement of capitalism. The £10,000 stamp has increased in value through scarcity; but it can still be seen, which was all it ever could be. The £10,000 bottle of wine started life as a challenge to the palate of the connoisseur. It might be drunk too soon, like an artist cut down before his prime; or it might be left too late, until it had gone "over the top" and its quality had started to decline. In either case the test is the test of the expert palate. But here the considerations are different. The £10,000 bottle of wine illustrates the ability of capitalism to create wealth, not merely out of the collection of stamps and other objects whose values are always artificial, but also out of the collection of objects whose value, originally utilitarian, is transformed either by the growth of an autonomous cult or by the activities of governments so hostile to business and industry that almost any competitive investment may prove more productive to the investor.

The £10,000 bottle of wine also shows in quintessential form the ability of the capitalist system to create wealth out of thin air. Unlike the £10,000 stamp, it cannot be admired visually; it can merely be seen through a glass darkly and cannot be tasted at all. But the attribution of value to the bottle of wine by the market involves no deception and is a form of wealth creation through the appreciation of history that compares well with the promotion of particular sites in order to attract visitors. The transformation is passive and not promoted by anyone; and it is not, as in Ovid's *Metamorphoses*, instantaneous, but gradual. It creates wealth as the result of a shift in sentiment, even though the cult object is artificial not merely in the sense of bearing no relation to the value of current goods and services, but also on a higher plane through no longer maintaining contact with the sense to which it was originally designed to appeal.

This paradox exemplifies strengths of capitalism which most of its potential supporters have belittled or ignored or even misrepresented as weaknesses.

## Industry and wealth

Stamp-collecting has been chosen as an example of wealth creation by changes in sentiment because the element of scarcity is not connected at all with current goods and services and is not closely connected with the beauty of art. Land is in limited supply, but it is required for current economic activity; Titians are in limited supply, but they are great paintings. In stamp-collecting, that is, in the collection of *old* stamps, the connection between scarcity, sentiment and the creation of wealth is seen in its purest form. Old stamps are not used in producing current goods and services. Some may be fine works of art; but the most valuable often are not. In general a valuable stamp has the same sort of beauty as a cheque for ten thousand pounds.

The distinction between stamp-collecting and other forms of investment is nevertheless a distinction of degree more than of kind. Land may be bought for investment as well as for use; so may old furniture; so may a Stradivarius. There are elements of "monopoly" (scarcity of supply) in the provision of many current goods and services, for example in the goodwill attaching to a name. A writer or composer may come to be more highly regarded during the course of his working life: this shift of sentiment creates wealth, even though it is closely connected with the provision of current services. The same may happen to a firm.

When wealth is created by a shift of sentiment, it is not created by labour or capital investment in any ordinary sense, perhaps hardly by economic activity at all. The wealth-creating activity of Wordsworth and Betjeman was not that of workers, but of entrepreneurs in ideas. Financial entrepreneurs can measure their success in money terms and their activity is directly economic; entrepreneurs in ideas may have little or no financial reward from the success of those ideas, and their activity is not directly economic or not economic at all, though it can have economic consequences. These consequences may be adverse rather than beneficial, and material losses may be recommended and justified for religious reasons or otherwise [17]. Entrepreneurs in ideas are artists, teachers, preachers, reformers, Saint Benedict sending out the call to religious poverty, Mozart creating the classical concerto, von Mises demonstrating the inefficiencies of socialism. Entrepreneurs in ideas, when acting in that capacity, bear their production costs themselves; their ideas are contentious, during their lifetimes and often afterwards; and the gains and losses from their activities, whether financial or spiritual, accrue largely to others and not to themselves.

When wealth is created by a shift of sentiment, this may be through a reassessment of what is beautiful or through a revaluation of what is scarce. In principle, the first process is independent of ownership: it is possible, though unlikely, that the beauties of the Lake District could be enjoyed without impairment even if the place had been turned into a People's Park, that the beauties of the Victorian churches would be equally evident even if they had all been reconstituted as Anti-God Museums. But it is a different tale for scarcity. Stamps are of no use to the government. Scarcity creates wealth only for individuals and not for the State. If the State tries to appropriate any of this wealth, it destroys more than it acquires (Chapter III, "The taxable capacity of saving"): the wealth created by scarcity is not merely wholly dependent, but more than wholly dependent, on the assets' being held held in private ownership, since otherwise the gains obtainable from scarcity are not just wholly destroyed but (through the capitalisation of losses) more than wholly destroyed.

Thus private ownership is a necessary condition for extracting the additional wealth created by scarcity. But private ownership is also a sufficient condition for extracting additional wealth even if there is no limitation of supply, provided that the assets are currently produced as well as currently used. Ordinary furniture in the home provides an everyday example. In a capitalist system this is owned by the occupier, tenant or landlord. In a socialist system it is owned by the State. In a socialist system it is owned by nobody and in a capitalist system it is owned by somebody. This difference represents a difference in economic wellbeing. In a capitalist system the owner feels better off and indeed is better off, even though he makes no additional demands on the provision of current goods and services. This distinction is not temporary or once-for-all; it is permanent. There are two dimensions of economic welfare, use and ownership. They are not in competition with each other. Use is in competition with use and is subject to the limitation represented by the maximum production of goods and services. Between private individuals, ownership is in competition with ownership: when Henry VIII confiscated the monasteries and gave them to friendly courtiers, the gains of the gainers were a large proportion of the losses of the losers, the difference being expenses of administration and costs of upheaval. Modern socialism is less neutral and more destructive. When private home ownership is replaced by government home ownership, the provision of current services is not necessarily affected (though in practice it is made more expensive); but the dimension of ownership is destroyed. Even if the cost and charge for rent and related services were the same in the council house as in the private house, the private system would have the advantage, because there would be a gain from ownership to be shared between landlord, owner-occupier and tenant; the economic value of ownership is lost if the owner is the State, although it is preserved if the owner is a co-operative or other organisation intermediate between the individual and the State, set up and maintained without State subsidy or compulsion. However the benefits of ownership are distributed between landlord, owner-occupier and tenant, they are to be had somewhere: they are reduced or destroyed by the impairment or destruction of private ownership, for example through the operation of rent control. Rent control is a partial destruction of the benefits of ownership and inflicts a loss on the whole population in their private capacities; any gains of one individual are more than offset by the losses of others (including those who cannot obtain or afford houseroom because of government-inflicted restrictions in the private and government sectors). The same argument that holds good for housing holds good for everything else: the impairment and destruction of ownership destroy wealth, and any incidental gain to one citizen is more than offset by consequent losses to others.

The creation of additional wealth through ownership is a magic peculiar to capitalism. It was unknown to Inca Peru and it is unacceptable to the USSR and Communist China. Socialism condemns the populations it controls to a lower standard of economic wellbeing as long as the system lasts. This has nothing to do with the relative merits of capitalism and socialism as systems for producing current goods and services (although there are reasons for considering capitalism the more efficient system [18]). Even if socialism were equally efficient in the production of goods and services, it would lack the dimension of ownership. Ownership, or capitalism, creates economic wellbeing out of thin air. This is because ownership, or capitalism, distinguishes spending from spending power: spending power represents economic wealth even when it is not exercised in spending, and the excess of spending power over spending is additional wealth beyond what is created by additional goods and services. I have used elsewhere the term "the banking principle" to describe the relationship between spending and spending power: the bank's customers accept spending power as the equivalent of spending as long as they have no doubt that the former can be translated into the latter [19]. The benefit of ownership, like the benefit of banking, depends on confidence and is substantial as long as this confidence can be justified by events, which may or may not be for ever. If all the depositors try to encash their deposits at once, the bank may be in difficulties. If all the owners try to realise their claims at once, prices will collapse. The art of banking is to prevent a run on the banks and the art of economic management is to reconcile ownership claims and use claims so as to maximise economic wellbeing.

The opportunity of increasing economic wellbeing through reconciling ownership with expenditure has not merely been neglected but thrown and kicked away in recent years by industrialists and trade union leaders, by Conservative and Labour politicians. To say this need not be a criticism. They have their own interests to pursue, their own constituents to satisfy; and it may not be the fault of any individual if the common interest that reconciles all parties is neglected, misunderstood or forgotten. But there are advantages for the general polity, and may even be advantages for particular parties and pressure groups, in seeking to harmonise apparently conflicting interests and realise the concept of One Nation.

This would involve a turnaround in conventional attitudes. *Our analysis has shown that there are at least three ways of creating economic wealth* [20]. *The first is by the use of brute force to come to terms with the curse of Adam: by using the sweat of the face and investment in machinery to produce what is needed for the sustenance and improvement of life.* Whether this is done by handwork, by brainwork or by investment in machinery, it is costly. It involves real economic cost or effort. Whatever any one party extracts from the system, he or another party has contributed by blood, toil, tears or sweat [21]. *But there are two other methods of creating wealth. The second is through the operation of scarcity; and the third is through the institution of ownership.* The second and third methods of creating wealth are clean and costless. The use of resources they involve is negligible and the desecration of the countryside that they cause is nil. They are self-contained in the sense that their effects are confined to the participants.

If there has been one question on which the good and the great have made common cause in recent years, industrialists and trade union officials, Labour politicians and Conservatives, it has been the superiority of method one (Adam's curse) over all other methods, or rather the diplomatic recognition of method one and the non-recognition of all competitors. Conventional opinion has preferred the creation of wealth by brute force and the use or exhaustion of natural and other economic resources. The distinction between "productive" and "non-productive" assets has customarily been drawn to the advantage of the former. But the truth is the other way round. Investment in real goods and services, like personal spending, imposes a real cost on society; it leaves less for everyone else. Its economic justification is the expectation of enough profit to defray the financial costs involved. Beyond this point, wealth is destroyed, not created, by investment in real goods and services. Further investment can be justified only by an improvement in profit expectations; if there is no such improvement, wealth is destroyed, not created, by exercises in investment solidarity, like those sponsored by the Wilson and Heath Governments and the Confederation of British Industry. The benefits are as transient as those of a stock exchange boom created by manipulation; but the damage done is more serious and more lasting because it involves the destruction of real resources, the materials and labour invested in capital goods for which there is no economic justification. Manipulated real investment flows and manipulated investment in stocks and shares have this in common that they can be falsified by the short-fall of income below expectations. Since stamps and similar assets yield no income, they are not exposed to any corresponding risk: all the determinants of success and failure are within the minds of the investors. The attempt to create wealth by exhortation to investment, which must be unsuccessful for real goods and services, might in principle succeed for old stamps, coins, books and Victorian paperweights; and this would at least be a less destructive channel for the surplus energies of the government and the Confederation of British Industry [22].

The creation of wealth by private ownership itself (as opposed to the creation of wealth by the appreciation in the value of assets in private hands) is perhaps best illustrated by the example of large houses ("stately homes"). Even supporters of wealth tax and capital transfer tax in Britain have generally recommended reliefs or even exemption for these assets on the ground that it would cost the State money to take them into public ownership even by confiscation. The reason is that the owners, in their capacity as owners, will do work for little or no remuneration in keeping these houses going. Ownership provides its own reward and its own wealth. If ownership is destroyed, by taxation or otherwise, this wealth is destroyed. But the argument is not peculiar to large houses; they merely illustrate it drama-tically and unmistakably. The argument holds good for assets in general. Owner-ship provides a dimension of costless wealth that can be had for the asking.

The potentialities of ownership and scarcity for wealth creation have been neglected; and some forms of scarce assets in private hands, especially land, have been visited with particular fiscal penalties. But "productive" assets may have sub-stantial taxable capacity merely by virtue of being productive; it is private owner-ship, and especially the private ownership of scarce assets, which creates wealth out of thin air and whose economic taxable capacity is negative in the sense that the wealth destroyed is at least as large as the tax collected. (Chapter III, "The tax-able capacity of saving").

Thus the creation of wealth through private ownership and the appreciation of scarce goods is particularly vulnerable to damage by taxation. Taxes on capital and capital gains destroy more of such wealth than they transfer to the fisc. But "productive" investment, though less vulnerable than the creation of wealth through ownership and the appreciation of scarce goods, is also liable to damage by taxation. Taxation can compound the curse of Adam.

## CHAPTER III

# SAVING AND INVESTMENT

## Wealth and investment: four methods of wealth creation

The foregoing anaylsis of wealth and the distinctions between the three meanings and methods of wealth creation apply directly to real and financial investment. The *first* of the three methods of wealth creation on page 39, the use of brute force, may involve investment — investment in income-yielding assets. The *second* does involve investment — investment in other assets. The *third* involves a transfer of assets from government hands into private hands. There is *fourth* method, described above as entrepreneurship in ideas, which differs from the other three because some of its principal manifestations are not economic at all. Investment in income-bearing financial assets does not constitute a separate category, since any of the four methods of wealth creation may take this form; but its principal role is to act as an intermediary between the individual saver and the investor in industrial assets.

Investment in industrial assets is the creation of wealth by brute force. More accurately, it is the creation of wealth by brute force if the assets are new. If the assets are second-hand, there is merely a rearrangement of portfolios, an exchange of existing assets for cash, so that the transaction has some of the characteristics of an investment in financial paper or old stamps: it resembles investment in financial paper because it yields an income and investment in old stamps because it makes no current claim on resources. An investment in things is "productive" if they yield an income-stream and "non-productive" if they do not. A "productive" investment is economic if it covers its financing costs and yields a profit and uneconomic if it does not; it is abortive if it yields no income-stream at all. It follows from the foregoing analysis that "non-productive" investments may create more wealth than "productive" investments, not merely because "productive" investments may be abortive or uneconomic, but also because "non-productive" investments are economically costless. "Non-productive" capital expenditure that makes a call on current resources is mostly investment for use, like expenditure on a new swimming pool in a private garden, though here as elsewhere the categories may overlap (an artist's current work may be bought as an investment).

"Productive" assets may be expected to create more wealth than "non-productive" assets (unless they are prevented from doing so) merely by virtue of their being "productive". When this relationship is reversed, as it has been in Britain in recent years, the instinctive reaction of many people, not only in the Labour Party but also in the Conservative Party and in industry, is to impose fresh burdens and restrictions on the creation of wealth through investment in "non-productive" assets in order to restore the competitiveness of the creation of wealth through brute force. But this is to impose on "non-productive" assets the same burdens that have made "productive" assets unproductive and to impede the creation of wealth still further. The wiser reaction is to ask oneself why "productive" assets have proved less productive than "non-productive" assets in recent years and indeed often counterproductive, so that the industrial hardware they embody might as well have been dumped in mid-Atlantic for all the good they have done to the economy. The obvious answer is that "non-productive" assets have flourished for the same reason that services have flourished: because they are less vulnerable than manufacturing and heavy industry generally to trade union restrictive practices, "employment protection" (read *employment destruction*) and similar consequences of legislative and other interference by government, so that the creation of wealth by capitalism can proceed with relatively little obstruction. It is much to be desired that manufacturing and heavy industry should be released from the handicaps which government interference imposes on them at present. But it is useless and indeed destructive to anticipate this happy day. While the present situation persists, it is both selfishly wise and socially expedient to invest in "non-productive" assets if they are expected to yield the highest return; the British Rail Pension Fund may well have created wealth for others as well as for itself by investing a large tranche of employees' pension contributions in paintings and *objets d'art* rather than in British industry.

Investment in non-income-yielding assets may create or destroy wealth; but these terms require care in interpretation. If the value of old stamps doubles on Monday and halves on Tuesday, the majority of investors in old stamps will be unaffected; a few will have gained and a few will have lost and, apart from taxation and costs of dealing, the gains will exactly match the losses [1]. Tuesday's losses destroy the wealth that Monday's gains created. But the long-term increase in the value of stamps is pure wealth creation. Indeed, for investors collectively (again apart from taxation and costs of dealing) all investment in existing or second-hand goods creates wealth. The man who invested his money in stamps on Monday lost some of it on Tuesday; but, provided that profits cover dealing costs (which may be negligibly small), society cannot lose from investment in second-hand assets except through the operation of taxation. As we noted earlier (page 37), any taxation of these profits diminishes the social gain or even turns the social gain into a social loss. But, apart from the obstacles interposed by taxation, the argument is general and admits of no exceptions: all investment in second-hand assets, whether real or financial, creates a gain for the economy (a social gain), even though some individual investors may lose and even though the social gain may be diminished or turned into a loss through the operations of the fisc.

Financial investments are intermediate except for those where one party is the State. The placement of a new debenture or equity issue merely brings together willing lenders and borrowers of funds: the lending may be done on terms of financial participation and the function of riskbearing may be shared between existing shareholders, new shareholders or even other parties. If the funds raised by a new issue are hypothecated for a particular use, the financial merits of this use determine whether it is socially desirable that the new issue should succeed. If the money would have been spent on a loss-making factory, it would be socially preferable that the new issue should fail and that the money should instead be spent on consumption. If the end use was well judged, it is socially desirable that the new issue should succeed. But new issues are not passive: they can be the servant of society. New issues cannot raise money without the voluntary participation of investors. In aggregate they screen out the projects for loss-making investments involuntarily supported by the taxpayer, which have in recent years been comparable in aggregate with the amount of funds for new investment raised privately: in so doing they save the economy the additional losses that would be incurred if all funds for investment were raised by force from the taxpayer. Similarly, "speculation" in the sense of buying when goods or financial assets are cheap and selling when they are dear is socially useful like any other trading activity; it evens out price variations, as has been noted by the socialist author A. P. Lerner [2]. But, like any other trading activity, "speculation" in this sense creates wealth out of resources, not out of thin air. "Speculation" in the sense of investment in second-hand goods with an eye to long-term gain creates wealth out of thin air for the reasons explained earlier (page 22); and it is notable that "speculation" in this sense, for example speculation in land, has been a particular target for conventional criticism. Here, as elsewhere in the economics of public finance and taxation, the consensus of established wisdom is largely erroneous [3].

Although new-issue markets between private persons are merely intermediaries, secondary financial markets are not. In the short term they enjoy the same potential for wealth creation as secondary markets in goods. In the short term a rise in the price of ICI shares creates wealth in just the same way as a rise in the price of Penny Blacks. The difference is that the rise in the price of Penny Blacks, although it creates real wealth, is not determined by other current events: it can be self-sustaining for ever. But a rise in the price of ICI shares is ultimately controlled by the capacity of the company to generate current profits. Thus in the long term the capacity to generate wealth autonomously is confined to non-income-yielding assets (or to paper representing such assets). There is no limit to the potentialities of non-income-yielding assets for the autonomous creation of wealth. The attractions of investing in non-income-yielding assets are increased by inflation and diminished by taxation; but ultimately sentiment is no less important as an arbiter.

Different considerations apply to financial investment transactions in which the principals are the private investor and the government. The difference from transactions between private persons is that the government has the legal power to use the sword in order to have its way with the citizen. It can raise money from voluntary subscribers on the credit of its power to do violence to its own citizens. This power has the financial consequence that a change in the terms offered to the investor by the government may create or destroy wealth autonomously. It is customary for the government to use its monopolistic borrowing power in order to offer the worst possible terms to the investor on the pretext that it is thereby obtaining the best possible bargain for the taxpayer. But the truth may be the opposite: the taxpayer may lose as well as the investor. Given the amount of government spending on goods and services, government financing requirements may be satisfied alternatively by taxation or borrowing. The volume of borrowing varies with the rate of interest on government securities. An increase of £10 m. in interest disbursements in year 1 may attract an inflow of £100 m. in additional borrowing. If the inflow is the same in all subsequent years, it is eventually exceeded by the additional interest payments required to service the additional borrowing; but this will never happen if the additional borrowing grows as fast as the additional interest.On the other hand, the amount of additional borrowing is subject to the restraints of financial prudence. As a simple criterion, additional borrowing should not grow faster than monetary national income (national income before adjustment for inflation). This is the long-term limitation. The short-term limitation is that the new, higher rate of interest should not exceed the "social rate of return" (the pre-tax return from private investment). Provided that these two requirements are satisfied, the taxation of saving can be replaced by borrowing for ever. The reduction in the taxation of saving represents the continuous and cumulative creation of wealth which must eventually exceed the wealth destroyed by the fall in the capital values of existing government securities when the return on new government securities rises [4]. All that has happened is that private individuals own assets (government securities) that would otherwise not exist. The use of resources and the distribution of current spending need not be affected. The replacement of taxation by borrowing creates wealth by creating ownership, which is the subject of the next section.

The creation of wealth through the replacement of taxation by borrowing illustrates the way in which the institution and extension of ownership in the market economy creates new wealth from existing resources. Wealth is created by restricting the compulsory (governmental) sphere of activity and expanding the voluntary (private) sphere. New wealth can also be created from existing resources by diminishing or removing monopolistic powers enforced by the state, both those of public bodies like nationalised industries and those of private bodies like trade unions: if restrictive practices are not supported by state compulsion they can be attacked by competition. Here again, new wealth is created by an extension of the market or voluntary sector of activity.

The replacement of taxation by borrowing can destroy wealth instead of creating it if the restraints of financial prudence are disregarded. Excessive borrowing can lead to monetary incontinence and profligate spending. To avoid these results, the funds raised on the market must be returned to the taxpayers, not spent, and the holdings of government debt must be long-term and stable. The rise in long-term interest rates required to attract the additional borrowing from the market can with advantage be complemented by a general funding operation (a lengthening in the average maturity of government debt). Funding reduces the supply of money, so that the replacement of taxation by borrowing can form part of a conservative financial policy. The policy may appear to be benefiting the present generation at the expense of the future, but this is not really so. Provided that the restraints and limitations are respected, the system is stable for ever and each generation gains in its turn.

The logic of the argument is not confined to the replacement of taxation by the sale of government debt in traditional forms. It extends to any long-term, stable purchases by private persons with funds made available by tax cuts. It provides the rationale for the financing of profit-sharing by the Revenue. Through taxation, the Revenue has a large interest in business profits; but the capital value of that interest is not owned or enjoyed by anyone. Profit-sharing financed by tax cuts can put this capital value to work without costing the Revenue anything in terms of the present discounted value of future taxes. Indeed, the Revenue can make a profit (though not in terms of the cash flow in the first year). The essence of the idea is that money put into a trust fund for employees is to be free of tax both in the hands of the company (for whom it is a deductible expense) and in the hands of the trust; the arrangement is voluntary, and the initiative lies with the company, not with the government.

## Wealth and ownership

Spending and ownership are in different dimensions. Ownership is spending power. *Posse iuvat*, says Ovid, power itself is pleasing; and this applies to power in general, to political power, for example, as well as to purchasing power. The power is agreeable as well as its exercise. This means that purchasing power is valuable, is an economic good, has "utility"; that the creation of additional purchasing power is as rational an aim of economic policy as an increase in the standard of living, although the two are quite distinct and may even be in conflict.

Conventional economics, Western and communist, has missed the dimension of ownership, partially or even entirely. The communists and their supporters in the

West have had their own reasons for belittling or ignoring the capacity of owner-ship to create economic value additional to that created by expenditure on consump-tion and investment goods. But the performance of Western economics has not been much better. Ownership has been ignored by welfare economics [5]. More remar-kably, the wealth-creating potential of ownership has generally been neglected, both at academic and political levels, in arguments about the relative merits of pri-vate ownership and nationalisation, even though nationalisation destroys wealth and denationalisation creates wealth out of thin air. There are no statistics of national wealth analogous to those of national income. The greatest single advantage of capitalism over socialism has received little attention.

Indeed, in the one area where ownership has been treated as a separate dimen-sion, namely the economics of taxation, the conclusions adduced for policy have been perverse. The notion of taxation according to "capacity to pay" has been taken to imply that the additional dimension of ownership should be visited with additional tax charges. In a tautological sense, the notion of taxation according to "capacity to pay" justifies any confiscation of property, large or small, partial or total, at death or during life. The trouble with the notion of taxation according to "capacity to pay" is that it appears to say something while really saying nothing. It justifies any rate of tax between zero and a hundred per cent on any asset and any owner at any time with or without warning. It is the ultimate enemy of private ownership, and if it were taken seriously the institution of private ownership would be at an end. In reality, the notion of taxable capacity is not used in any valid economic sense but as a slogan supporting arbitrary capital taxes on a limited number of politically vulnerable taxpayers [6].

Economic logic points in the opposite direction. The concept of taxable capacity connotes policies by which wealth is destroyed; a just and rational tax policy imposes the least possible hindrances on its creation. All taxation destroys wealth by weaken-ing incentives and distorting the price pattern of the free market; taxation accord-ing to taxable capacity destroys wealth in the less subtle manner of a medieval monarch plundering monasteries or expropriating Jews. The creation of wealth by the the first of our four methods, brute force supported by investment in real first-hand assets, is the least vulnerable to taxation according to "taxable capacity", though the damage may still be severe; for example, if corporation tax is levied at 50 per cent, this suggests that 50 per cent of the new wealth created by the market is des-troyed by the government. This is the sort of price that has to be paid for a situa-tion in which the government spends about half the national income. But this is the traditional argument about incentives which cannot be proved or disproved in either direction [7]. The worst criticism of the taxation of earnings from labour and investment by brute force is that at any rate of tax it *may* diminish national income, at some higher rate it *must* diminish national income, and at some still higher rate it *must* diminish tax revenue itself, when the rate begins to be *prohibitive* in the sense of a prohibitive customs tariff. The only trouble with this argument is that it cannot be demonstrated either logically or empirically that a particular tax is or is not reducing national income or tax revenue. The question is not susceptible of empirical proof in either direction; and the *a priori* arguments, though powerful and persuasive, are confined to probabilities and cannot achieve certainty [8].

It is another story when taxes are imposed on the second and third forms of wealth creation, on investment in second-hand goods and on ownership. All these taxes destroy wealth even if they are below the point of maximum revenue yield. They may not reduce national income; but national income is only a partial indicator of economic prosperity. A tax on earnings from labour may reduce output by reducing incentives or increase output by making people work harder to achieve any given standard of living; in either case the tax reduces welfare, but national income may rise because the cost of the reduction in welfare may be borne by a reduction in leisure, which is not a component of national income or indeed measurable in money terms at all. Taxes on investment in second-hand goods, by contrast, are unequivocally destructive. They must reduce national wealth by more than the amount of the tax yield even if the tax is below the point of maximum revenue. ("The taxable capacity of saving", below). There is no analogue to the increase in national income through a reduction in leisure. National wealth itself is reduced; and this is in principle a measurable magnitude, just like national income, even though in practice statisticians measure the one and not the other. Taxes on ownership and on investment in second-hand goods are necessarily destructive because these forms of wealth creation have a negative economic taxable capacity, in the sense that the wealth destroyed exceeds the tax levied. ("The taxable capacity of saving"). The wealth created by ownership and investment in second-hand goods is real but not material. It is in the mind. The attempt to tax such wealth is an attempt to turn immaterial wealth into material. This attempt must necessarily fail. In addition to the destruction of wealth by the amount of the revenue raised, the damage to confidence due to the intrusion of the State into a private affair causes further destruction of wealth through the reduction in value of the assets remaining in private hands. This damage to confidence is of a different order from the damage to confidence that may reduce investment in industry. Industrial investment is investment in income-yielding assets; the investment decision is based on an appraisal of costs and returns that may be objective and depend little on confidence. But investment in second-hand goods depends entirely on confidence because the wealth it creates is immaterial. The wealth created by ownership is also immaterial, and the taxation of ownership not only reduces wealth by the amount of the tax but also diminishes the value of the assets remaining in private hands.

Taxes on ownership and on investment in second-hand goods are wealth tax, capital gains tax, and capital transfer tax and its equivalents (estate duty, legacy duty, succession duty, gift tax), All these taxes are levied on capital irrespective of the income it yields and indeed of whether it yields any income at all. It follows from the foregoing analysis that these taxes are more destructive than income taxes:

for income-yielding assets, taxes on income and its parent capital are all equivalent in the sense that they can be translated into each other[9], but for non-income-yielding assets, taxes on income are impossible and taxes on capital are the only option. For non-income-yielding assets the impossibility of income taxes correctly reflects the lack of any positive economic taxable capacity: taxation is not a participation in the creation of wealth by others but the pillage of wealth already created, like a series of raids to plunder the monasteries. This fiscal pillage has been generally supported by the conventional wisdom.

Taxation of ownership and of investment in second-hand assets is taxation without economic taxable capacity. Taxation of investment in new income-yielding assets draws on positive economic taxable capacity only if the saving is temporary. The presence or absence of positive economic taxable capacity thus leads to the subject of the next section, the distinction between temporary and permanent saving and its fiscal implications.

## Temporary and permanent saving

The words "saver" and "investor" overlap but differ in meaning. A saver is a non-spender. In an absolute sense, a saver is someone who could spend current income but does not; the same is true in a relative sense of owners who could draw down existing assets for spending but refrain from so doing. But, as the Parable of the Talents points out[10], the wise saver is not the one who keeps his money under the bed but the one who invests it to yield a return. So the saver is also an investor. He may invest in government bonds, in private financial paper, in income-yielding industrial assets or in second-hand goods. Government bonds have already been discussed on page 44 and second-hand goods on page 42. Private financial paper is primarily an intermediary between the individual saver and the investor in industrial assets.

The industrial investor is a spender as much as the individual consumer. He makes a call on real resources. In his capacity as an investor, he is a spender. If he saves what he invests the two roles offset each other. The saver, in his capacity as saver, provides the resources which the industrial investor spends; again, the same person may combine the two roles[11].

The process of spending through industrial investment represents a postponement of present consumer spending in the interest of higher consumer spending in the future. The productivity of industrial assets provides the means of increasing consumption in the future over consumption in the present. This process is the creation of wealth by brute force; with its successes or failures in practice, it is the intellectual framework common to Western and communist economic analysis[12]. In this analysis, saving must be realised through expenditure on new assets because saving is temporary: all saving is for future consumption. The industrial investor spends the wealth that the temporary saver creates. All the creation of wealth through this method is temporary, although there is an optical illusion because the process is continuous and is spread out over the years.

Permanent wealth creation is caused by enterprise in ideas, the spread of ownership and investment in second-hand goods (assets other than second-hand income-yielding paper assets, investment in which creates wealth only temporarily). Enterprise in ideas has been discussed earlier (page 36): in its economic manifestations, it provides the counterpart in a free economy to the creation of wealth by brute force in a socialist economy. It is the creation of wealth through the removal of government controls and restrictions, through effort and risk-taking, and it has nothing to do with permanent saving. But permanent saving has everything to do with the creation of wealth through the spread of ownership and investment in second-hand goods. Permanent saving is the permanent maintenance or increase of spending power in preference to the realisation of spending power in spending. For the collectivity of savers or owners, the maintenance of ownership requires the maintenance of permanent saving and the extension of ownership requires the extension of permanent saving. For example the *maintenance* of private home ownership requires that collectively citizens *remain* willing to own rather than sell a given amount of real property; the *extension* of private home ownership (whether through purchase or the gift of council houses to their tenants) requires an *increase* in the willingness to own rather than sell.

Permanent saving by the citizens collectively is to be distinguished from permanent saving by individuals. In a stationary economy there may be a pool of houses owned by the occupiers during their lifetimes but confiscated by the state when they die. This is permanent saving collectively but not individually: the pool of private ownership is maintained only by a constant inflow of new saving to match the outflow through confiscation. Similarly for funded pensions; and the same principle holds good in a growing economy for a steadily increasing pool of private ownership that is collectively permanent but individually temporary. Permanent individual saving is a different concept. Individual saving is permanent if it is neither drawn down by the saver nor confiscated by taxation. The stock of permanent individual saving need not be replenished by fresh saving of succeeding generations. It represents a constant stock of physical assets and potentially an increasing stock of real wealth. The flow of fresh permanent individual saving adds to this stock. Saving is permanent not by virtue of an irrevocable decision but simply by being left undisturbed in perpetuity [13].

Temporary saving creates wealth by the postponement of consumption. It is the counterpart of industrial investment. It is the creation of wealth by brute force. Permanent saving creates wealth out of ownership. It makes the same asset work twice, once for the user and once for the owner. It is the creation of wealth out of thin air. Wealth can be created out of thin air either by permanent saving or by investment in second-hand assets. They are two separate processes although they overlap when second-hand assets are the investment medium chosen for the permanent saving. The creation of wealth through permanent saving corresponds to the creation of wealth through the institution of ownership. Wealth can in principle be created by permanent saving even if there is no investment in second-hand assets. In a free economy, that is to say, an economy without a State sector, this result is achieved by the simple operation of the system: owners enjoy claims on resources which they do not and could not all exercise simultaneously. In a largely socialist economy, these advantages are diminished or destroyed by the taxation of ownership as such, through the levying of taxes on wealth, capital transfers and capital gains; as we have noted above (page 47), taxes on ownership destroy more wealth than they yield revenue. But wealth cannot be created by investment in second-hand assets unless there is permanent saving: although each investment in second-hand assets is necessarily matched by a sale, wealth is not created by investment in second-hand assets unless the pressure of buyers over sellers drives up the price.

Thus all saving creates wealth by making the same goods and services work twice, once in use and once in ownership. If saving is temporary, it gradually destroys the wealth it has created: the wealth that is built up by saving is drawn down by additiona consumption. But the wealth created by saving is never totally destroyed. Even in a stationary economy additional wealth is created by the double function of capital required in the process of production: the more capital-intensive the production process, the more the wealth created by this duality of function. This is a dimension of the argument neglected by conventional Western and communist analysis, which concentrates on output and misses the creation of wealth by ownership.

Wealth is also created by investment in second-hand goods. The investor in second-hand goods may also be a saver; but he need not be a saver, as when investment in second-hand goods is financed by borrowing.

The investor in new industrial assets, by contrast, is not creating wealth but spending it; the buildings, plant, machinery and vehicles that he purchases are not useful in themselves but merely a means of making money. Wealth is created if the investment is profitable and destroyed if it is unprofitable.

Investment in new industrial assets consumes resources; investment in second-hand goods does not, because the assets are already in existence. It is therefore notable that the thrust of fiscal policy has been to favour the former over the latter. Investment in second-hand goods is a certain method of creating wealth, not an uncertain method, and attempts to tax investment in second-hand goods necessarily destroy more wealth than they yield tax revenue; for both of these reasons investment in second-hand goods deserves to be taxed more lightly than industrial investment, not more heavily, and indeed not to be taxed at all.

Thus all saving creates wealth by creating a double function for the same money, once in ownership and once in use. This wealth created by saving can be destroyed by subsequent spending or it can last for ever. If the rate of return is positive (that is, unless the economy is in long-term decline), the postponement of consumption through temporary saving enables the eventual volume of consumption to be larger. The increase of consumption through its postponement, like the increase of consumption through work or enterprise, is a possible object (or base) of taxation [14]; but the simplest method of taxing it is to tax consumption itself. There are only two outlets for saving: one is spending and the other is a continuation of the act of saving itself, which constitutes permanent saving unless the funds are drawn down for spending. So, although temporary saving has positive taxable capacity, it has no taxable capacity in excess of that represented by the taxation of the addition to consumption which it makes possible. Permanent saving has negative, not positive, economic taxable capacity. Permanent saving creates permanent wealth; but this wealth is not taxable: taxes levied on it destroy more wealth than they yield revenue[14].

Traditionally, opinion has been divided between those who accept the concept of permanent saving and those who regard all saving as being destined for eventual consumption [15]. The concept of saving for consumption, or temporary saving, implies the existence of taxable capacity (though not beyond what is provided by the additional consumption which temporary saving makes possible). But saving never spent is never taxed by taxes on consumption. That is why Simons was so critical of the assumption that all saving is temporary [16]. He could see that this was not so and that permanent saving yielded economic welfare. But it is wrong to infer that this additional welfare represents additional economic taxable capacity: in reality, the economic taxable capacity of permanent saving is negative.

## The taxable capacity of saving

The taxable capacity of saving is a concept with more than one meaning. There are different kinds of saving and different senses of taxable capacity.

In the *first* or naive sense, taxable capacity is positive if the yield of a tax is positive. Thus, if a tax is levied at 98 or 99 per cent and still yields revenue, the taxable object is considered to have taxable capacity at this level of tax. Very high rates of tax on foreign trade or investment may be prohibitive because of domestic competition; but equally high rates of tax on work and saving may fall short of prohibition.

In the *second* sense, taxable capacity is treated *marginally*. Thus a tax rate of 98 per cent may be broken down into a succession of cumulative 1 per cent rates, each 1 per cent being regarded as a separate tax. If 98 per cent is past the point of maximum tax yield (Appendix V), the yield of an additional 1 per cent is negative and marginal taxable capacity is negative at this point.

The *third* sense is also marginal but differs from the second in taking the rest of the tax system into account. If one tax is raised or lowered, how much will other taxes have to be raised or lowered in order to keep the total revenue yield the same? The marginal or even total taxable capacity of a taxable object is negative in this sense if an increase in the tax on it requires compensating increases, not reductions, in the rest of the tax system in order to keep total tax revenue the same.

The *fourth* sense concerns a situation in which the government's borrowing requirements are determined independently of the level of interest rates and are met by genuine borrowing from the domestic market and not by printing money. A shortfall in borrowing must thus be made good by an increase in taxation (and a surplus provides room for tax cuts). Increases in taxes on the lending of money to the government require an increase, not a reduction, in other taxes in order to make good the government's cash flow (in any one year or in a succession of years). (Page 44). Lending to the government has negative taxable capacity. The fourth sense thus resembles the third but applies to *cash flow* not *tax flow*. The argument can be extended to the financing of any given volume of productive investment from taxation by comparison with voluntary subscription [17].

The *fifth* sense is *economic* or social rather than *financial* as in senses one to four. Economic taxable capacity is negative when the tax collected is less than the wealth destroyed by the levying of the tax. Onerous taxation of key foreign workers provides one example. Economic taxable capacity turns negative before the tax rate reaches the point of maximum yield, since at this point even the fisc itself is no longer gaining. *If economic taxable capacity is negative, the loss of wealth to the rest of the taxpaying community exceeds the loss to the taxpayer from the payment of tax.*

Financial taxable capacity in the first sense cannot fall below zero if administrative expenses are ignored. It cannot rise above zero in the fourth sense. In the second and third senses it may be positive or negative. If financial taxable capacity is negative, economic taxable capacity must be negative. If financial taxable capacity is positive, economic taxable capacity may be negative; but if economic taxable capacity is positive, financial taxable capacity must be positive also.

Temporary saving is part of the production process and has positive taxable capacity, not only in senses one to three but also in sense five, provided that rates of tax are sufficiently low. Taxable capacity in all senses *must* be annihilated at or below a tax rate of 100 per cent and *may* be annihilated at any rate, however low. Taxable capacity is larger in so far as the savers' response is "perverse" (the higher the tax, the more the saving).

Permanent saving is not part of the production process. It has positive taxable capacity in senses one to three, though at lower rates than for temporary saving (since permanent saving is more sensitive to variations in price). Its taxable capacity in sense five is negative. This is because the permanent saver's response to taxation is not "perverse". The amount of saving falls. Money which was formerly working twice, once in ownership and once in use, now works only once, in use: this applies both to the tax paid and to the reduction in saving. The difference from temporary saving is that temporary saving is building up a fund to defray the cost of spending later: the money is committed to this purpose and has not the double function it has when saving is permanent.

In practice, saving is a mixture of temporary and permanent. It is proved retrospectively to have been temporary by being drawn down; it is proved to have been permanent by being left unspent for ever. Thus, as permanent saving has negative economic taxable capacity and temporary saving has positive economic taxable capacity, and as saving is a mixture of temporary and permanent saving, we may say as an approximation that *saving has no economic taxable capacity*. Both temporary and permanent saving have negative taxable capacity in the fourth of the five senses above, where the criterion is cash flow year by year, unless the response of temporary savers to taxation is "perverse".

For the creation of wealth through investment in second-hand goods, the logic of the argument is the same as for permanent saving even though the saving represented by the investment in second-hand goods need not be permanent. Both permanent saving and investment in second-hand goods create wealth out of thin air. In permanent saving, money works twice; and when a tax is levied, the amount of money working twice falls by more than the amount of tax revenue. In investment in second-hand goods, wealth is created by capitalising over the existing stock the increase in value due to the additional demand; and the loss from a tax on the increment is partly or wholly capitalised back into a reduction in the value of the existing stock, not only for the taxpayer himself, but also for his fellows. A tax of 40 per cent on the increase in value of stamps may cause an economic loss not only of 40 per cent of future increases but of 40 per cent of the existing value; this latter may be a large multiple of the tax yield, and all future growth is from the lower base. Thus the creation of wealth through investment in second-hand goods has a negative economic taxable capacity even if the saving in question is temporary.

An example of the way in which the taxation of ownership and perpetual saving has a negative economic taxable capacity is provided by "perpetual roll-over" of capital gains tax when a productive asset is sold and replaced by something similar. The difference between roll-over and exemption of the gain is a potential charge hanging over the head of the taxpayer. This makes the taxpayer poorer and makes him feel poorer; but as long as the business continues, it confers no benefit either on the fisc or on the taxpayer's fellows: it is pure loss to the economy. And the potential tax charge on the migration or liquidation of the enterprise causes further loss to the economy by distorting decisions to the advantage of continuity and the disadvantage of change. The potential charge to tax embodied in the United Kingdom 1974 system of stock relief (relief from tax on illusory profits due to inflation) is open to similar objections and has gradually been qualified and circumscribed as the economic damage it does becomes increasingly obvious. But the damage done by taxes on ownership is not always so evident to the senses.

## Consumers and producers

In reality, the permanent saver is everyone's friend and no one's enemy. He is not competing with spenders for scarce resources. The wealth that he enjoys is created out of thin air by his own actions. If he is taxed, the rest of the economy is made poorer, not richer.

This is not the message that has come through in the universities, in public opinion or in fiscal policy. The academic tradition has generally supported the doctrine of taxation in accordance with "taxable capacity", a doctrine which annihilates the creation of wealth by ownership and puts saving, like labour, in thrall to the curse of Adam. Nor have most of the capitalist leaders been much better. The principal superiority of capitalism over communism, the costless and indeed limitless creation of wealth through the institution of ownership, has been neglected and ignored. Industrial leaders have generally supported discrimination in favour of "productive" assets by comparison with "non-productive" assets and have preferred the creation of wealth by brute force to the creation of wealth by the magic of capitalism, the secret of the market economy which permits savings in private hands to work twice, once in use and once in ownership. Nor has the private saver received any support even from those who are paid to look after his interests. The investment institutions have been content merely to make money out of the private saver; they have neglected any representational activity on his behalf [18] and have not lifted a finger to defend him from ideological attack. The personal saver has been abandoned by those who should have supported him from intellectual or material motives and even by those with a duty to defend his interests. It has been a *trahison d:; clercs.*

One reason why the most powerful weapon of capitalism has been left rusting in its scabbard is the tendency of so many in public life as well as ordinary citizens to think of the economy as a struggle between producer interests rather than a econ ciliation of consumer interests. Producer orientation causes conflict and consumer orientation creates harmony. Perversely, this is why producer groups are important in our public life and consumer groups are not. The business of producer groups is to promote the real or imagined interests of their constituents, as the TUC tries to promote the interests of labour and the Confederation of British Industry tries to promote the interests of manufacturers and investors in industrial assets. These interests are potentially or actually in conflict. There are no similar conflicts between consumers and savers. Consumption and saving are the purposes of economic activity, and a free economy in which each consumer or saver can dispose of his money as he pleases provides an automatic reconciliation of interests between all consumers and savers. Individual consumers and savers have not a sectional interest in conflict with the common interest, and they therefore have no need of pressure groups like producers. Because producer groups are important in our public life, producer-oriented thinking is common. The potential for harmony within the capitalist system has been ignored even by those who would have gained from it most. The potential for the costless creation of wealth by ownership has been neglected. The fiscal consequences have been destructive as well as unjust.

## CHAPTER IV

# PROSPERITY VERSUS JUSTICE?

## The conventional wisdom

There have been two main opinions in recent years about the relationship between the creation of wealth or income and its distribution. First, there are those who belittle the effects of taxation (and other forms of government interference) on incentives to work, save and take risks. These people assert that the volume and growth of activity are little affected by taxation, however high, and that in consequence the government can levy whatever taxes it pleases on income and capital without thereby reducing the taxable base. Second, there are those who believe incentives to be important and think that for this reason egalitarian fiscal policies, though desirable in themselves, should not be pushed too far. There is a "trade-off" between prosperity and justice; prosperity and justice are in conflict [1]. The two opinions differ only about the magnitude of incentive effects; and since these effects cannot be measured empirically (page 16), the argument between the two is condemned to futility. The argument between socialists and their opponents in recent years about the philosophy of taxation and its implications for policy has generally taken place within this conceptual framework. The public have become used to hearing socialists arguing from the side of equity and their opponents arguing from the side of economics; and they have learnt to believe that the two criteria conflict but that the importance of incentives can apparently never be proved in particular situations. Since conservatives and liberals have generally accepted their opponents' arguments about equity and equality, the socialists have won hands down with the results we see around us today [2].

The present book argues that the conventional wisdom is false as well as futile. Prosperity and justice are allies rather than enemies. This conclusion follows from a logical concept of prosperity and a logical concept of fairness [3]. Earlier chapters have explained how real but immaterial wealth can be created out of thin air if the process is not frustrated by the tax system. The present chapter discusses the relationship between wealth creation and equity, whether in an egalitarian sense or otherwise.

## Conflict and reconciliation

Distributive justice, equity and fairness may be taken as variants of the same idea. In economic literature and political discussion they are generally interpreted as having something to do with equality. But this is not the only sense of fairness; nor is it the sense most commonly found in everyday life. Moreover, "equality" may mean different and even contradictory things, some of which are the allies of fairness even if others are enemies.

Distributive justice in the egalitarian sense is a quality of distributive results, of distributions themselves. If "social justice" requires that A should not receive more than twice as much as B, this remains true however little work and saving may be done by B and however much by A. But there is an entirely different sense of distributive justice, real justice and not "social justice", in which the distribution is assessed by the relation it bears to the activities of the agents. The distribution of punishments is normally assessed like this, even if the distribution of rewards often is not. In this sense, if it is fair for A to be paid the same as B when he does the same amount of work, it is fair for him to be paid twice as much when he does twice as much work; gross-of-tax piece-rate payment conforms with this principle, but the income tax and "social security" systems bear no relation to it at all. Justice may be assessed in terms of results in matters of taxation and public finance; but it is arguably a false criterion even there, and it is a criterion accepted in hardly any other area of human activity [4].

Financial return according to activity may be interpreted as reward according to merit. This in turn may be held to imply that the President of the European Commission, with some £100,000 a year, is twenty times as meritorious as a junior employee with £5,000. But such Calvinistic arithmetic is difficult to swallow. The trouble is that it confuses economic merit with personal merit. These are distinct concepts, even though they overlap. The real argument is that in a free economy everyone is rewarded according to his economic usefulness to his fellows. The company chairman with £50,000 a year is ten times as useful as the employee with £5,000. This says little about the personal merits of either, just as the value of the work done by poets, artists and composers bears little relation to their merits as individuals. The private lives of artists are useful background to the interpretation of their works, not their assessment. But economic activity is a less personal matter than artistic creation; and the personal qualities of the agents, inside as well as outside working hours, are best left out of account altogether in assessing the economic value of what they do. Relevant personal qualities receive their economic reward and should not be counted twice; irrelevant personal qualities deserve no economic reward and should not be counted at all. The difficulty comes where the economy is not free, where the incomes in question are the salaries of nationalised industry chairmen, for example, or senior civil servants or the President of the European Commission. Arguments from economic freedom provide no justification for the salaries paid to these people; arguments from personal merit are even more difficult in the State sector than in the market economy (because in the State sector "personal merit" is not assessed through voluntary trading transactions but through operations backed by force or political skulduggery); and the principles justifying promotion in the State sector are of quite a different order — survival, Buggins's turn, old school tie, jobs for the boys, last in first out, you scratch my back, if you can't beat them join them, blood's thicker than water. These are the problems of socialism, not of a market economy, and concern the consumption of wealth, not its creation.

In a market economy the alleged conflict between justice and prosperity not merely disappears but is reversed: economic justice is distribution according to what each has contributed to prosperity. There is no conflict between prosperity and distributive justice in the sense of economic merit or economic freedom. But there may be a conflict between prosperity and distributive justice in the sense of equality, or rather in certain senses of equality: "equality" has its ambiguities, and these may even reverse the direction of the argument.

What does "equality" mean? Equality of what (income? wealth? expenditure? saving?)? Equality between whom (individuals? husband and wife treated as one individual? parents and minor children treated as one individual? tax penalty on marriage?)? Equality over how long (a day? a year? a period of years? a lifetime? eternity?)? Interplay of these different dimensions (for example, equality of income measured over one period, equality of transfers over another)? Equality measured how? (The measurement of equality is a technical question and different measures give different answers [5]).

The list of questions in the last paragraph is not exhaustive; it merely gives a few examples of the difficulties. But it indicates the ambiguities and logical complexities of equality as a principle informing fiscal policy [6]. Distributive justice between citizens and taxpayers is not an intuitive matter but complex and even ambiguous in direction; and this is true not only for the subject in general but even if distributive justice is construed in the narrow sense of egalitarian results.

Thus the pursuit of equality may be internally inconsistent; reducing the inequality of wealth may increase the inequality of expenditure and this must be so for present-day Britain. (Appendix III). But there is a related paradox for the inequality of income: reducing the inequality of income may reduce the income of everyone; this argument depends on the efficacy of incentives. The same argument applies more powerfully to the inequality of wealth: reducing the inequality of wealth may reduce both the income and the wealth of everyone; the argument depends not only on the efficacy of incentives but also on the concept of wealth.

Even for the poorest citizens there can be a sharp conflict between prosperity and equality: the more the equality, the less the prosperity. For wealth, the argument that equality reduces prosperity is true at all income levels: saving has no economic taxable capacity. (Chapter III, "The taxable capacity of saving").

57

Against all this, the old practice of raiding the monasteries has retained its appeal in modern form, now dignified with a social purpose by the concept of (financial) taxable capacity. Its appeal is its simplicity and the gratification it offers to envy. We have already noted (page 46) that taxation in accordance with ability to pay is deeply in conflict with prosperity, since the slogan can be used to justify any confiscation of income or capital [7]. The following sections explain why taxation based on ability to pay is also deeply in conflict with equity in important senses of that term, including even egalitarianism.

## The creation and distribution of wealth

"The wider distribution of wealth" is a phrase that can be interpreted in two opposite senses. In the first sense, which is also the common sense of the matter wealth is more widely distributed if there is more wealth and people now have wealth who had no wealth before; in this sense the distribution of wealth can become at the same time wider and more unequal. In the second or perverse sense, wealth is more widely distributed when it is more equally distributed even if there is less wealth in total and everyone has less than before. There are intermediate meanings of "the wider distribution of wealth" between these opposites.

In the first sense, the creation and wider distribution of wealth are different elements in the same process of creating wealth by the spread of ownership and by investment in second-hand goods. No one becomes worse off in this process (except through the emotion of envy). Wealth is created out of thin air by the operation of permanent saving which makes the same money work twice, once in use and once in ownership. Those without wealth become wealth owners for the first time either by purchase (because the increase in prosperity attracts new saving) or by donation (for example, through the gift of council houses to sitting tenants).

The process is different for investment in industrial assets. No new wealth is created by the act of investment itself. Wealth is created if the investment is profitable and destroyed if it is unprofitable. If the investment is profitable and new wealth is created, it is shared between shareholders, customers and employees by the normal operations of voluntary exchange in a free market. But for customers and employees this wealth is merely potential wealth in the form of lower prices and higher pay; it may be spent and never become wealth at all. Moreover, the benefits may not accrue to the workforce immediately; for example, they may become redundant through the introduction of labour-saving machinery. On both counts, the spread of ownership and investment in second-hand goods are superior to investment in industrial assets: wealth is necessarily distributed more widely and all the participants benefit immediately.

The thrust of British fiscal policy in recent years has been towards the second sense of "wider distribution" (less inequality at the expense of less wealth). Ownership has attracted special fiscal penalties like capital transfer tax; and the yield of taxes on ownership has not been redistributed to other citizens but spent by the government. "Productive" assets have received privileged treatment for capital transfer tax and income tax, even though they have a positive economic taxable capacity, which ownership and investment in "non-productive" assets have not. The thrust of fiscal policy has been in the wrong direction. The removal of tax obstacles to the creation of wealth by ownership and investment in second-hand goods also leads to its wider distribution in the common sense of this expression.

Finally, inequality has a number of different dimensions — earned income, investment income, wealth, new saving, consumption. The same policy that reduces inequality in one of these dimensions may increase it in another. In particular, any policy that seeks to reduce the inequality of wealth or investment income by increasing taxes at the top of the scale must in present-day Britain be expected to increase the inequality of expenditure. This is because taxes on investment income and its parent capital are so high at the top of the scale already that the only rational response to further increases in these taxes is capital consumption (spending out of capital): taxes on investment income and its parent capital become prohibitive over this range of income or wealth. Increases in these taxes make the distribution of wealth or income more equal but the distribution of expenditure more unequal; the creation of wealth is frustrated but the gap between living standards of rich and poor increases. By contrast, the tax policies that lead to similar patterns of spending between different income classes are policies that diminish or remove the present fiscal obstacles to the creation of wealth [8].

## Income and outgo

Income is the sum of investment income and income from earnings. Outgo is the sum of spending and saving. Income equals outgo in any period, since all income must be either spent or saved. The accounting identity between income and outgo is not affected by the addition of consumption out of the saving of past periods, because on the outgo side the same amount is subtracted from saving as is added to consumption. Thus on the outgo side the net new saving of each period is permanent unless it is drawn down later; and if net saving is positive in all periods, the new saving figures are in practice figures of saving in perpetuity [9].

The identity of income with outgo makes it possible to translate taxes on earning, on spending and on saving from one to the other. For example, a tax of 10 per cent on earnings is equivalent in its effects to a tax of 10 per cent on all spending and all saving financed out of earnings. A tax of 10 per cent on permanent saving may be levied either once-for-all on the original act of saving (the acquisition of the asset) or on the income in all subsequent periods [10]. There are similarities between this classification of taxes and the distinction between direct taxes and indirect: at least taxes on spending are indirect and taxes on saving are direct. But taxes on earnings are not pure direct taxes but a mixture of spending and saving taxes in which the spending element predominates. More generally, the classification into taxes on earning, spending and saving shows the logical relationships between them and the possibility of substituting one for another. It also indicates that there are only three degrees of freedom in a consistent system of personal taxation: the height of taxation, the relative taxation of spending and saving, and the pattern of tax graduation or proportionality [11]. Graduation can be taken only once — in earning, in spending or in saving: in other words, any tax pattern can be obtained by the graduation of one tax only; if more than one tax is graduated, the system is more complex and costly to administer, but no rational result is achieved which could not be achieved with a single graduated tax. Similarly, for any taxpayer at any level of income (or outgo) there is only one price (or rate of exchange) between spending and saving. Everything that is not spent is saved and everything that is not saved is spent. Saving and spending have a relative price in terms of each other, like the pound and the dollar, even though both may decline in purchasing power, like the pound and the dollar. If a 10 per cent tax is imposed on both spending and saving, the purchasing power of pre-tax money declines but the rate of exchange between the two is unaltered. If a 10 per cent tax is imposed on saving but not on spending, the purchasing power of pre-tax money declines for saving but not for spending and the rate of exchange between them alters.

It follows that any tax system which makes saving expensive makes spending cheap and any tax system which makes saving prohibitively expensive makes spending costless. This is the position for the rich in Britain at present. Saving at the top of the scale is prohibitively expensive and spending in consequence costs nothing. The rich man's spending costs him nothing in terms of opportunity cost, which is real economic cost; it costs him less than his own saving and less than the poor man's spending. This paradoxical and inequitable result is the consequence of a system that taxes saving (and earning) at graduated rates while the various components of expenditure taxation are all proportional to purchases [12].

If taxes on saving are cut right through the scale and top graduated rates are reduced, the rich man's saving is made cheaper but his spending is made relatively more expensive. This is a more equitable state of affairs. Indeed, graduation of expenditure taxes is more equitable or less inequitable than graduation of taxes on saving (or on earning, which is in effect a mixture of spending and saving). The target is then what the rich man takes out of the economy, not what he puts in, the wealth he consumes, not the wealth he creates.

For every taxpayer, at every level of income and wealth, there is a relative price or rate of exchange between spending and saving. This is the same for all taxpayers if the taxation of both spending and saving is proportional; it varies between taxpayers and between different slices of the same taxpayer's income or wealth or spending if taxation is graduated. It might seem at first sight that the system was neutral between spending and saving if the two were taxed at the same proportional rates — for example, 20 per cent on spending and 20 per cent on investment income [13]. But this is not so. It is true that taxes on saving fall only on saving and not on spending. But it is false that taxes on spending fall only on spending and not on saving. In a closed economy where emigration is impossible, taxes on spending are fully borne by saving. The value of saving is what it will buy, just like the value of spending: the value of saving is real spending power. If taxes on spending rise, savers lose as much as spenders. Increases in taxes on spending constitute a once-and-for-all tax on wealth, and reductions in taxes on spending generate a once-and-for-all capital gain. If emigration is possible, then in principle it provides a means of avoiding the burden of consumption taxes on saving; but most taxpayers do not emigrate or even consider emigrating, so that this is no more than a minor qualification (especially if emigration is more or less offset by immigration) [14].

It follows that there is no need for any tax on investment income or its parent capital in order to achieve neutrality of treatment between spending and saving. Whatever the taxation of spending, neutrality is most nearly achieved when there are no taxes on investment income and its parent capital. The achievement of neutrality between the taxation of earned income and investment income through the abolition of the investment income surcharge, although in present circumstances it would be a move in the right direction, is in principle irrelevant to the achievement of tax neutrality between spending and saving [15]: tax neutrality between spending and saving requires that taxes on investment income and its parent capital be abolished.

Not everyone may wish to have a tax system that is neutral between spending and saving; it is a matter of opinion. But our previous analysis enables us to identify the costs which departures from this neutrality impose. All taxes on the acquisition and ownership of non-productive assets destroy more wealth than they yield tax revenue. For ownership, this is because the benefits of private ownership are immaterial and additional to the benefits of use: if ownership is reduced by taxation or its extension is restricted, prosperity is reduced at a given level of national income (in other words, welfare is reduced at a given total output; output must be increased to compensate for the loss of welfare caused by the taxation of ownership); and the revenue yield cannot be spent by the State on goods and services without causing at least as much inflationary pressure as if the money had been printed rather than raised in taxation. For investment in second-hand goods, it is because each act of investment drives up the price not only of the asset purchased but of the whole existing stock; and every fiscal discouragement to investment has a gearing effect on the price of the whole stock as well as on the price of the items which are candidates for a marginal purchase. There is a large overlap between the taxation of investment in second-hand assets and the taxation of ownership as such, and similar considerations apply to both.

The argument holds good for the distinction between "productive" and "non-productive" assets if "productive" is taken to mean "productive of a money

61

income": money income from temporary saving has positive economic taxable capacity. ("Money income" here means money income as opposed to imputed income, like the rent from an owner-occupied house, not money income as opposed to inflation-adjusted income, which is the subject discussed under the heading "Inflation" in Chapter VII). The argument for not taxing the imputed income from owner-occupied houses is entirely separate, though in my opinion it is equally valid. An owner-occupied house is not "non-productive" in the same sense as a stamp collection. An owner-occupied house generates an annual imputed income (the rent otherwise payable) which is in principle a candidate for taxation and is in practice sometimes taxed. The argument for leaving the income from owner-occupation untaxed is not that it is not a tangible annual benefit nor that it has no economic taxable capacity but solely that it is not paid or received in cash. The distinction between cash payment and do-it-yourself by the household is a lifeline to economic sanity that should be grasped with both hands. If the imputed income from owner-occupation is taxed on the ground that the householder would otherwise have had to pay a taxable rent to a landlord, why should not his wife's imputed income from cooking be taxed on the ground that the family would otherwise have had to go to a restaurant? Why should not his work in his own garden be taxed on the ground that he would otherwise have had to employ a gardener? Similarly for home laundering, cleaning, mending, baby-sitting and the whole range of services normally provided without payment from within the household.

If non-income-producing assets that are "productive" in the sense of owner-occupied houses or furniture or apparatus are ignored for the reasons just explained, we are left with the distinction between "productive" assets like plant and machinery and "non-productive" assets like stamp collections. For reasons already explained (pages 51—53), "non-productive" assets in this sense have a negative economic taxable capacity; indeed, as is shown by the example on page 53, the destruction of wealth (the social loss) may be a large multiple of the gain to the fisc. But investment in "productive" assets in the sense of industrial assets has a positive economic taxable capacity. Taxes on these assets and the profits therefrom indeed reduce prosperity and welfare even if only in the sense of impelling people to work harder in order to attain the same level of money income; but this effect is exactly the same as that of an income tax on any employee. It diminishes his welfare; but it may or may not diminish the money value of his output. The similarity between industrial investment and the labour of employees is not accidental: both represent the creation of wealth by brute force, a subservience to the curse of Adam. There is not, and never has been, any superiority of industrial investment over the use of the finger nails as a means of creating wealth: either may be a success and either may be a failure. Economic wealth is created exclusively by profit: profit from labour or profit from wealth. Even if this profit can be assessed retrospectively, it is unknown and intangible prospectively: it cannot be taxed at the time decisions are taken, whether decisions to invest one's money or decisions to invest one's working time. True profit has no financial taxable capacity; if it yields tax revenue in practice, this is due to a breach of faith by the State, an element of retro-spection in the tax system, which is likely to be counterproductive for the future. Nor has ownership any economic taxable capacity. What has economic taxable capacity is sheer hard work and (its equivalent in terms of industrial hardware) investment in industrial assets and the return on this investment at the going rate. It is true that survival is a powerful motive: as the standard of living declines, for fiscal or other reasons, the taxpayer may be willing to work more or even save more in order to keep himself where he was. But this has nothing to do with the creation of wealth: it is the argument of a pharaoh wondering if he could build more pyramids by taxing his workers more or paying them less. This is not the most interesting question for the ordinary citizen and taxpayer: for him the most inte-resting question is whether he will be more prosperous, immediately and in the long term, under the one system or the other. Since the spender has a higher rate of discount than the saver, the interests of both are frustrated by the taxation of pure discount income: this is an attempt to tax ownership as such; it yields a modest return in so far as ownership is temporary, but it is necessarily counterproductive in so far as ownership is in perpetuity.

Some industrial pressure groups, like the Confederation of British Industry, have argued explicitly or implicitly for a distinction between "productive" and "non-productive" assets to the advantage of the former and the disadvantage of the latter. Our analysis shows that this distinction is exactly the opposite of what the public interest requires. There is of course nothing unusual, or even perhaps reprehensible, in a pressure group's promoting a sectional interest at the expense of the community; the irony here is that the sectional interests would gain rather than lose if instead of merely seeking privileges for assets of particular importance to themselves they broadened their horizons and achieved lower taxation of assets in general. If there were a justifiable distinction between productive and non-produc-tive assets, productive assets should be taxed more heavily, because they have a positive economic taxable capacity. But no such distinction can be sustained. The productivity of productive assets should be taxed, if at all, through their yield; no separate tax is required on the assets. The distinction that is useful in terms of equity and efficiency is not between productive and non-productive assets but between assets that are owned by individuals (capitalist assets) and assets that are owned by the State (socialist assets). Capitalist assets are more valuable than socialist assets: socialist assets are valuable once, in use, whereas capitalist assets are valuable twice, in use and in ownership. This principle is simply illustrated by the "historic houses" argument (page 40). It has been conceded even by spokesmen of the Labour Party that historic houses can be more cheaply maintained in private ownership than in the ownership of the State because private owners will do for love what hirelings would do only for money. The same principle applies to small firms. Pride of owner-ship is a cheap and efficient economic motive. Indeed, "cheap" is too weak a word:

63

ownership is costless. It is not an accident that even in communist countries small-scale private enterprise is generally permitted: the cost of state-run alternatives would be prohibitive. But the same principle applies, although to a lesser degree, to larger enterprises as well. Privately-owned unquoted companies have made a creditable showing in recent years by comparison with public companies, to say nothing of nationalised industries. Unquoted companies would be proportionately more important today were it not for the continuance over many years of tax policies specifically designed to make substantial private shareholdings difficult or impossible to maintain. Ownership creates wealth out of thin air; and the destruction and dilution of ownership destroy wealth without offering any compensating benefit. It is not only unquoted companies, but the population in general, that have lost from a tax regime hostile to private ownership beyond the level of a peasant plot or its Western equivalent. And similar considerations apply to public companies. It is thanks to "progressive" taxation that the influence of shareholders on the management of companies is so weak and the influence of employees [16] so strong. Hence the erosion of support for the limited liability company, which is still much the most efficient form of large-scale corporate organisation. The public interest is best served, not by coercive worker participation nor by increasing government interference, but by the maintenance and increase of private participation through voluntary ownership. Private ownership is costless to the rest of society; and the private owners have more interest in efficient management than any other effective owners or controllers, so that their supervisory functions are provided free — more accurately, at negative cost.

The Confederation of British Industry and other producer pressure groups would thus serve the general interest better if they abandoned special pleading for assets in which they are particularly interested ("productive" assets) and argued for lower taxation of assets in general. A change of policy in this direction would serve not only the general interest and the corporate interests of producer pressure groups but the private interests of their members as well (or at least those private interests which the spokesmen are paid to represent). Both the community and its richer members gain not only from a reduction in the taxation of ownership but also from a reduction in the preference accorded to "productive" over "non-productive" assets at any given level of taxation on ownership.

Income from labour and income from industrial assets should be distinguished from income from entrepreneurship and income from investment in "non-productive" second-hand goods. Income from labour and industrial assets has taxable capacity, if only from the taxpayer's instinct for survival and self-preservation. Income from entrepreneurship has no taxable capacity apart from its labour content, which may be negligible; income from investment in "non-productive" second-hand goods is intangible and its economic taxable capacity is negative. The conventional tax discrimination in favour of "productive" assets flies in the face of common sense: the "productive" assets enjoying favours may be destroyers rather than creators

64

of wealth; ownership and investment in "non-productive" second-hand goods, which cannot fail to create wealth, are the victims of fiscal discrimination. Similarly, it is by definition the "productive", not the "non-productive", assets that increase the inequality of income and expenditure.

If any alternative to taxes on expenditure is acceptable, the foregoing argument implies the superiority of taxes on (money) income over taxes on capital. Taxes on money income are vulnerable to the effects of inflation ("Inflation" in Chapter VII, below); but otherwise they are superior to taxes on capital at any given level of revenue yield. They are less arbitrary and more objective; they are less destructive of wealth creation; and they are less unjust. The least destructive taxes on enterprise and economic freedom are taxes on income (adjusted for inflation). All taxes on capital, capital gains and capital transfer should in the collective interest be replaced by taxes on income (adjusted for inflation). If any taxes on saving other than taxes on income are maintained, instead of being replaced by taxes on income, prosperity will be reduced, not only for the taxpayers in question but for the rest of the community as well [17].

## Once-for-all spending and sustainable spending

Appendix I argues that conventional concepts of wealth have the serious failing *inter alia* of representing as gains the losses caused by a fall in the rate of discount to all savers in perpetuity if taxes are levied on capital and to current savers in perpetuity even if no taxes are levied on capital.

An alternative concept is proposed in which wealth is a flow, not a stock, and is measured by the maximum level of spending per unit of time which it can support in perpetuity.

The substitution of the alternative for the conventional concepts approximates more nearly to the truth, first, by increasing the importance of capital relatively to labour as the means of defraying current expenditure and, second, by reducing the measure of inequality in the distribution of income and wealth. In particular, the wealth statistics of the Royal Commission on the Distribution of Income and Wealth were compiled on a basis which systematically and grossly exaggerated the inequality of its distribution [18].

## Labour and capital

The foregoing analysis can also be used to show where the interests of labour and capital coincide and where they conflict. They coincide in the extension of private ownership, both because workers become owners and because the surplus value created out of thin air by ownership can be shared with non-owners [19]. For the same reasons the interests coincide in the creation of wealth through investment in second-hand goods. The interests likewise coincide in the encouragement and increase of personal and corporate saving, since additions to saving make room for additions to consumption. Again, the interests coincide at national level in the avoidance of unprofitable investment; at the level of the firm the avoidance of unprofitable investment is a common interest if it is financed from private sources, although its acceptance may be a common interest if it is subsidised by the governement. The interests conflict temporarily in industrial investment, because resources are invested which might otherwise be used for additional consumption; this conflict is reconciled in time if the investment is profitable, because in a free economy the profits from voluntary exchange and collaboration are shared between the parties.

The leaders of organised labour have consistently worked against their members' interests as set out in the last paragraph. They have supported industrial investment financed by public subsidy, although these subsidies are largely paid for by their members and reduce their members' standard of living. They have been lukewarm or hostile to profitable investment because they have been lukewarm or hostile to profit. They have been generally hostile to the creation of wealth out of thin air and have supported the frustration of this process by taxation.

Trading profits are a form of earned income and have a positive taxable capacity like other forms of earnings. But the economic taxable capacity of pure ownership, saving in perpetuity, and investment in second-hand goods is negative: the more they are taxed, the less the wealth not only of the taxpayers in question but of the rest of the community as well. A policy that permits capital to be accumulated and capital ownership to be extended is as much in the interest of labour as of capital; reductions in taxes on capital and investment income would increase the living standards of the ordinary worker and consumer as well as those of the investor.

## Impact and incidence

Tax may not always lie where it strikes. It may be passed forward to customers or backwards to suppliers. Estate duty and capital transfer tax, which are levied on the testator or donor, may be borne by the beneficiary. Rates may be charged on the landlord but paid by the tenant. This is the distinction between impact and incidence. The impact of a tax is determined by the legal obligation to pay. The incidence is determined by the comparison between the situation with the tax and the situation without. This is the comparison of a real situation with a hypothetical situation. All such comparisons can be disputed, and there is much room for argument.

Wherever the real burden may lie in any particular situation, tax is always a barrier dividing donor from beneficiary, employer from employee, buyer from seller, customer from supplier. The concept of tax as a barrier is independent of both impact and incidence. A 20 per cent tax remains a 20 per cent barrier whether it is levied on buyer or seller (impact) and whether it is borne by buyer or seller (incidence). On the principle that voluntary trading is beneficial to both parties, it may be assumed that the burden of a tax is normally shared between the parties, in proportions varying from case to case.

The impact cost of a tax yielding £100 is £100 plus costs of collection. The incidence cost cannot be less than this and will generally be more, often many times more. It is possible for the burden on each party simultaneously to be many times the yield of the tax. The *excess burden* is reduced in so far as the tax system is *neutral*, that is, it taxes competing activities at similar rates [20].

It follows from the foregoing analysis that all taxes impose a burden on consumption: in general, saving has no positive economic taxable capacity, and taxes on earning are substitutes for taxes on spending and saving: thus ultimately, only spending has an independent economic taxable capacity [21]. Taxes on earning and saving have an incidence on spending as well.

At any given level of government spending on goods and services, the tax that does least to frustrate the creation of wealth is a tax at the same proportional rate on all consumer spending. Incidence is substantially confined to the area of impact. Excess burden is minimised. The ordinary worker and consumer gain if all taxation is levied on consumer spending, partly because consumer spending is taxed no more heavily than if taxes are levied on saving as well and partly because they are savers as well as consumers. The tax on earned income resembles a tax on consumer spending because a large proportion of earnings is spent. The real contrast is between the taxation of spending and the taxation of saving. Reductions in the taxation of saving impose no costs elsewhere, because in general saving has no positive economic taxable capacity. Reductions in the taxation of saving remove barriers to the creation of wealth and thus increase the prosperity of the consumer as well as the saver. The acceptability of these reductions depends on political considerations, not economic.

### The economics and equity of tax reduction

On economic grounds there is wide scope for tax reduction. No economic purpose is served by taxes on saving and there are no economic obstacles to their abolition, within a short period or even overnight. The obstacles, such as they are, are political. But for political obstacles, taxation could be levied solely on personal consumption: this is substantially the system in the USSR and East Europe, and it is a strong point of the communist system in comparison with the West. A tax on earnings may be used instead or in addition as a substitute for further taxation on personal spending, since much the greater part of earned income is spent; in particular, a graduated tax on earnings is easier to administer than a graduated tax on personal spending [22].

In a fully socialist system, where saving is prohibited, a graduated tax on earnings is equivalent to the same graduated tax on spending [23]. The graduation of tax on spending is the easiest form of graduation to justify, in terms of both economics and equity [24]. In a system where saving is permitted, graduated taxation of earnings and of spending are no longer equivalent: there are losses of efficiency and equity in graduating the taxation of spending indirectly, through the graduation of the tax on earnings. Graduation of the tax on earnings has the perverse effect in terms of equity that not only leisure but also spending becomes cheaper for the richer taxpayer than for the poorer when measured in opportunity cost (or real economic cost). The result is also perverse economically, since graduation of the tax on earnings increases the taxation of net saving, even though saving has no positive economic taxable capacity.

If the tax system is to be graduated, not proportional, and for administrative or other reasons the graduation is to be effected through the tax on earnings, not spending, it is at least a move in the right direction to abolish all taxes on saving (all taxes on investment income and its parent capital). Saving will still be fully taxed through the taxation of spending [25]; but the discrimination against saving will be limited to the graduation of the tax on earnings and not multiplied by additional taxes on capital and investment income [26].

There are similarities and differences between the taxation of saving and sumptuary taxation (the taxation of "luxuries" at higher rates than "necessaries" or "necessities"). The two are similar, firstly, because saving is a "luxury" in the technical sense of an outgo absorbing proportionately more net-of-tax income for rich than for poor, and, secondly, because the effective burden of taxation on luxuries and saving is heaviest, not at the top of the scale, but in the middle. A sumptuary tax on large cars, for example, makes little difference to the millionaire. He pays the tax by reducing or drawing down his savings; if saving is heavily taxed, the cost may be negligible [27]. The poor taxpayer is not directly affected, at least as a purchaser, because he is not in the market for large cars. The taxpayer who bears the heaviest burden is the man in the middle, who is prevented by the tax from buying the car [28]. The argument for saving, though not precisely analogous, is similar. The poor taxpayer is not a saver and is not, in that capacity, affected by taxes on saving. If the taxation of saving at the top of the scale is already confiscatory [29] (as in present-day Britain), the rich taxpayer is immune from further tax *increases*: you cannot be deader than dead. The taxpayer who bears the full weight of *increases* in taxes on saving is the man in the middle, who is prevented from saving by the *increase* in taxation. The differences between sumptuary taxation and the taxation of saving are, first, that the man in the middle is most affected by *absolute* levels of sumptuary taxes and by *increases* in taxes on saving, and, second, that luxuries use real resources and saving does not; this latter distinction suggests that sumptuary taxation should be more sharply [30] graduated than the taxation of saving (if graduation is acceptable at all), whereas in reality the taxation of saving is graduated very sharply (especially in Britain) and the taxation of spending very little.

Our discussion of fiscal politics has shown that the subject has its own logical structure connecting the different opinions of what is fair in personal taxation. The three principal dimensions of fiscal politics are the *height* of the tax system (the maximum rates of the various taxes); the *basis* of the system (the taxation of saving relatively to spending); and the *intension* of the system (graduation — the taxation of richer relatively to poorer). A method of measuring these political qualities of a tax system has been explained in detail elsewhere [31]. Height and basis are counterproductive for the creation of wealth: the higher the level of taxation and the more the bias against saving, the more the obstacles to wealth creation. For intension, the argument is the opposite: given the maximum rate of tax, wealth creation is frustrated less if there is a larger gap between the lower rates and the maximum than if the gap is smaller. But it would be unrealistic to allow for this difference arithmetically. If the top 1 per cent of taxpayers pay tax at 90 per cent and the rest pay at 40 per cent, it is unrealistic to argue that the 90 per cent rate is of negligible importance for the creation of wealth because it is paid by so few taxpayers: these taxpayers may have a potential for wealth creation far out of proportion to their numbers. So the numerical comparisons below (Chapter IX and Appendix IV) are confined to height and basis, in other words, to the levels of maximum tax rates and to the taxation of saving relatively to the taxation of spending.

Our analysis has shown a close connection between the economics and equity of tax reduction. There is little or no merit in the traditional idea of a conflict (or "trade-off") between prosperity and a single concept of equity, egalitarian and generally agreed. This is because there are a variety of opinions about what constitutes fairness in taxation, some of them not egalitarian at all [32]; and equality itself is a complex and not an intuitive concept, so that the same policy that reduces equality in one sense increases it in another [33]. The only irreconcilable conflict between prosperity and "equity" is the diametrical opposition of prosperity to the maxim of taxation in accordance with "ability to pay" (itself a variant of equality). This maxim is an unqualified licence to plunder, since it serves to justify any levy on the creation of wealth: whatever the State succeeds in seizing comes by definition from within the taxpayer's "taxable capacity" [34]. The damage done by the idea of "taxable capacity" is kept under some control because it is seldom taken seriously; other more substantial considerations determine when it is to be applied in practice and when it is not. These operative ideals of equity (freedom, reward according to contribution, wider distribution of property, even some conceptions of equality) are in harmony rather than conflict with the creation of wealth.

Although the relationship between justice and prosperity may be debatable for the creation of wealth by brute force (through earnings from labour and investment in new industrial assets), the relationship is clear for the creation of wealth through the extension of ownership and investment in second-hand goods. The wealth is distributed as it is created. The wealth created by uncompensated denationalisation (as in the gift of council houses to sitting tenants) lies where it strikes. The wealth created by investment in second-hand goods accrues in the first instance primarily to existing holders of comparable goods. Whether these policies further the "wider distribution of wealth" depends on the construction of the word "wide". Uncompensated denationalisation can be tailored to satisfy almost any sense of the word. Again, investment in second-hand goods need not make the distribution of wealth more unequal or even alter it at all. If a house or a plot of land or a stamp collection worth £ 100,000 rises in value to £ 200,000, it may be that other assets are rising comparably, or even that consumer prices and wages are rising comparably; if other assets are not rising comparably, prices of assets generally may be falling behind inflationary price rises or increases in living standards. Nothing in all this suggests that wealth is less widely distributed as a result of rises in the prices of second-hand goods; that would require a relatively high increase in the price of assets whose ownership is relatively unequally distributed. Criticisms of profits from ownership of second-hand assets such as land, buildings, Old Masters and coins are really a criticism of wealth creation itself: wealth creation is in principle neutral in its effect on the distribution of wealth (though in practice it will sometimes make the distribution more unequal and sometimes less unequal), and any attempts to transfer the wealth created from the taxpayer to the government destroy more wealth than they yield tax revenue.

The process of *trading* is in conflict with equality. Trading is a form of work. Not all workers are paid the same and not all traders are paid the same. In a free economy, the largest incomes go to those who are most economically effective, in other words, to those who create the most wealth. It is a different tale for the creation of wealth from *passive ownership* (the extension of ownership as such and investment in second-hand goods). The extension of ownership through government policy can be tailored to make the distribution of wealth less unequal or more. When the monasteries were nationalised by Henry VIII and then denationalised by donation to courtiers and landowners, it is likely that the beneficiaries of denationalisation were already wealthy above the average, so that the inequality of wealth was increased; no attention was paid to such arguments in those days, which may reflect well on their common sense by comparison with ours. If council houses are given to their tenants, the inequality of wealth may well be reduced. Which way the kite flies is a question of political power. But in either case wealth is created by uncompensated denationalisation, just as it was destroyed by the uncompensated nationalisation of the monasteries. When wealth is created by the other form of passive ownership, investment in second-hand goods, the effect on the inequality of wealth is in principle again neutral, just as it is for the extension of private ownership through denationalisation or tax reductions: the result may go either way, but here it depends more on the market and less on the government. Thus, the creation of wealth by trading creates inequality whereas the creation of wealth by the extension of ownership and investment in second-hand goods does not.

The emotional sympathies of the egalitarians have been back to front. Those who make money out of thin air have been regarded as parasites; those who make money by the sweat of their brow have not. This is doubly mistaken — both by egali-

70

tarian standards and otherwise. By the egalitarian criterion it is mistaken in general (although from time to time it can be true in the particular, and journalists and politicians have in this area of policy preferred the particular to the general). But by the more general and objective criterion of which citizen gains and which loses from the direction of government policy, the distinction between traders on the one hand and passive owners and investors on the other has been taken amiss. Trading, as a form of activity, imposes costs — demands for labour, for materials, for space. These costs have to be borne by the rest of the community, whether the trading is profitable or unprofitable and especially if it is unprofitable. Ownership, including ownership of second-hand goods, imposes no costs: it is pure gain; nothing has to be borne by the rest of the community.

In present tax policy there is a theme, often ham-handedly realised, of preferring the creation of wealth by brute force to its creation by less painful means. Hence the investment income surcharge; hence the capital gains tax; hence the capital transfer tax. Our analysis indicates that this distinction is misconceived, both by egalitarian criteria and also in the interest of the ordinary citizen. In an egalitarian sense, the distinction ought to be the other way round: income from earning and trading should be taxed more than income from passive investment (and "productive" assets should be taxed more than "non-productive" assets). In the more general sense of the ordinary citizen's interest, income from passive investment should be taxed less than income from trading because it makes no call on real (or scarce) resources.

We can ignore the alleged conflict between equality and prosperity. The egalitarian argument can be left to take care of itself, especially as the same policies that increase equality in some senses reduce it in others [35]. What remains is the sharp conflict between prosperity and socialism. The essential difference between socialism and capitalism is not the distribution of rewards from labour, including active trading: the tax systems of the communist countries are much more favourable to inequality than those of the West (page 67). The essential difference between socialism and capitalism is that capitalism permits, and socialism frustrates, the creation of wealth through the institution of ownership itself. It is indeed true that socialism may thus in a certain sense and in certain circumstances promote equality; but in other senses and other circumstances it may do the opposite. Socialism reduces the importance of ownership and may thus reduce inequality in total if it is empirically or even necessarily true that the inequality of wealth exceeds the inequality of income [36]. But this is a particular sense of "inequality", which has nothing to do with the ordinary sense, namely the inequality of living standards; indeed, when inequality of ownership increases, inequality of living standards declines [37]. And, whether socialism increases or reduces inequality in particular senses or circumstances, our analysis indicates that its assault on ownership must necessarily reduce prosperity. This is the subject of the next chapter.

CHAPTER V

# SOCIALISM AND INFLATION

Socialism and inflation, like taxation, are measures of government policy that may be supported on distributive grounds or even on grounds of efficiency. Socialism has been recommended as superior to taxation for the achievement of equality [1]; and its alleged contribution to economic efficiency has been among the grounds on which it has been supported from time to time, particularly in the nineteen-thirties — before there was as much evidence to the contrary as there is now. Inflation also has distributive consequences, though there has been less consensus about what they are; and the expropriation of debt ownership which it achieves has been recommended as an incentive to investment and growth. The purpose of this chapter is to compare taxation with socialism and inflation in their effects both on the creation of wealth and on its distribution.

## Taxation and socialism

There are two ways of extending socialism. One employs the armed force of the state to seize from private citizens without recompense property that the government wishes to keep or use for its own purposes. This was the method by which Henry VIII nationalised the monasteries and the communist governments of Russia and East Europe nationalised the religious and secular property which they expropriated. The second also employs the armed force of the state to effect the seizure, but it offers other assets in part exchange; these other assets cannot of course provide full recompense (otherwise the transaction could be voluntary and violence need not be used), so that the difference from the first method is one of degree and not of kind. The second was the method used by Ahab to nationalise Naboth's vineyard (I Kings XXI 2) and by British Labour Governments to nationalise such industries as gas, steel and electricity. The first may be called the communist method and the second the socialist method: the difference between communism and the "democratic" variants of socialism is one of degree, and the one shades into the other; what starts as exchange under pressure or expropriation with recompense (I Kings XXI 2) may finish as unrequited plunder (verses 15, 16).

Taxation provides one method of communist expropriation without recompense. Taxation is expropriatory in this sense when it cannot be defrayed out of trading profit or other current income; taxation that absorbs the majority of current income is like expropriation with small or derisory compensation. Thus taxation, like non-fiscal expropriation, varies from something bordering on a situation of voluntary exchange at one extreme to retrospective confiscation of capital at the other. At the top of the scale, where taxes multiply and rates of tax are highest, British taxation absorbs the whole of the current yield or more; the only difference from communism, one of little importance in the long term, is that the process of expropriation is spread out over a period of years instead of being carried through overnight.

In British politics the nominally non-socialist parties have strained at the gnat of nationalisation with recompense and swallowed the camel of uncompensated nationalisation through the tax system. This is the wrong way round. That is not to deny that "democratic" socialism is unjust and inefficient; but taxation is in both respects worse. The substitution of public for private industry diminishes wealth creation and economic and political freedom; but some of the industries taken into the State sector are large-scale industries where the feeling of private ownership is less personal and intense and where the destruction of wealth by nationalisation is more a matter of money than of political values. Most important of all, the destruction done is limited by the compensation paid. But taxation is by definition uncompensated; and it falls with especial weight where the excess of wealth destroyed over revenue raised is highest.

This argument does not apply to all taxes equally. Taxes levied at the same proportional rates on consumption and on income from labour and from manufacturing and other forms of trading are the State's cut out of current activity; like the extortion of protection money, they are damaging, but they need not be prohibitive. Business may be able to carry on, albeit on a smaller scale. In this sense, some taxes on trading profits may be less damaging than some forms of socialism, which annihilate these profits or turn them into losses. But, equally, some forms of a tax-ridden though nominally capitalist economy may be less just and efficient than some forms of socialism which combine nominal state ownership of industrial assets with devolution of economic decision-taking and liberal taxation of privately-owned assets. East Europe provides some useful precedents — for example, the liberal taxation of personal assets in the Soviet Union and the devolution of decision-taking in Yugoslavia. Each system should be judged on its merits item by item, irrespective of labels.

Taxation may be more or less damaging than socialism to the creation of wealth by brute force — by personal labour and industrial investment: this depends on

73

the form and degree of socialism and on the height and basis (the level and nature) of taxation. But taxation of wealth from "non-productive" assets is inevitably more damaging than any form of socialism with compensation, per million pounds of revenue yield or asset value: socialism with compensation leaves some positive amount, however small, whereas taxation of ownership and investment in second-hand goods destroys more wealth than it yields tax revenue.

The implications for tax policy are diametrically opposed to the conventional wisdom. There is indeed a valid distinction between making things and making money, between the creation of wealth by brute force and the creation of wealth effortlessly through the market economy; but it is drawn in the wrong place and in the wrong direction. Traditionally, a distinction is drawn between earned income and investment income in favour of the former. More properly considered, there is no logical relationship between earned income and investment income [2]; and the distinction between the creation of wealth by brute force and the creation of wealth through the operation of the market economy should for tax purposes be drawn in favour of the latter, since any tax raised from the capital values or capital gains of "non-productive" assets destroys more wealth than it yields tax revenue. Thus (1) the best tax system is levied only on personal consumption; (2) if tax is to be levied on anything other than personal consumption, it should be levied only on income from work; (3) if tax is to be levied on anything other than income from work, it should be levied only on income from investment and not on the parent capital; (4) if tax is to be levied on privately-owned capital other-wise than through the income it generates, any wealth tax, capital gains tax or capital transfer tax should discriminate against "productive" assets and in favour of "non-productive".

This fiscal programme might not be everyone's favourite. It would mean the abolition of taxes on income and capital; if any taxes on income or capital were retained, they would be taxes on income; if there were any discrimination within taxes on income and taxes on capital, it would be discrimination against the creation of wealth by brute force and in favour of its creation through the operation of the market economy.

The opposition to this programme is based, first, on a scepticism about incentives in general; second, on a neglect of the distinctions between different kinds of wealth creation; and third, on a refusal to accept the distributive consequences of wealth creation, whatever the cost of this refusal in wealth destroyed. The first of these cannot be confirmed or refuted empirically. (Page 16). The third is beyond cure if it represents pure relativist egalitarianism (a preference for equality even at the cost of prosperity forgone for every member of society); otherwise it is negotiable. The core of the argument is the second ground of opposition, which is apparently due to faulty analysis. Opposition to tax reductions may diminish if it is understood that they are costless or better than costless and that their creation of additional wealth is inseparable from its wider distribution.

74

## Wealth and liberty

Although the theme of this book is the destruction of wealth by taxation, the damage done by taxation is not confined to the destruction of wealth. The libertarian argument for tax cuts is independent of incentives. It reposes on something deeper — the harmfulness of government spending as such and of the forcible separation of the taxpayer from his money.

This is the difference between the libertarian position and supply-side economics [3]. Supply-side economics argues that wealth is destroyed because tax rates are too high: a reduction in tax rates would increase tax revenue as well as increasing wealth in general, and it is sometimes explicitly proposed that the increase in tax revenue should be used to increase government spending. For the libertarian, the increase in government spending would undo much or even all of the good done by the tax cut (not least because any increase in government spending is a spring-board for a further increase): the purpose of the tax cut is to reduce government involvement in the economy, and government spending is a form of government involvement. Similarly, the libertarian puts much more emphasis on the moral dimension of the argument, whereas the interest of the supply-side economist is primarily or entirely material. For the supply-side economist a tax reduction that had little or no effect on incentives would be a failure; for the libertarian it would still be a success because it necessarily reduces government economic involvement in general and in particular the compliance and other hidden costs of taxation [4].

The libertarian argument for tax cuts is stronger and wider than the argument from supply-side economics. All the supply-side arguments against high tax rates are compatible with the libertarian position; and in addition the libertarians have the advantage of a moral and political dimension of which supply-side economists have generally made little use.

The present book is libertarian in outlook, even though its subject matter is oriented towards supply-side economics (not least in Chapter IX), rather than towards moral and political arguments for lower taxes (about which I have written elsewhere [4]). I hope that the moral arguments which are not the subject of this book will be complemented by the material arguments which are.

## Taxation and inflation

Just as taxation is more socialist than socialism, so inflation can be more socialist than taxation. For saving in perpetuity, nationalisation without compensation does no more than is done by expropriatory taxes on assets and the income they generate ("expropriatory" taxes being defined in the sense of "confiscatory", as taxes the combined burden of which exceeds the yield, if any) [5]; and nationalisation is sometimes partially compensated. But inflation magnifies and distorts taxation itself; and, whereas nationalisation and taxation in kind cannot take more than

75

the value of the asset itself, the combination of taxation with inflation can take more in tax revenue than the whole real value of the investment income or capital gains that are the object of the tax. Inflation is thus an efficient engine of socialism.

The distributive effects of inflation have been widely misunderstood, and it is worth spelling them out. For earned income, graduation inflicts the heaviest losses at the top of the scale; the *addition* of inflation (the *combination* of inflation with a given graduated scale) inflicts the heaviest losses in the middle of the scale (where the ratio of marginal to average net income is lowest), because the taxpayers at the top of the scale lose most from graduated taxation *without* inflation and have correspondingly less to lose from the *combination* of inflation with a graduated schedule. For investment income, the argument is entirely different. The effect of inflation depends on the rate of tax, not on tax graduation. The higher the rate of tax, the higher the yield required to achieve a break-even real return of zero: for example, a price rise of 10 per cent a year requires a gross-of-tax yield of 20 per cent to break even if income tax is 50 per cent and of 50 per cent if income tax is 80 per cent. In the nineteen-seventies prices were often rising faster than even gross-of-tax yields so that taxation of investment income was expropriatory from top to bottom of the income scale and not merely at the top. Similarly, capital gains tax is systematically levied on nominal gains even when they represent real losses. Since the effect of inflation on investment income varies with the rate of tax, even if it is proportional, the combined effect of inflation and graduated taxation is most severe at the top of the scale where the rate of tax is highest: if the gross-of-tax yield is 25 per cent and prices are rising at 5 per cent, a 50 per cent rate of tax reduces real net income to $7\,{}^1/_2$ per cent and an 80 per cent rate reduces it to zero [6].

Thus inflation increases both the height of the tax system (the aggregate level of the maximum rates of tax) and its basis (the taxation of saving relatively to spending). Both of these processes are inimical to the creation of wealth, since they shift the burden from the taxation of what the taxpayer takes out of the economic system to what he puts in. The government is related to the private sector as debtor to creditor: inflation reduces the real value of debt and credit, which shifts wealth from the private sector to the government; and this shift of wealth represents its partial or total destruction, both because it is a shift from the productive sector to the dependent sector and because it reverses the process whereby the mere institution of private ownership creates wealth out of thin air.

Both taxation and inflation can make the creation of wealth not merely difficult but impossible and worse than impossible: in other words, they can make the destruction of wealth profitable [7]. If there is no inflation, taxation has this effect only at the top of the scale (though there alone it is damaging enough, since that is where the creation of wealth is concentrated). But inflation can have this effect even if there is no taxation; and if there is taxation the effect is intensified. For example, it has been easy since 1945 to save for years to buy a house and be further away from this achievement at the end of a decade or more than at the beginning, net-of-tax compound interest combined with an inflow of new saving year by year being insufficient to match the inflationary rise in house prices. This has been true even at the most modest income levels, where no income tax was payable; and income tax has aggravated the problem. For many people the only way to acquire a house has been to borrow much the greater part of the price. If inflation makes the creation of wealth through saving unprofitable, it must make the destruction of wealth through spending profitable; and this effect is aggravated by taxation.

A tax adjustment for inflation is no less requisite for the creation of wealth than the reduction of tax rates and of the taxation of saving relatively to spending. The Sandilands Committee considered this problem as it concerns manufacturing industry (the production of things) and recommended solutions whose benefits are confined to firms trading in things, as manufacturers or dealers, and to other firms only in so far as they use depreciable assets (fixed assets consumed by economic use, not financial assets wasted by monetary erosion) [8]. The present book is not the place to discuss whether the Sandilands formula can be adapted to accommodate financial assets; or whether it cannot and so another formula should be found for financial assets; or whether it cannot and so the Sandilands formula should be scrapped in the interest of uniformity of treatment between financial and real assets. But what emerges unmistakably from our analysis is that the correct inflationary adjustment against tax liability is not less important for monetary assets than real assets, but even more important. The damage done by the government to the creation of wealth through inflation and taxation is doubly destructive to monetary assets, to ownership and to investment in second-hand goods.

If all taxation on saving is levied in the form of income tax, and none in the form of tax on wealth, capital transfers and capital gains, no adjustment is required for "non-productive" assets in the sense of assets that yield no income stream; this is a major reason for taxing saving only through the income it yields. Income from monetary assets (including shares) should be adjusted for inflation, whether by deducting the rise in consumer prices from the yield or otherwise. Any capital taxes levied on either "productive" or "non-productive" assets should allow for a similar adjustment.

The need for inflationary adjustment reinforces our earlier preference for income taxation over the taxation of capital, if any form of taxation is considered desirable beyond the taxation of spending. (Page 74). If taxation is levied only on spending and income, there is no need for any distinction between productive and non-productive assets in the taxation of capital; and the need for inflationary adjustment in the taxation of income is confined to income-producing assets, where this adjustment is in any rational system indispensable.

CHAPTER VI

# THE BURDEN ON INDUSTRY

## Wealth and production

There are two different senses of "the creation of wealth". One is the production of consumer goods and services; the other is the creation of wealth proper, through the extension of ownership, investment in second-hand goods and enterprise in money and ideas. Investment in first-hand industrial assets resembles the former rather than the latter. "Living standards" may and "prosperity" does include the ownership of wealth as well as the level of consumption; if the value of wealth doubles while consumption remains unchanged, prosperity increases and living standards rise in the one sense but not in the other. Production for consumption raises living standards but does not permanently increase the ownership of wealth, since the wealth created by production is soon destroyed by consumption. Industrial assets resemble consumer goods rather than durable wealth; they are consumed over a period of years, and whether or not they create any wealth depends on whether or not they yield a profit [1].

There are two different senses of "industry" corresponding to the two different senses of "wealth creation". One is the creation of wealth by brute force — by manual or mental labour or by an increase in the level of investment. The other is the creation of wealth by ownership, enterprise and investment in second-hand goods.

## Rates of tax and tax take

The burden of tax may be measured in tax take (ratio of tax yield to national income) or in rates of tax. *The Camel's Back* explained how the burden varies qualitatively as well as quantitatively and pointed out the crudity of tax take (especially aggregate tax take) as a measure of the tax burden.

The three reasons why taxes do not always weigh the same per pound of tax revenue are, first, that they are not similarly perceived: taxes on income and capital are felt personally more than taxes on expenditure [2]; second, that taxes on income and capital are levied disproportionately on wealth creators; and, third, that tax avoidance, which imposes an *excess burden* on the creation of wealth [3], is caused by high tax rates, not tax take, and is therefore missed by the statistics of tax revenue.

The tax statistics in Chapter IX and Appendix IV start with comparisons of tax take and move on to comparisons of tax rates. The tax rates compared are maximum rates, which cause the most distortion and impose the heaviest excess burden of avoidance.

## Tax take and the burden on industry

Table 6 in *The Camel's Back* showed tax revenue including social-security contributions but excluding tax revenue from goods and services as a percentage of gross national product for 1972. This percentage is a measure of international competitiveness since taxes on goods and services (and only taxes on goods and services) are normally chargeable on imports and rebatable on exports. Table 4 below gives the corresponding figures for 1975, 1978 and 1979, which are discussed in Chapter IX and Appendix IV.

These figures offer a crude measure of international competitiveness, just as the ratio of aggregate taxation to national income offers a crude measure of the total tax burden. Both ignore the qualitative dimension: some taxes are more keenly felt than others, and these are the taxes with a disproportionate effect on the creation of wealth. Moreover, wealth is created by the intangibles of enterprise and ownership rather than by industrial brute force. When all this is taken into account, a more sensitive measure of the tax burden on industry is provided by the index of tax awareness in Table 11 of *The Camel's Back*, which excludes social-security contributions as well as taxes on general consumption but includes taxes on specific commodities. This is updated to 1979 in Table 4 below and is discussed in Chapter IX and Appendix IV.

The burden on industry is still more sensitively measured by maximum rates of tax instead of revenue yield. This is the procedure followed in the remainder of Chapter IX and Appendix IV.

## Earning and owning

The distinction between earning and owning or investing in second-hand goods is the distinction between the creation of wealth by brute force and its creation through the operations of the market economy. It is the distinction between trading and non-trading, between an active and a passive role in economic transactions. Earning and owning can both produce wealth; but the creation of wealth by production is closely connected with its destruction by spending, which the creation of wealth by ownership is not.

The distinction between trading and non-trading and between active and passive ownership has been expressed capriciously in British tax legislation, sometimes working in one direction and sometimes in the other. The distinction has mostly been drawn in favour of activity. Earned income has enjoyed "earned income relief" by comparison with investment income (or investment income has suffered an "investment income surcharge" by comparison with earned income). "Productive assets" have enjoyed reliefs from estate duty and capital transfer tax. Individuals with income from work or trading have been able to purchase pension income on preferential terms. But sometimes the discrimination is reversed. Business profits are exaggerated for tax purposes, and thus overtaxed, by the disallowance of expenses like entertainment, depreciation of commercial buildings and the costs known as "nothings" (pre-trading costs, abortive costs of mining exploration etc.). A gentlemen-versus-players distinction informs the tax treatment of occasional capital profits: they are taxed as income if they are of a trading character and at the more favorable capital-gains-tax rates if they are not. And in the measures providing relief from international double taxation, income from trade is sometimes treated better than income from portfolio investment and sometimes worse.

We have noted earlier (pages 46—47, 51—53) that there is indeed a distinction between income from work and benefits from ownership that is relevant for tax purposes. Income from work has positive economic taxable capacity: the tax collected can exceed the wealth destroyed, although this result becomes less likely as the rate of tax increases. The same holds good for temporary saving, like saving for a holiday or a pension, at rates of tax below a critical maximum, which may not be much above zero. But the economic taxable capacity of ownership itself is negative: and attempts to tax perpetual saving, ownership as such, the income from ownership and profit from investment in second-hand goods not only damage the effortless creation of wealth but also increase the cost of providing a given level of consumption by brute force, because taxes on passive ownership spill over into taxes on investment for later consumption. Similarly, enterprise (or entrepreneurship) has no taxable capacity, since the insurable value of enterprise at any time is nil.

The implication for tax policy is that there is indeed a valid distinction between active income from work and the passive benefits of ownership, to be drawn against the former and in favour of the latter, but that this has little to do with the haphazard and inconsistent distinctions drawn in practice at present. Positive economic taxable capacity is a characteristic only of personal consumption, and of income from trading and other work in so far as it constitutes an alternative means of levying on consumption. Earning and saving have no economic taxable capacity additional to the taxable capacity of consumption.

Although our main finding is that active wealth creation has positive economic taxable capacity, whereas passive ownership has not, tax is always and necessarily damaging to the creation of wealth, since it represents an artificial barrier between the creator and his achievement. The damage done increases as the rate of tax rises. The damage is done partly by the impoverishment of wealth producers and partly by the discouragement both to work and to investment; and the damage per million pounds of revenue yield is less to active investment in trading assets than to passive investment in ownership as such.

## The burden on enterprise

It was argued in the last section that enterprise (or entrepreneurship) has no taxable capacity, since the insurable value of enterprise at any time is nil. But the term "enterprise" has other meanings in which the pure concept of instantaneous and costless moneymaking by the exploitation of ideas is diluted with smaller or larger admixtures of brute force — waiting for investment income and working for earnings. An example is what was officially described as the "enterprise package" in the British Budget of March 1981 — a mixture of measures designed to make active trading less unattractive to small business than it would have been otherwise.

Since enterprise has no taxable capacity, the incidence of any taxes or tax reliefs aimed at enterprise is either on work or on saving. Heavy and graduated taxes on work and saving impede and frustrate enterprise; when this process goes so far as to have a major effect on employment, remedial action becomes attractive to politicians. Fiscal countermeasures may also be required to offset non-fiscal barriers to industry. ("Fiscal and non-fiscal barriers", Chapter VIII).

But no tax concessions are required for enterprise if there are no taxes on saving (investment income and its parent capital). Taxes on work are a minor obstacle to the creation of wealth, by comparison with their yield. There is a limit to what anyone can earn with his own two hands, a limit at present represented by the most successful professional people or entertainers: and the destruction of this income is the maximum damage that can be done per person by even confiscatory taxes on work. There is no limit to what anyone can earn as an entrepreneur; and taxes on work may be no great barrier to the realisation of this potential provided that taxes on saving are sufficiently low. Reductions in taxes on saving have more effect on incentives per million pounds of nominal revenue cost than reductions in taxes on work; the tax burden on industry is at bottom a tax on ownership, and the ultimate "enterprise package" is the abolition of taxes on saving.

## Enterprise and environment

The thrust of our argument is that the creation of wealth through enterprise and capitalism is preferable to its creation through brute force and that the clean and costless processes of the market should not be frustrated by taxation. The advantages of financial dealings for the participants are also advantages for third parties. It is therefore notable that the environmental lobby have missed this dimension of the argument entirely.

The environmentalists' attitude to non-monetary capitalist activity (and likewise to the industrial activity of State-owned concerns) is generally hostile. This hostility is often unavoidable: there are real clashes of interest between industry and its neighbours which cannot be avoided without a refinement and elaboration of the present system of property rights [4]. But financial business confers the advantages of capitalism without the offenses to eye, ear and nose that for non-financial business are often inevitable. This might suggest that environmentalists would favour financial as against non-financial methods of creating wealth. No such luck. The attitude of environmentalists to the creation of wealth has in general been wholly negative and destructive. Indeed, some of them are, in a paradoxical other capacity, among the sternest critics of making money out of money, even though any advantage of "financial" over "real" activities is the result of government economic intervention, fiscally or otherwise.

The logic of the environmentalist position implies a fiscal preference for passive over active investment income, and for investment income over earnings and for saving over spending; in practice, such environmentalists as interest themselves in these matters are generally on the wrong side and support the elements in the tax system that discriminate in the opposite direction.

The explanation of the paradox is partly shortsightedness but partly the constitutional inability of pressure groups to follow a remoter general interest in preference to a nearer particular interest, even when the general interest ultimately coincides with their own. Capitalism, as an institution serving the economy in general, is exposed to attack by every interested pressure group. What counts is often less the strength of argument than the ease of organising a lobby. Producers and consumerists are easier to organise than the consumers and savers who constitute the general interest.

Despite the confusion of the issue by the activities of pressure groups, the interest of the citizen as consumer, saver or environmentalist is best served by a system with a minimum of government involvement and a maximum exposure to external competition. Even if this principle is not carried to its logical conclusion of abolishing taxes on income and wealth, the environmentalist has good reasons for favouring a tax system which prefers passive to active investment income, investment income to earnings and saving to spending.

## CHAPTER VII

# THE BURDEN ON CORPORATIONS

## Tax take and tax rates

The tax burden on corporations is a narrower concept than the tax burden on industry. If personal investment companies are excluded, the tax burden on corporations is a burden on one form of trading entity; and trading is only one means of creating wealth.

Corporations are important because they are the principal form of large-scale trading entity in private hands and because trading is a principal means of creating wealth. Moreover, their attribute of legal personality is sometimes misinterpreted as implying an economic identity separate from that of natural persons: and it makes possible the subdivision of tax revenue statistics between revenue from income of individuals and revenue from income of corporations. The OECD statistics and the UK statistics both give this subdivision [1]. There is thus a temptation to use the distinction between corporate and individual income tax yield as though it corresponded to a distinction between yield from trading and from non-trading income or as though the yield from corporations represented the yield from productive activity or entrepreneurial wealth creation. Quite apart from the fact that there are many non-corporate entrepreneurs, the subdivision conveniently provided in the revenue statistics cannot be used for these purposes. First, the yield from taxes on trading income, whether paid by corporations or otherwise, is an ambiguous magnitude: if it is low, this may be because taxes are low or because profits are low, and similarly if it is high. This ambiguity is not characteristic of the yield from taxes on employment income, which is always a large proportion of national income. Second, the yield from corporate taxation is not a simple concept, but depends on the system of corporate taxation in force. (See below under the heading "The analysis of corporate tax structure"). If there is any form of relief from the economic double taxation of dividends, this relief may be shown in the corporate tax yield or the personal tax yield as a result of nominal differences in the tax system that are of little or no economic importance. Third, the statistics of tax revenue distinguish between tax yields from corporate and non-corporate income, although this distinction is of little economic significance; the economically significant distinction, which is not so often made in the statistics, is the distinction between income from individuals' earnings and income from individuals' investments [2].

For these reasons, statistics of the yield from corporation tax mean just that and cannot safely be interpreted to shed light on questions of greater economic significance. But the distinction between tax take and tax rates is once again to the point. The structure and level of corporate taxation are both a manageable and a significant subject of study: manageable for reasons explained in the next section and significant because economic decisions are determined not by average rates of tax but by maximum rates and what happens at the margin. Taxation can be a serious deterrent even if it yields little revenue [3]. This general proposition is especially apposite to corporate taxation. When corporate profits are too low to absorb tax-allowable expenses from investment, the real cost of investment to the taxpayer rises: and this phenomenon of "fiscal starvation" is intensified if the taxation of corporate profits is artificially divided into two streams, the withholding tax (advance corporation tax) on dividends and the residual tax on dividends and total tax on retentions, advance corporation tax being purposely made ineligible to absorb otherwise tax-allowable expenses. This is the situation in the United Kingdom: investment by a large proportion of manufacturing companies was being made much more expensive in the late nineteen-seventies and early nineteen eighties than was originally intended because the legislation was drafted to include unnecessary restrictions on the availability of advance corporation tax to absorb otherwise tax-allowable expenses [4].

It is worth noting in this connection that manufacturing and other industrial companies were in the early nineteen-eighties mostly paying no corporation tax (and the nationalised corporations were mostly operating at a loss). Such corporation tax as was still being paid was coming partly from financial and service concerns and partly from the withholding tax on dividends (withheld from the profit on the financial operation of shareholding). This provides empirical confirmation of the conclusion of the earlier analysis that there ought to be a fiscal preference for passive ownership over economic activity and for financial transactions over non-financial since wealth can be destroyed as well as created by investment in new real assets [5].

One reason why the taxation of profit income is economically destructive out of all proportion to its yield is the graduation of taxes as between different individuals and as between individuals and corporations. The principle that expenses are tax-deductible at the taxpayer's marginal rate ensures that the first effect of engaging an additional employee or sub-contractor is a reduction of tax liability (a charge on the Inland Revenue). The employee or sub-contractor is normally paying tax at a lower rate than the employer, whether individual or corporation; so the first effect of engaging staff or outside assistance in the United Kingdom is a reduction

84

in the tax bill of up to 60 per cent of the amount paid out in salary or fees. The Revenue may or may not ever see any of this money back again. The whole principle of making business expenses tax-deductible, which is economically neutral when the entrepreneur is paying the same rate of tax as his staff and sub-contractors, constitutes a gigantic haemorrhage in the normal situation where the entrepreneur is paying more. The damage done by the taxation of profit income should be measured, not by revenue yield, but by tax rates, as is explained in the next section. The foregoing argument gives the reason for concentrating on tax rates, which operate at the margin, rather than on intra-marginal differences such as variations in the tax treatment of depreciation.

## The analysis of corporate tax structure

The conventional classification of corporate tax systems divides them into classical, two-rate and tax-credit systems (variants of the last being known as imputation and *avoir fiscal* systems) and the integrated system of total imputation. The classical system levies the same rate on distributed and undistributed profits at the level of the corporation and gives no credit for this tax against the tax on dividends at the level of the shareholder; it is the system in the United States and the Netherlands, for example, and was the system in the United Kingdom from 1965 to 1972. The two-rate system gives no relief against dividend taxation at shareholder level for taxation at corporate level, but distributions are less heavily taxed at corporate level than retentions; this was until the end of 1976 the system in Federal Germany. The tax-credit, imputation and avoir-fiscal systems give no relief for dividends at the level of the corporation but allow credit for some of the tax paid at corporate level against tax chargeable on dividends received by the shareholder; this is the system in France and the United Kingdom and was the system in the United Kingdom before 1965. In the integrated system no tax is charged at the level of the corporation and both retained and distributed profits are taxed at shareholders' marginal income tax rates; as a variant, retained profits may be taxed at an average composite rate, rather than at rates varying with the circumstances of individual shareholders. In the imputation system the credit at the level of the shareholder is calculated as a proportion of the tax on the dividend, whereas in the French *avoir fiscal* system it is calculated as a proportion of the tax on the corporation.

The disadvantage of this classification is that it is nominal rather than real. A two-rate system may be equivalent to a tax-credit system in everything but name. A classical system may be almost identical with either. The differences of substance may be within the categories rather than between them.

An economically significant classification of corporate tax systems should start from the principle that they may include double taxation in up to three dimensions: double taxation of corporations as such; double taxation of dividends; double taxation of income from abroad. Double taxation of dividends is sometimes called "economic double taxation" to distinguish it from international double taxation; but double taxation of corporations as such is economic double taxation also. The three forms of double taxation are interrelated: if there is no double taxation of corporations there is no economic double taxation of dividends; if there is no economic double taxation of dividends, international double taxation is diminished or eliminated.

All corporate tax systems can be analysed numerically in terms of the three components (1) the definitive tax on distributed and undistributed profits at the level of the corporation; (2) the additional tax on undistributed profits; (3) the withholding tax on dividends. If (1) is zero, there is no double taxation of corporations as such and dividends are taxed under the system of total imputation. If (2) is zero, we have the classical system, which represents the maximum discrimination against dividends. If (2)=(3) we have a system neutral between distributions and retentions for shareholders whose marginal income tax rate is the same as the rate of withholding tax, as in the United Kingdom before 1965 and after 1972; higher-rate taxpayers are liable to additional taxation on their dividends and lower-rate taxpayers are entitled to a refund.

Appendix II analyses the principal systems of corporation tax in terms of these three variables [6]. The third paragraph of the appendix distinguishes between nominal and effective rates of corporation tax levied on dividends at the level of the corporation and translates from one to the other. In a two-rate or imputation system with neutrality between retained and distributed profits, the additional effective tax on undistributed profits and the withholding tax or tax credit on dividends are equal as a proportion of gross-of-tax profits (or as a proportion of the dividends gross of the withholding tax). Table 1 [7] analyses the corporate tax systems of the nine pre-1981 European Community Member States and nine other OECD countries at the start of 1981 in terms of these effective tax rates. Business tax, wealth tax, local taxes and church tax are excluded in part A of the table and included in part B.

Column (1) in Table 1 is both the nominal rate of corporation tax and the total tax on retained profits. Column (2) is both the discrimination against companies as such and the corporation tax on dividends as a proportion of pre-tax profits. Column (3) is the excess of column (1) over column (2) and is thus both the additional corporation tax on retentions and the relief from corporation tax on distributions, both as a proportion of pre-tax profits. Column (4) is column (3) as a proportion of dividends after deduction of tax at the level of the corporation but before deduction of tax at the level of the shareholder.

The discrimination against dividends as a proportion of dividends gross of the shareholder's income tax is the excess of the weighted average of marginal income tax rates on dividends over column (4). This discrimination is at a maximum under the classical system (where column (4) is zero) and is negative where column (4) is above the average rate of tax on dividends and zero where column (4) equals the average rate of income tax on dividends (which is approximately the situation in most of the other countries). This concept of discrimination against dividends at

# TABLE 1

Corporate tax structures of OECD countries 1981

Percentages

| | (1)<br>Nominal rate of<br>corporation tax | (2)<br>Corporate tax<br>on distributions | (3)<br>Additional cor-<br>porate tax on<br>retentions | (4)<br>Tax credit<br>or relief |
|---|---|---|---|---|
| A. Exclusive of business tax, wealth tax, local taxes, church tax | | | | |
| Belgium | 48.00 | 24.08 | 23.92 | 31.5 |
| Denmark | 40.00 | 31.00 | 9.00 | 13.0 |
| France | 50.00 | 25.00 | 25.00 | 33.3 |
| Germany | 56.00 | — | 56.00 | 56.0 |
| Ireland | 45.00 | 21.43 | 23.57 | 30.0 |
| Italy | 25.00 | — | 25.00 | 25.0 |
| Luxembourg | 40.00 | 40.00 | — | — |
| Netherlands | 48.00 | 48.00 | — | — |
| United Kingdom | 52.00 | 31.43 | 20.57 | 30.0 |
| B. Inclusive of business tax, wealth tax, local taxes, church tax | | | | |
| Austria | 71 | 71 | — | — |
| Belgium | 48 | 24.1 | 23.9 | 31.5 |
| Denmark | 40 | 31 | 9 | 13.0 |
| Finland | ·45 | 45 | — | — |
| France | 50 | 25 | 25 | 33.3 |
| Germany | 58 | 34 | 24 | 36.4 |
| Greece | 38 | 38 | — | — |
| Ireland | 45 | 21 | 24 | 30.0 |
| Italy | 36.3 | 15 | 21.3 | 25.0 |
| Luxembourg | 57 | 57 | — | — |
| Netherlands | 48 | 48 | — | — |
| Norway | 42 | 42 | — | — |
| Portugal | 40 | 50.8 | −10.8 | — |
| Spain | 33 | 23 | 10 | 13.0 |
| Sweden | 57 | 57 | — | — |
| Switzerland | 23 | 23 | — | — |
| United Kingdom | 52 | 31.4 | 20.6 | 30.0 |
| United States | 46 | 46 | — | — |

(1) = total tax on corporate retentions.

(2) = definitive dividend tax at the level of the corporation as a proportion of pre-tax profits.

(3) = corporate tax on retentions additional to corporate tax on distributions, both as a proportion of pre-tax profits; also = shareholder tax credit as a proportion of pre-tax profits. If negative, (3) = additional withholding tax on dividends.

(4) = tax on dividends at corporate level imputable as a credit to shareholders, as a proportion of dividends net of (2) above but gross of the credit itself.

$(1) = (2) + (3)$

$(4) = 100 \times (3) \div (100 - (2))$

Source: Part A of the table updates Table 7 of *Investment Incentives* for the nine members of the European Community; updating from *Supplementary Service to European Taxation* (International Bureau of Fiscal Documentation, Amsterdam), Section A (Corporate Tax Rates in Europe), March 1981. Part B is compiled from *The Taxation of Private Investment Income* (*Guides to European Taxation*, Volume III, International Bureau of

Fiscal Documentation, Amsterdam), taxation of cash dividends in the table "Dividends: Residents" in Section E for each country ("Effective total tax burden on dividends and interest"), Supplement 22, November 1980.

Notes: (1) The amount of 52 available for distribution in Belgium after deduction of 48 corporation tax is subject to withholding tax at 20 per cent, leaving 41.6. This 41.6 is accorded a credit of 57.5%, giving 23.92. The sum of 41.6 and 23.92 is 65.52, to which the withholding tax of 10.4 is added back, giving 75.92, which is the excess of 100 over the figure in column (2).

(2) The Portuguese system includes schedular taxes on dividends in addition to the taxes on all profits, both retained and distributed.

the level of the shareholder is to be distinguished from discrimination against dividends at the level of the corporation; it is the latter, with which we are primarily concerned, that is discussed in the following section.

By international standards, the United Kingdom *rate* of corporation tax is high, but not very high: at 52 per cent, it is some 14 per cent above the 17-country average of 45.47 per cent in Table 1B. What makes the United Kingdom corporation tax *structure* unusually high by international standards is the degree of discrimination against corporations as such, against dividends and against income from abroad.

## Three kinds of double taxation

### Discrimination against corporations as such

Table 1A, column (2), shows that the nine countries fall into three groups: Germany and Italy, where discrimination against corporations is zero; Luxembourg and the Netherlands, where the discrimination against dividends inherent in the classical system varies from 40 per cent of pre-tax profits to 48 per cent; and five countries with the imputation system, where the range of variation is from 21.43 to 31.43 per cent. Discrimination against corporations in the United Kingdom is higher than in any of the other countries with relief from economic double taxation of dividends. Table 1B shows similarly that after business tax, wealth tax, local taxes and church tax have been included, the discrimination against the corporation as such is higher in the United Kingdom than in any of the other countries with relief from economic double taxation of dividends except for Germany.

### Discrimination against dividends

Discrimination against dividends as a proportion of pre-tax profits is maximised when columns (1) and (2) of Table 1 are equal and columns (3) and (4) are zero; it is minimised when column (2) is zero and columns (1), (3) and (4) are equal. A measure of this discrimination with a minimum of zero and a maximum of unity is thus provided by the ratio of column (2) to column (1): whereas column (2) gives discrimination against corporations as such, the ratio of column (2) to column (1) gives discrimination against dividends. Discrimination against dividends may therefore be low either because column (2) is low or because column (1) is high.

The United Kingdom is in a better position than the five countries with classical systems, which by definition have discrimination against dividends of 100 per cent. Among the other countries only Denmark and Spain have more discrimination against dividends than the United Kingdom; and that is entirely due to their nominal rates of corporation tax, at 40 and 33 per cent respectively, being so much lower.

### Discrimination against income from abroad

International double taxation is a more complex matter than the two previous forms of discrimination and is not directly represented in Table 1. Under the principle of fiscal imperialism by which the fisc in the country of residence seeks to levy on residents' foreign income, income taxed abroad is still fully taxable at home unless there is some form of relief from international double taxation. Combined taxation can approach or even exceed 100 per cent of income: for example, if foreign tax is 50 and domestic tax is 55, combined tax is 105 on gross-of-tax income of 100. There are three main methods of improving on this situation. The first is the *deduction* method: home tax (at 55 per cent) is levied on foreign income (100) after deduction of foreign tax (50). But tax is still $77^1/_2$ ($= 50 + 55 \times .50$) which is far in excess of either foreign tax (50) or home tax (55). The second method, the *tax credit* method, is an improvement. Foreign tax paid (50) is deducted from domestic tax payable (55), so that the net tax due at home is only 5. This method has the disadvantage that tax is always charged at the higher of the two rates, home and foreign; it is not neutral but represents a barrier to international investment by comparison with domestic investment in either country. The third method, the *exemption* method, charges no domestic tax on foreign income; this method removes the tax barrier to international investment by providing neutrality between international investment and domestic investment in either country [8]. This result is impaired if exemption is granted only under *réserve de progressivité*, in other words, if the foreign income, though not taxed as such, is taken into the taxpayer's domestic tax base, thus causing his domestic income to be taxed at higher graduated rates [9]; neutrality is fully realised if exemption is granted without *réserve de progressivité* or under the territorial principle which makes exemption unnecessary because the pretensions of the fisc never extend beyond domestic income.

The barrier to international investment represented by any system other than exemption without *réserve de progressivité* (or the territorial principle of confining the claims of the fisc to domestic income and not extending its pretensions to worldwide income) is the combined result of the *height* of taxation and the *difference* between the rates in the two countries. For the tax credit method of relief from international double taxation I have explained elsewhere an algebraic method of analysing the *yield variance* (the attractiveness of domestic relatively to foreign investment due to taxation) as the sum of the *tax variance* (the difference between home and foreign tax rates, as defined) and the *height factor* (the level of tax at home and abroad, as defined) [10].

*The discrimination against income from abroad in the United Kingdom tax system is narrow but intense.* It interplays with discrimination against corporations and against dividends. In so far as United Kingdom companies retain profits instead of distributing them, they are indifferent between foreign rates of tax up to the United Kingdom rate of 52 per cent (unless tax-sparing (tax-exemption) articles have been inserted in the relevant double-tax treaties). In so far as profits are distributed instead of being retained, United Kingdom companies with interests abroad gain relatively to their domestic competitors from an increase in the rate of United Kingdom tax on corporations as such up to the level at which they have paid tax abroad. I have provided elswhere an algebraic analysis of United Kingdom tax prejudice on income from abroad [11]. Discrimination is most intense against companies with relatively little domestic income, facing high tax rates abroad and distributing a large proportion of their income: and oil companies operating in the seas around Britain are subjected to additional discrimination by the Petroleum Revenue Tax [12]. The more liberal system prevailing before 1965 permitted credit for taxes paid abroad to be carried through to dividends. The present system is a fiscal barrier to international business and his little or no economic justification. The only argument in its favour is that it satisfies certain non-economic standards of fiscal propriety that are favoured by senior Inland Revenue officials; and the dissatisfaction of these officials would be a small price to pay for the introduction of a system that was both more just and more economic than the system in force today [13].

Short of the territorial principle (or exemption without *réserve de progressivité*), any method of relief from international double taxation is more effective if it is multilateral rather than merely bilateral. The European Community draft directive on company taxation of 23 July 1975 (COM (75) 392 final) gives some recognition to the multilateral principle between member states, but it is mostly of an administrative character. The lopsidedness of the tax-credit method of relief from international double taxation is maintained in full: if the tax credit from the country of source is less than the tax chargeable in the country of the taxpayer's residence, a supplementary tax is levied by the latter country, but in the contrary case there is no refund. Likewise, dealings with third countries are still bilateral [14].

### Investment incentives

Investment incentives are negative taxation. Just as discrimination against corporations, dividends and income from abroad represents a burden on corporations and thus on industry, investment incentives are an alleviation of this burden.

It is sometimes suggested that investment incentives are a "tax expenditure", a subsidy by comparison with the tax that would have been levied otherwise. The

90

standard of comparison is the "normal" pattern of taxation, if indeed this norm can be identified.

It has been argued elsewhere that this approach to the subject is misleading [15]. Even if a "normal" pattern of taxation is identifiable, it may have little or no economic significance. The "norm" may incorporate discouragements to investment which the "investment incentives" do no more than partially redress.

The economic and indeed the political significance of investment incentives can be assessed only against the background of the discouragements to investment inherent in the rest of the tax system. It is shown in Chapter IX that these discouragements, which affect individuals as much as corporations, are exceptionally severe in the United Kingdom.

## Inflation

Corporations are a narrower interest than traders and a much narrower interest than industry as a whole. For example, the temporary tax relief on stock appreciation introduced in the United Kingdom in November 1974 was confined to companies and was thus an offset to the taxation of companies as such. But it was not an offset to the taxation of industry. On the contrary, any advantage obtained by companies was relative to the position of individual traders and non-trading individual investors. A tax advantage of this kind has little or nothing to do with the encouragement or even the toleration of industry in the sense of effort, risk-taking and saving by comparison with idleness, security and spending.

Inflation adjustments should not be confined to companies or even to traders. There is no relevant boundary between companies and non-corporate traders nor between traders and private individuals. Any concessions to companies or traders that are not extended to individuals or non-traders merely distort economic activity into corporate or trading form.

This principle is not confined to inflation. If there is to be any distinction between corporate and non-corporate income, it should be to the advantage of the latter (as it is under corporation tax). If there is to be any distinction between trading and non-trading income, it should be to the advantage of the latter (as it is for purposes of the distinction between income tax and capital gains tax, although the advantage is in the opposite direction for purposes of capital transfer tax). Passive investment income deserves an advantage over active investment income, first, because it involves no use of real resources, and, second, because it provides no taxable object in the form of work. If work is not regarded as offering additional taxable capacity, and all taxation is levied on the outgo side (on spending and saving), the case for discriminating against work and effort disappears; but the case for treating investment by non-trading individuals no worse than investment by corporate and individual traders is still equally strong.

It is individual, non-trading investors who create wealth out of thin air. Paper investors use no resources and bear all their own risks. Investors in fixed assets (machinery and buildings) use real resources, and it is reasonable that they should be taxed on the use of these resources at rates similar to those levied on private consumption. What happens in practice is the opposite of what is just and economic. Investors are taxed on what they put into the economy, not on what they take out. Taxation of income and profits is higher than taxation of spending. Even if there were no inflation, the efficient use of real resources is penalised by a much higher rate of tax on business profits than on private consumption. Similarly for the contrast between fixed and paper assets. The investor in fixed assets whose mistakes destroy real resources, enjoys an inflation adjustment; the paper investor, whose mistakes diminish only his own paper assets, does not.

An economic tax system would favour paper investment by comparison with investment in fixed assets (because it uses no real resources) and non-trading income by comparison with trading income (for the same reason and perhaps additionally because trading income is regarded as a form of earned income and earned income is considered to be taxable as such). The present United Kingdom system favours real relatively to paper investment and, for purposes of capital transfer tax, trading relatively to non-trading assets. The biases in the United Kingdom tax system are discussed in Chapter IX. With or without inflation, the fiscal penalisation of individual non-trading savers in the United Kingdom by comparison both with individual spenders and with individual and corporate traders has served to frustrate and prevent the effortless creation of wealth that only capitalism can offer.

## CHAPTER VIII

# CONFLICT AND HARMONY

The last two chapters discussed the burden on industry and the burden on corporations. The next two will discuss the current arithmetic of taxation and the policy implications of the whole analysis. The present chapter discusses the gains and losses from the present situation as compared with a system less burdensome to corporations and industry in general. Which interests are in harmony with a system less burdensome to industry and which are in conflict?

## Fiscal and non-fiscal barriers

We start from the position that taxation destroys wealth or hinders its creation by interposing a barrier between one free agent and another. This proposition is quite general and is true even of a minimal state whose functions are confined to defence, law and order. Taxation is in itself a destroyer [1], even though a certain minimum of taxation is unavoidable. A certain minimum is unavoidable if some form of state is preferable to anarchy. Economically, taxation is always an evil, even if it is a necessary evil. Wealth is created by dealings between free agents; and taxation keeps them apart. If the marginal rate of income tax is 50 per cent, for example, the taxpayer must be twice as productive in paid employment or self-employment as in his own house or garden in order to surmount the fiscal barrier; if he is less than twice as productive, he is better off at home. If the tax rate is 80 per cent, he must be five times as productive in paid work as in his own demesne. Wealth is destroyed whenever these high barriers prove insurmountable. Para-fiscal charges like "national insurance" or "social-security" contributions are, pound for pound, as much a barrier as taxation.

But taxation is not the only form of government intervention by which wealth is destroyed. The argument applies equally to any other form of legislation or administrative action which prevents or impedes voluntary dealings between free agents. Incomes policies, prices and dividends policies and a mass of legislation prescribing conditions of employment come under this category. So does interference with private "monopolies", in the sense of firms with significant shares of a market, even though these shares may be relatively modest and fully exposed to international competition. If two "monopolies" charge the same price, they may be accused of collusion; if they charge different prices, the more profitable may be accused of profiteering and the less profitable of inefficiency. No large firm is safe from official harassment when "monopoly policy" is based on these comprehensive and contradictory principles.

The damage done by intervention may be partially offset by the provision of subsidies, in cash or in kind. Although subsidies are not costless and have to be paid for by taxpayers in general, £1 m. spent on subsidies to industry may be less destructive of wealth than £1 m. spent on subsidies to consumers. But the distinction goes further. A subsidy to consumers is an unrequited payment which ends where it begins. A subsidy to producers need not be so: it is less destructive of wealth if it incorporates an element of self-help. The producers who need subsidisation most, in the sense of being most dependent on the subsidy, are the ones who use it least economically; a given sum in subsidy is expended most economically if it is paid disproportionately to the producers who do most to help themselves. The principle of economy is directly opposed to that of need. The marginal firm, whose needs are least, will use a given subsidy more economically than the firm at death's door whose situation is the most desperate. The argument is general and holds good for subsidies both to current and to capital costs; I have explained its application to capital costs more fully elsewhere [2]. As long as subsidies are provided for ailing firms as such, the application of market principles to the subsidy would at least limit the damage. At present, ailing firms are subsidised on one or other of the opposite principles of paying where the need is greatest or paying where there is most hope of an economic return. Economically, the subsidies might as well be decided by lottery; the real determinants are political, from the level of the individual Parliamentary constituency upwards.

## Purpose versus outcome

Fiscal and non-fiscal obstacles to industry are intended to confer a benefit on someone else. Explicitly or implicitly, the idea is always that if industry produces less by reason of government interference, the loss to society from this destruction of wealth is more than compensated by the gains enuring to consumers or workers.

This is not necessarily unreasonable. The maximum creation of wealth may not be the highest value for all purposes. For individuals, human or even animal, the relief of need and the alleviation of distress have a cogency which they entirely lack for legal entities like companies. Government interference is damaging to the crea-

94

tion of wealth; the interesting question is therefore whether, and what, benefits are obtained from this process by sentient individuals.

It is generally doubtful whether the alleged beneficiaries of government intervention gain rather than lose. "Progressive" taxation may yield less revenue than if the higher rates of tax were reduced [3]. Minimum wage legislation prevents the weakest members of the workforce from finding jobs. There is also the distinction between the short term and the long [4]. In the short term "job protection" may create a benefit for existing employees at the expense of their employers; in the long term the existing employees all die or retire and the losers are not merely the employers but the employees whom the employers would have taken on but for "job protection". Similarly and a fortiori for rent control. The losses of existing landlords are capitalised and the landlords gradually disappear from the scene; in the long term the cost of rent control is largely borne by frustrated tenants (potential tenants who are prevented from obtaining accommodation by the legislative barrier between tenant and landlord).

It is not only governments who can devise policies which defy the proverb and blow no good to anyone. If sufficiently ill directed, private organisations can inflict losses both on their members and on the rest of society. The Confederation of British Industry's price initiative of 1971—72, under which members were inveigled into holding their prices down, not only incited the monetary profligacy which followed and thus helped to start the runaway inflation of the following years; it also instigated and authorised all the subsequent price controls, from which consumers lost no less than producers. (Price controls soon fall on consumers and potential consumers, just as rent controls fall on potential tenants.) Subsequent governments of both Parties were able to argue: how can industry object to our intensifying and perpetuating price controls when they brought in the first round of controls themselves? This example shows how industry can come under attack not only from its adversaries but also from its nominal representatives [5].

## Conflict and harmony

### Tax producers and tax consumers

The primary conflict of interest is between tax producers and tax consumers (or *tax eaters*, in William Cobbett's graphic phrase from *Rural Rides*). Tax producers are those whose compulsory payments to the State exceed their gratuitous receipts from the State; there is little ambiguity in this definition within a given year, even though a taxpayer might move in or out of this category over a period of years. Direct tax consumers are officials whose incomes come from taxes (from levies exacted by the sword); officials must, in that capacity, be tax consumers (although they might be net tax producers if they had other sources of income, for example from investments). Indirect tax consumers are citizens or firms receiving more in gratuitous handouts from the state than they contribute in taxes.

Officials performing hard-core government functions, such as those of the armed forces, the police and the judiciary, are not tax consumers to the same degree (if at all) as the miscellaneous tribe of bureaucrats, official advisers, experts and other gold-diggers.

Thus, although there is in principle a conflict of interest between tax producers and tax consumers, this need not mean that tax producers are discontent. Taxes might be used with the agreement of tax producers, for example, to defend the country from external threat or to support victims of catastrophic illnesses; tax producers might judge that taxes had been efficiently and economically spent for these purposes. But such acceptance by tax producers is a logical extreme. There is generally likely to be disagreement about both policy and administration; and taxes are not voluntary contributions but forced levies. So there is generally in practice a conflict of interest between tax producers on the one hand and officials and indirect tax beneficiaries on the other. To put the same point another way, tax producers produce taxes by their own efforts and at their own risk; tax consumers consume taxes whether the policies concerned are well-conceived or ill-conceived or even counterproductive, and whether their administration is efficient or inefficient.

### Spenders versus savers?

Here the situation is the opposite. There is harmony, not conflict, between spenders and savers. The capitalist principle of saving makes money work twice. The saver postpones his call on resources and leaves more for spending. At any given level of government expenditure or productive investment, the more the saving of the saver, the more the spending of the spender [6]. Each contributes to the prosperity of the other. Conventional doctrine is exactly the opposite, namely that capitalist and wage-earner are competitors in the distribution of a given quantity. The reason why conventional doctrine has been diametrically wrong on this central question is that it has ignored the critical distinction between temporary and permanent saving [7]. Permanent saving creates wealth; but its economic taxable capacity is negative.

The same holds good not only in total but also by income group. An increase in saving benefits the poor as well as the rich. Appendix III shows that any tax that is proportional or "progressive" on saving is "regressive" both on spending and in general; in other words, both the inequality of spending and inequality in general are increased by any proportional (and *a fortiori* any graduated) tax on saving [8]. And if taxes on saving are effective in reducing the inequality of wealth, non-savers as well as savers lose from the reduction of general prosperity.

### Spenders versus earners?

There are two differences between *spenders versus savers* and *spenders versus earners*. The first difference is real: it is that earnings are partly spent and partly saved, so that the distinction between spenders and savers is reproduced in diluted form in the distinction between spenders and earners; the foregoing arguments about the harmony of interest between spenders and savers apply similarly to spenders and earners, though in a lesser degree. The second difference is merely apparent: if there are no savings out of earned income, the distinction between the taxation of earnings and the taxation of spending disappears, whether the taxation is proportional or graduated. If there is no new saving out of earnings, leisure and idleness are subsidised just as much by taxation whether tax is levied on earnings or on spending. The conventional distinction between direct and indirect taxes on earnings is valid only in so far as saving is taxed at different rates from spending. If spending and saving are taxed similarly, or if there is no new saving, direct and indirect taxation of earnings are equivalent. The conventional distinction, by contrast, has treated these equivalents as though they were different and has paid little attention to the essential distinction between the taxation of spending and the taxation of saving.

*Rich versus poor?*

Our analysis has shown three separate ways in which the poor (as well as the rich) lose from "progressive" taxation (taxation of savings and graduated taxation in general):— (1) The poor lose from the reduction of incentives (the increase in the barrier between saving or earning and spending). (2) The poor lose from any tax on saving because it increases the burden on spending[9]. (3) The poor lose relatively as well as absolutely because the inequality of spending and inequality in general are increased by any proportional or graduated tax on saving. (Appendix III). By contrast, there is one way in which the poor may gain from "progressive" taxation. This is through graduated taxation of expenditure: even after allowing for costs of administration (direct tax consumption) and effects on incentives, it is possible that the poor may gain rather than lose (even though the gains of the poor are necessarily less than the losses of the rich). This outcome is the less likely if tax graduation is applied to earnings rather than expenditure. Earnings exceed expenditure by the amount of new saving out of earnings; graduated taxation of earnings is disproportionately burdensome on new saving, and the taxation of saving has in general no economic taxable capacity[10].

*Government versus people?*

We have seen that there is a conflict of interest between tax producers and tax consumers; harmony between spenders and savers and between spenders and earners; and harmony between rich and poor, with the important qualification that the poor can in principle gain (subject to deduction of administrative expenses and losses due to destruction of incentives) from graduated taxation of spending; the poor can gain from graduated taxation of earnings only if any gains from the graduated taxation of spending are not offset by any losses from the taxation of saving inherent in the taxation of earnings. The scope for the government to aid the poor by raiding the rich is thus at best limited and at worst negative; at best the poor may gain and at worst everyone will lose. For those interested in distributive conflicts, a more promising line of enquiry is, not *saver versus spender* or *rich versus poor*, but *government versus people*. This conflict embraces (1) unavoidable administrative costs, (2) administrative inefficiency, (3) ill-considered policy aims or conflict of aims, (4) destruction of wealth through adverse effects on incentives, (5) destruction of wealth through diminution of permanent saving, (6) empire building by government agencies at the expense of private individuals. These conflicts between government and citizen are far and away more substantial than any conflicts between one group of citizens and another, however much the present conventional wisdom may assert the opposite.

Industry is under attack not so much from its nominal adversaries or even its own spokesmen as from governments of both Parties, even when government policies enjoy widespread support. Proudhon proposed a third as the maximum of the government's tax take: "Toute famille qui devrait payer, pour sa quote-part des frais d'Etat, un quart ou un tiers de son revenue, pourrait se dire pressurée; mieux vaudrait, comme en certaines localités de l'Amérique, courir le risque de l'anarchie" [11]. More recently, Colin Clark has suggested "that the level of budgetary expenditure acts by a more or less automatic procedure, as the final determinant of the value of money, the cause taking perhaps two or three years to work out its full effect" and "that the critical limit of taxation is about 25% of the national income, or possibly rather less" [12].

The next chapter and Appendix IV give an indication of how far the limit of a quarter has been exceeded both in Britain and elsewhere [13]. And the figures do not show the full extent of the damage, since they give taxation, not government expenditure, and thus ignore inflationary deficit financing. But the figures do illustrate an additional dimension, namely how far the tax burden has been concentrated on industry (through tax graduation and taxes on saving and earnings) instead of being broadly spread through proportional taxes on consumption. By this criterion industry is under fiercer attack in Britain than anywhere else in the developed world [14].

## CHAPTER IX

# THE TAXATION OF INDUSTRY QUANTIFIED

This chapter and Appendices IV and V show in figures what the argument of previous chapters means for Britain and for the British economy. Limitations of space preclude a detailed international comparison here; readers who wish to do o can refer for definitions and further explanations to the sources cited. *(The Camel's Back* and *Short Measure from Whitehall* [1]).

## The Camel's Back **and subsequent changes**

In *The Camel's Back: An International Comparison of Tax Burdens* (1976) I compared the weight and pattern of taxation in Britain and the other countries of the OECD using figures for 1972 and earlier years. This comparison in terms of tax *yields* complemented an earlier comparison in terms of tax *rates*. *(The Measurement of Fiscal Policy: An Analysis of Tax Systems in Terms of the Political Distinction between "Right" and "Left",* 1971).

*The Measurement of Fiscal Policy* showed that in 1968 the British tax system was further to the political left than that of any other West European country by reason of the high tax rates at the top of the scale, the heavy taxation of saving relatively to spending and the extreme graduation (or *intension*) of the tax schedules (the difference between the highest rate of tax and the average of the lower rates). The general measure of political leftwardness used for the purpose of this comparison was called the *coefficient of fiscal policy.*

*The Camel's Back* showed that in 1972 Britain's tax burden in aggregate was only just above the OECD median but that the total *yield* of tax in Britain was derived disproportionately from taxes that were painful to the taxpayer or damaging to industry. It also showed that the portrayal of Britain in *The Measurement of Fiscal Policy* as a country with high maximum *rates* of tax, especially on saving, remained true in 1975.

Appendix IV updates the figures of tax yields for Britain and the rest of the OECD to 1978 and 1979 (Table 4) and the figures of tax rates to the beginning of 1981 (Table 5). For tax yields, the main difference between 1978—1979 and 1972 is that the tax burden as measured by the ratio of aggregate taxation to gross domestic product at market prices rose for the OECD on average every year from 1965—66 to 1977—78: in 1965 the percentage was 27.08, in 1978 it was 35.80. So although the British tax burden was almost the same in 1979 (33.79 per cent of gross domestic product) as in 1972 (34.06 per cent), the relative burden in Britain fell, because the relative burden was rising elsewhere. And similarly Britain's tax system was in 1978 and 1979 no longer more unfavourable than the OECD average to international competitiveness in the sense defined in *The Camel's Back* (the excess of aggregate taxation over tax revenue from goods and services, taxes on goods and services being generally charged on imports and rebated on exports). But otherwise the picture portrayed in *The Camel's Back* has remained correct: the British tax system has unusually high maximum rates of tax, is unusually burdensome on saving and puts more than average emphasis on taxes that are readily perceived and acutely felt.

We return to these characteristics of the British tax system in the next section but one ("The qualitative burden"). Meanwhile the next section considers the main official offering on international tax comparisons, the annual article by the Central Statistical Office in Economic Trends.

*Short Measure from Whitehall*

Appendix IV discusses changes made by the CSO in their annual Economic Trends articles *International Comparisons of Taxes and Social Security Contributions*, apparently in response to criticisms of mine in a pamphlet entitled *Short Measure from Whitehall: How CSO Statistics Understate the British Tax Burden* [1]. The understatement persists, although it is now on a much smaller scale. But as a result of the rise in aggregate taxation abroad, it is now not so much the total weight of taxation that makes the British tax system relatively onerous, but rather its *qualitative burden*.

**The qualitative burden**

This section summarises the findings under the corresponding headings in Appendix IV.

*Quantity and quality*

Whereas the quantitative burden weights all taxes equally per million pounds of revenue yield, the qualitative burden gives additional weight to taxes which are relatively painful or acutely perceived. Although the weighting process is inevitably subjective, the validity of the distinction between quantitative and qualitative burdens, which is always explicit or implicit in Conservative tax policy, appears to have both bipartisan political and official support.

The qualitative burden of United Kingdom taxation in 1979 was still relatively heavy by international standards, though less so than at the beginning of the seventies.

## Tax yields and tax rates

Still more sensitive measures of the qualitative burden can be provided by calculations based on tax rates. These calculations show the differences between the United Kingdom tax system and the systems of other OECD countries in sharper focus than calculations based on revenue yields: the United Kingdom tax system was in 1981 still exceptionally burdensome on saving (investment income and its parent capital).

## Tax height

Tax *height* is a technical term in *The Measurement of Fiscal Policy* (Chapter VII A) for the *total* weight of the *maximum* taxes on the various elements of spending, earning and saving. Table 6 shows that among twelve countries of the EC and Scandinavia, the United Kingdom was in 1981 second only to Sweden (by 5 per cent) for the height of its tax system and was 26 per cent above the average of the eleven other countries (including Scandinavia, which is rightly regarded as the most heavily taxed group of countries in the world).

## Tax basis

The *basis* of the tax system is a concept used in *The Measurement of Fiscal Policy* (Chapter VIIB) as an indicator of the bias against saving at the top of the scale. It is the tax burden on capital (and thus on industry) after allowance has been made for the level of taxation in general.

Table 7 shows that, by the criterion of tax basis, the tax bias against saving at the top of the scale was higher in 1981 In the United Kingdom than in any of the other eleven countries represented — 32 per cent higher than in Sweden (the nearest competitor), 88 per cent above the Scandinavian average, 108 per cent above the 11-country average and 122 per cent above the average for the rest of the EC.

## Numerical and conceptual neutrality

The fiscal bias against saving in the United Kingdom and elsewhere is understated by ignoring the indirect effect on saving of taxes whose impact falls on the consumption of goods and services.

*Agrgegate tax burden on saving*

The aggregate burden of taxes on saving in perpetuity (the burden of taxes on investment income and the parent asset) is their aggregate present discounted value as a proportion of the asset's value at the time of its acquisition.

*Fiscal prohibition of saving*

The aggregate tax burden on saving is prohibitive if its income equivalent absorbs more than the whole of the yield and its capitalised value exceeds the value of the asset on acquisition.

A measure of fiscal prohibition is provided by a comparison of commercial rates of return with the minimum or break-even rate of return required to preserve capital when spending out of investment income is nil.

The break-even rate of return in the United Kingdom, at 22.8 per cent, is higher than in any of the countries in Scandinavia or the EC except Sweden and is far in excess of commercial yields. It is 70 per cent above the Scandinavian average and over five times as high as the average for the rest of the EC.

The point of fiscal prohibition in the United Kingdom in 1981 was not much over £100,000 at full rates of capital transfer tax even under conditions of stable prices: it was lower on the more realistic assumption that prices were rising so that the real value of the asset must be made good out of the net-of-tax yield.

## The burden on corporations

The main tax burden on industry in the United Kingdom is imposed tnrough the taxation of saving, which is prohibitive for a substantial proportion of taxpayers and for a much larger proportion of funds for wealth creation. No other country in the European Community comes within miles of imposing such a burden. In the other countries, the break-even yield required for the preservation of capital is near or within the range of what is commercially attainable. The United Kingdom's relatively generous incentives to industrial investment are a partial and inadequate recompense for the overtaxation of financial investment by individuals [2].

By international standards, United Kingdom corporations are much less overtaxed than United Kingdom financial investment by individuals. But we noted in Chapter VII ("Three kinds of double taxation" and Table 1) that discrimination against corporations is higher in the United Kingdom than in any of the other EC countries with relief from economic double taxation of dividends (Table 1A); that, apart from the countries with classical corporation tax systems, the United Kingdom imposes more economic double taxation on dividends than any of the other seventeen OECD countries represented except Denmark and Spain (Table 1B); and that companies affected by discrimination against income from abroad are affected severely.

The burden imposed on corporate and non-corporate enterprise by legislation and other forms of government interference can at the level of the enterprise be as heavy a burden on industry as taxation itself (pages 93—94). But it generally falls short of prohibition; and it is in this sense a lighter burden on industry than the taxation of saving at the level of the individual, not least because smaller businesses suffer most from legislation and government interference whereas larger family businesses, whether corporate or not, suffer most from taxation.

## Maximum tax yield

Even if taxes fall short of prohibition, it is possible to improve on a sceptical assessment of the effect of taxation on industry. In the Appendix to *The Camel's Back* I proposed a method of estimating the diminishing returns to the fisc from increasing tax rates. As tax rates rise, the chance that the fisc will lose from the rise increases and the chance that it will gain diminishes. But the probabilities are relative to the rates of tax, and the weakness of this method is that the fisc cannot be proved to lose *anything even at 99 per cent or more* even though it must necessarily lose *everything at 100 per cent* (when all business ceases, just as imports cease when a tariff becomes prohibitive). An import tariff is *prohibitive* at less than 100 per cent gross (or less than infinity as a proportion of the net-of-tax price); in practical terms it will be prohibitive at far lower levels and discouraging at lower levels still, and the authorities recognise this truth for the good reason that the movement or non-movement of goods through customs provides factual evidence that is susceptible to at least rough-and-ready measurement. For taxes on work and saving there is unfortunately no comparable test as long as the yield remains positive; and the fisc argues that an increase in the rate of income tax from 98 to 99 per cent will produce another 1/98 of tax even though it is compelled to admit that an increase from 99 to 100 will destroy the yield from the previous 99 per cent entirely.

*Magnum vectigal est parsimonia* [3]. Heavy taxes are a false economy. As tax rises from zero to 100 per cent (confiscation), the revenue yield rises from zero to a maximum and falls to zero again, since a tax rate of 100 per cent frustrates economic transactions that are both rational and voluntary. No one can be certain at what point the fisc maximises its own advantage at the expense of the citizens. But if the rate of tax is raised above this point, the fisc loses as well as the people. As the rate is reduced from 100 per cent to the level of maximum revenue yield, the marginal gain of the fisc falls gradually to zero; but the fisc continues to gain absolutely as long as the tax rate remains above the point of maximum revenue yield. *Present rates of tax on saving in Britain are so high that they certainly inflict losses not only on the people but also on the fisc itself; the fisc as well as the people would gain from the reduction in the tax on saving to below 100 per cent, and this gain would continue until the rate of tax fell to the point of maximum revenue yield.*

The rate of tax that maximises the advantage of the fisc must be expected to vary over space and time and from tax to tax. But it is possible to strengthen the argument with figures, especially if the figures err on the side of understatement. Appendix V gives the tax rate at which revenue yield is maximised for plausible assumptions about the pattern of fiscal discouragement and the rate of tax at which incentives start to be affected. It shows that increasingly implausible assumptions are required as the maximum revenue yield rises beyond a tax rate of about 58 per cent gross. *Appendix V indicates how much the fisc as well as the people could gain from reducing the aggregate tax burden on saving to this level or below.* The maximum rate of UK tax on individuals' earnings was reduced in 1979 to approximately this level (60 per cent); and the maximum-revenue rate of tax on saving is unlikely to be higher than on earning [4]. The reduction of the aggregate tax burden on saving to this level requires the abolition of capital transfer tax, capital gains tax and the investment income surcharge.

## Conclusion

With one major exception, it is in principle impossible to prove or disprove the frustrating effect of taxation on industry [5]. The exception is that fiscal *prohibition* is in a different dimension from fiscal *discouragement* (or *disincentive*). Discouragement to industry is like discouragement to work when the rate of tax rises from 30 per cent to 50, to 70, to 90 . . . . But the frustration of industry through the prohibition of saving is as though the tax on work rose through 100 per cent to 120, 140, 160 . . . . In face of a prohibitive tax system investors will invest only if they are not numerate, and that would be a poor augury for commercial success.

Since under the British tax system in 1981 the fiscal prohibition of saving could be reached at little over £100,000 (which was in turn far below the capital value of a senior civil servant's index-linked pension [6]), there are reasons for expecting the British tax system to frustrate the creation of wealth which would not hold good if British taxes on industry were merely heavy in the sense in which a tax of 80 or 90 per cent on earnings from work is heavy. But the British tax system also bears heavily on industry lower down the scale as well as being prohibitive at the top.

The creation of wealth *must* be *frustrated* by prohibitive taxes unless the taxpayer is irrational; it is *likely* to be *frustrated* and *certain* to be *impeded* by heavy taxes falling short of prohibition.

The comparison of the United Kingdom's economic performance in recent years with those of other industrialised countries shows just this result. Britain's taxes have been higher and economic achievements more meagre than in any other major developed country. The tax comparisons are spelt out in this book. Britain's poor showing in the economic league tables is well known and need not be explained in detail here [7].

## CHAPTER X

# THE IMPLICATIONS FOR POLICY

## White magic and black magic

Wealth can be created and destroyed both by brute force and effortlessly. It is created by brute force through profitable labour or industrial investment. It is destroyed by brute force through the losses of nationalised industries, for example, which are as harmful as dumping the same value of industrial machinery in mid-Atlantic, or by the vandalism of local authorities, as when good houses are demolished in the name of slum clearance. It is created effortlessly by the extension of ownership and by investment in second-hand goods. It is destroyed effortlessly by inflation, by socialism (the restriction of ownership) and by the taxation of saving outside the production process. Saving inside the production process is temporary saving later drawn down and spent, such as saving for pensions. Saving outside the production process is permanent saving for investment in financial assets and second-hand goods.

The destruction of wealth by socialism and taxation illustrates the more general phenomenon of the destruction of wealth through government interference in the economy: for example, wealth is destroyed as well as employment by the Employment Protection Act. The initial effect is negative even if the interference occasionally has redeeming qualities which justify it on balance.

The white magic of capitalism, which is able to create wealth out of thin air in so far as the government permits it to do so, is in contrast with the black arts attempting to create something out of nothing by government regulation and manipulation of the economy. But capitalism has a monopoly of effortless wealth creation. The creation of wealth by government economic control and interference is as impossible as the projection of base metal into gold by alchemy. The downfall of Keynesian economic management is one of the more recent illustrations of this truth. Economic black magic, like the attempt to influence events by sorcery, is not merely useless but damaging through its concealment of the truth and its diversion of effort into futile activities.

Although black magic is dangerous superstition, white magic is real. The one destroys, the other creates. The effortless creation of wealth can be achieved not only through the extension of ownership and investment in second-hand goods but also through the reduction of government interference in the economy, which exemplifies the creation of wealth through enterprise in ideas.

## Industry and its enemies

Everybody's business is nobody's business, and the truths and benefits of capitalism are so general that they are often ignored. Capitalism is based on the interests of consumers and savers, whereas most pressure groups represent the interests of producers. Given the British dislike of abstract and general argument, it is perhaps not surprising that the general interest has so often been ignored even by its potential beneficiaries.

The open enemies of industry, the Communists and their sympathisers, have done less harm than some who should have been its friends, including politicians and spokesmen for industry itself. Some of the deepest wounds have been self-inflicted. The inflationary measures of 1971, of which industry and the whole economy are still suffering the consequences, were brought in at the urgent insistence of the Confederation of British Industry among many others. And it was the CBI's own "price initiative" of the same year that inaugurated what eventually amounted to eight years of increasingly damaging price control.

## Wealth versus privilege

A major reason for blunders like this was the belief in some CBI circles in the first half of the nineteen-seventies that the CBI should not put forward policy proposals which would benefit the rich. This stultifying limitation is a recipe for general and permanent penury. The rationale of capitalism is that decisions are not taken by officials but by individuals voting with their own money. The engine of capitalism is personal enrichment. Capitalism cannot work unless the rewards of success remain in private hands. Capitalism cannot create wealth out of thin air unless its beneficiaries are enriched.

The alternative to wealth is privilege — special concessions to small firms, discrimination in favour of "productive" assets and so forth. These measures undo only part of the damage done by taxes on the creation of wealth; and they are difficult to justify in terms of equity, not least because their beneficiaries are frequently rich. They are equally difficult to justify in economic terms, since wealth can be created by "non-productive" assets as much as by "productive". There is no valid distinction in equity or economics between "productive" and "non-productive" assets. The only way to avoid frustrating the creation of wealth by capitalism is to reduce the taxes on saving in general and without distinction between one asset and another.

106

## "Progressive" versus "progressive"

The "progressive" policy of squeezing the rich till they squeal has consequences its advocates do not always recognise or even understand. There is not merely a conflict between "progressiveness" and prosperity: "progressive" policies themselves are in conflict with each other. "Progressive" goodwill is not enough: there is no substitute for understanding the logical machinery.

The dedication to a recent book on economic inequality runs as follows: "To Antara and Nandana with the hope that when they grow up they will find less of it no matter how they decide to measure it" [1]. Read "underemployment" or "sin" instead of "inequality" in this passage and you will see the problem. Inequality is not something tangible and unmistakable like a person's height or weight. It has a number of dimensions in each of which there is a wide variety of possible measures. The choice of measure can reverse the order of inequality (A being more unequal than B by measure X but less unequal by measure Y) [2]. The order of inequality can likewise be reversed by the choice of dimension (the inequality of spending being larger in C than in D but the inequality of wealth larger in D than in C). Measures intended to reduce inequality in one dimension may increase it in others. Above all, the desirabiliy or undesirability of inequality is not independent, but substantially the result, of the meaning attributed to the concept and the method of its measurement [3].

The section on "Purpose versus outcome" in Chapter VIII discussed the need to choose between competing aims of policy, however "progressive" the policy-maker's credentials. I have explained in detail elsewhere the narrow logical limitations on the range of fiscal policy options [4]. There are also conflicts between equality and justice (Chapter IV, "Conflict and reconciliation") and between equality and political freedom [5]. Appendix V spells out the limitations on the fisc's ability to raise more revenue by raising tax rates, because the yield declines after the maximum is passed: British rates of tax on saving rise so high that the fisc must be losing money by not reducing them, and so the losers are not only the taxpayers subject to these high rates but also the taxpayers' fellows, including even the fisc itself. And Appendix III shows that taxes on saving are "regressive": they increase not only the inequality of spending but inequality in general.

## "Progressiveness" versus progress

These conflicts at the heart of "progressive" policy-making are additional to the more widely recognised conflicts between equality and prosperity [6], which have been a major theme of this book. In particular, we noted in Chapter III that the economic taxable capacity of permanent saving is negative, as is the taxable capacity of investment in assets that would otherwise be financed from taxation.

## Harmony

The harmony of interests in capitalism has been generally neglected. The real conflicts are between producer pressure groups and between government and people. (Chapter VIII). These conflicts are the antithesis of capitalism. Capitalism reconciles the interests of consumers and savers (or capitalists); and this reconciliation is comprehensive, since everyone is a consumer. It is a matter of economic logic, not personal merit, that the relationship of the capitalist to the consumer, or the saver to the spender, is that of Raphael to Adam and Eve in the passage cited from *Paradise Lost* at the start of this book. More accurately, it is the relationship of the saver as *taxpayer* to the spender as *voter*; and it is the relationship to the spender of the *permanent* saver, the quintessential capitalist, whose saving is never drawn down and spent. The economic taxable capacity of permanent saving is negative; so the rest of the community as well as the permanent saver loses from the policy or practice of concentrating the full fury of the tax system on permanent saving. The cost to the rest of the community of reductions in the taxation of permanent saving is not merely an illusion; it is negative. It costs the consumer and voter less than nothing to be generous; in the words of Adam,

> Well may we afford
> Our givers their own gifts, and large bestow
> From large bestow'd, where Nature multiplies
> Her fertile growth, and by disburd'ning grows
> More fruitful; which instructs us not to spare.

## The implications for policy

The simplest way to tax temporary but not permanent saving is to tax consumption only. Any increase in spending made possible by postponement bears the full weight of tax in due time. As long as saving is not drawn down, it is not liable to the taxes on spending; but it still bears their implicit burden, since taxes on spending reduce the value of saving [7].

The abolition of explicit taxes on saving is also the simplest way of solving the problem of adjusting for inflation in the taxation of saving. If saving is not taxed as such, no adjustment is required.

The taxation of spending to the exclusion of saving is the system least damaging to the creation of wealth. It is also the most "progressive" or least "regressive" system in the sense that it minimises inequality. (Appendix III).

The logic and advantages of an expenditure tax base are not confined to the choice between taxation of expenditure and taxation of income. They apply equally to the taxation of capital — taxes on wealth, capital gains, capital transfers. These taxes, no less than taxes on income, favour spending against saving; they frustrate the creation of wealth; and they are "regressive" in the sense of increasing inequality. Indeed, these taxes are more damaging per unit of revenue yield than a tax on investment income (at least if it takes account of inflation), because their incidence is more capricious and arbitrary — in timing or amount or both. The introduction or maintenance of taxes on wealth, capital gains or capital transfers can constitute a crippling limitation on the advantages otherwise obtainable from the principle of expenditure taxation in terms not only of prosperity but also (for egalitarians) of equality [8].

Appendix V argues that the maximum-revenue rate for any of the three aggregates spending, earning and saving may be put at less than 60 per cent, in the sense that increasingly implausible assumptions are required to raise it above this level.

The tax on saving to which the 60 per cent maximum applies is the income equivalent of income tax (including any investment income surcharge), capital transfer tax, capital gains tax and wealth tax in combination: in Britain in 1981 income tax alone, at 75 per cent, was far beyond this level, although capital transfer tax and capital gains tax were levied in addition at the highest rates in Europe. (Table 5). But the maximum-revenue rate of tax for saving is well below the corresponding rates for spending and earning: first, because permanent saving is a luxury in the technical sense and is therefore relatively sensitive to increases in price; second, because lending to the government has negative taxable capacity (page 52); third, because permanent saving has negative economic taxable capacity (page 52). In general, saving (unlike spending and earning) has no economic taxable capacity (page 53); and this limits its taxable capacity in the ordinary or financial sense.

I have not attempted in this book to quantify the maximum-revenue rate of tax on saving. The considerations in the last paragraph suggest that it is unlikely to exceed the basic-rate-of-income-tax range of say 25—35 per cent gross and could be lower. The only reason why the maximum-revenue tax on saving appears to be higher than this is that savings taxation in Britain has for many years been largely retrospective, obtaining much of its yield from attacks on capital accumulated in previous decades and centuries. This retrospective taxation is not only unjust in its effect on old saving but also uneconomic in its effect on new saving [9].

The argument that the economic taxable capacity of saving in general is zero and of permanent saving in particular is negative is unlikely to carry any weight with the tax-gatherers of the United Kingdom Inland Revenue. The Inland Revenue have never shown any interest even in maximising their own tax receipts, still less in anything that might reduce the fiscal barriers to the creation of wealth in the British economy; nor have Customs and Excise. The motivation and behaviour of tax officials at the policy level have been what I have described elsewhere as sacerdotal [10]: their aim has been and is to defend what they call "the integrity of the revenue" (in other words, to prevent the taxpayer from escaping what they regard as his proper charge). Labour Treasury Ministers have over many years had their own good political reasons for supporting the attacks on the capitalist system mounted by their own officials, through the closing of "loopholes" and otherwise; and the course of events has been little different during the periods when Conservative Ministers were theoretically in charge of the Revenue Departments.

Nevertheless, the argument that the economic taxable capacity of saving in general is zero and of permanent saving in particular is negative ought to weigh heavily with the general public even if it does not interest Revenue officials at the policy level or the Treasury Ministers who act as their spokesmen. The argument from economic taxable capacity means that any revenue from taxes on saving causes at least an equivalent loss to the economy as a whole, so that the taxpaying community loses at least twice the amount of tax revenue instead of just once: in other words, the *excess burden* is at least as large as the tax revenue.

If the maximum-revenue criterion is replaced by the more socially justifiable criterion of economic taxable capacity, the maximum rate of tax on saving falls from say 25—35 per cent gross to nil. This argument from economic taxable capacity supports the conclusion of the argument from neutrality (in the first paragraph of this section) that saving is fully and properly taxed through the taxation of spending and that no form of separate tax on saving is required to achieve neutrality between saving and spending.

The reduction of the fiscal barriers to the creation of wealth should start with the abolition of the taxes on saving — income tax on investment income, investment-income surcharge, capital transfer tax, capital gains tax and wealth tax, or such of these taxes as are levied at present. Their combined yield is generally modest and has in recent years been of the order of the annual *increase* in total tax yield or less in a number of industrialized countries. There is no serious financial obstacle to the abolition of these taxes, at least in stages over a period of years.

The argument is different for taxes on earning and spending. For these aggregates, the maximum-revenue tax rate is of the order of 60 per cent or less; the UK tax on individual earnings was reduced to 60 per cent in June 1979, and the tax on spending is far below this level, except for a few commodities with a price-inelastic demand. Even if the taxes on earning and spending are combined, as they should be, their combined burden, at some 65 per cent, is much less in excess of the maximum-revenue rate than the combined burden of taxes on saving.

The argument for abolishing the higher rates of tax on individual earnings is, not that they are beyond the point of maximum yield, but that the revenue they yield is small and their potential for damage enormous. Their abolition would cost little and would enable the tax system to be radically simplified, not least because a large part of the present anti-avoidance legislation would become superfluous.

Since earnings are used partly for saving, a thorough-going policy of taxing saving only through taxes on spending requires the abolition of the basic rate of income tax on individual earnings. Desirable though this is as a long-term aim, it is extremely expensive in revenue lost to the fisc; and it does not offer the same high ratio of benefit to nominal cost as the abolition of the taxes on saving and the higher rates of tax on individual earnings. It is not clear that the basic rate of income tax on earnings, even when supplemented by social-security contributions, is much more damaging to industry than the raising of equally vast sums in taxes on spending. Here the problem is not so much the form of taxation as the high level of government expenditure it has to support: the reduction of this barrier to industry must start with the reduction of government spending through the "privatisation" of services at present provided by the government.

Corporation tax is a mixture of tax on earnings and tax on savings. If taxes on saving are abolished and the tax on earnings is confined to income tax at the basic rate, there is no point in charging more than this basic rate on corporations; and partial or total exemption from this charge would be appropriate for non-trading corporations that merely serve to hold investments.

The form of taxation that does least to frustrate the creation of wealth is a low equiproportional tax on consumer spending; and the ultimate aim of policy should be so to control government expenditure that all taxation can be raised in this form. High rates of tax on particular commodities, like the excise duties on drink and tobacco in the United Kingdom and elsewhere, are inimical to the industries concerned and would be reduced to the level of tax on spending generally, at which consumer choice between commodities is no longer distorted. The taxpayer's choice between taxable work and the autarkic activities of the household would still be distorted, but not seriously if the general rate of tax on spending were sufficiently low. This distortion would be the only remaining barrier to industry when the abolition of taxes on individuals' savings and earning had been complemented by its corollary, the abolition of the tax on corporations.

# ONCE-FOR-ALL SPENDING AND SUSTAINABLE SPENDING

### Spending power and present discounted value of future income

The section headed "Meaning of 'wealth'" in Chapter II compared and contrasted the two principal concepts of wealth in the traditional sense. The first is spending power and the second is the present discounted value of future income (future income discounted at the present rate of interest or yield).

Both these concepts have serious defects. The spending-power or naive concept of wealth values it at what it would be worth if it were all realised at today's values and spent at today's prices. This concept, on which conventional capital taxation is based, is doubly absurd. First, owners of capital (*existing saving* or *old saving*) do not wish to realise their holdings totally and simultaneously; otherwise, they would not have built their savings up. Second, if *per impossibile* owners of capital did wish to realise their holdings totally and simultaneously, they would be unable to do so: there would be no buyers, and capital values would plummet. Thus the apparently common-sense concept of wealth vastly overestimates its taxable capacity as a result of systematic double counting. The naive concept of wealth, for all its appeal to common sense, is based on an internal inconsistency.

The concept of wealth as the present discounted value of future income is at the opposite logical extreme from the naive concept discussed in the last paragraph: it implicitly values wealth as permanent saving, not immediate spending. Admittedly, if all assets had the same current and expected yield, the two concepts would give the same result, and the two concepts would also give the same result if any variations in yield were self-compensating at a given rate of discount (a higher current yield being commanded by riskier investments and a lower current yield by investments with growth potential). But yields vary for two other reasons as well: first, because an asset may be held partly or entirely for personal use and enjoyment and, second, because taxpayers may not all be paying the same rates of tax.

There are two variants of the concept of wealth as the present discounted value of future income. The first discounts future gross-of-tax income at gross-of-tax discount rates or net-of-tax income at net-of-tax discount rates. This variant gives the same result as the naive concept of wealth if gross-of-tax discount rates are the same. For example, if all current yields are 10 per cent, the value of wealth is the same whether calculated gross of tax at a 10 per cent yield or at 10 per cent for a tax-exempt taxpayer or net of 30 per cent tax at a 7 per cent yield or net of 70 per cent tax at a 3 per cent yield. But this variant has the paradoxical quality that the real (that is, net-of-tax) discount rate varies from taxpayer to taxpayer in accordance with variations in the graduated rate of tax, whereas the market value of wealth is determined by a weighted average rate of discount (the average of the net-of-tax rates weighted by the amount of wealth in the hands of each taxpayer). Moreover, this variant creates paradoxes when market yields vary by reason of differential risk or growth potential. These variations can be brought into equilibrium at only one rate of discount (the gross-of-tax market rate or, what is equivalent after tax, the average of the net-of-tax rates weighted by the amounts of wealth); but under the first variant the real (or net-of-tax) discount rate varies between taxpayers, so that risky investments are worth more to the poor than to the rich and investments with growth potential are worth more to the rich than to the poor.

The second variant of the concept of wealth as the present discounted value of future income discounts future net-of-tax income at gross-of-tax rates of discount (net-of-tax income being income net of taxes on investment income and its parent capital). The rationale for this procedure is that taxes form no part of future net income and that discount rates are the same between taxpayers, like any other market prices. If the gross-of-tax yield is 10 per cent, there is no rational pretext for discounting the 90 per cent taxpayer's future income on the basis of a 1 per cent yield merely because he is taxed at 90 per cent. The discount rate is logically independent of the rate of tax, as is the consumer's proclivity for goods and ser vices in particular and in general. But this variant, though offering a more logical concept of wealth as the present discounted value of future income, is radically at variance with the naive concept of wealth if tax rates differ: by comparison with the naive concept of wealth, this variant of the concept of wealth as the present discounted [value of future income reduces the wealth of the 90 per cent taxpayer by comparison with the wealth of the 50 per cent taxpayer to one-fifth of its former value ($=(100 - 90) \div (100 - 50)$).

The second variant of the concept of wealth as the present discounted value of future income is not only more logical than the first for the reasons explained in the last paragraph (because it reduces the relative valuation of wealth in the hands of high-rate taxpayers); it also brings the relative valuation between tax-payers of risky investments and investments with growth potential into line with their relative valuation by the market. Moreover, if wealth is constituted by the present discounted value of income from investment, it would appear to be constituted also by the present discounted value of income from labour ; not the least of the merits in this concept of wealth is the support it gives to a reduction in the taxation of saving relatively to earning. But even the second variant of the concept of wealth as the present discounted value of future income has a major weakness. Under this variant the value of wealth doubles if the discount rate halves and halves if the discount rate doubles. But a taxpayer saving in perpetuity ("Temporary and permanent saving", Chapter III) is worse off, not better off, if the discount rate falls and taxes are levied on wealth or capital transfers. His permanent income stream diminishes, and it is a serious defect of the traditional discounting method that this deterioration is represented as an improvement. Similarly, *mutatis mutandis*, if the discount rate rises. Even if no taxes are levied on wealth or capital transfers, the permanent saver who is also a *buyer* (that is, the *current* saver in perpetuity) *loses* from a fall in interest rates although the conventional concept of wealth regards him as *gaining* from the increase in the value of any existing holdings [1].

## Wealth as a cash flow

Different concepts of wealth may be useful for different purposes. The naive concept of wealth as the value obtainable on disposal has the advantage of conformity to the common sense of the matter, since the virtue of the capitalist system is precisely to multiply utility through ownership ; but as a criterion of taxable capacity it is a disaster, since in a consistent tax system the economic taxable capacity of permanent saving is negative. The second variant of the concept of wealth as the present discounted value of future income (the variant in which income is net of tax but the discount rate is gross) has the advantage of subtracting from the market value of wealth the part of future income that will be taken in taxes on income and capital ; but it has the disadvantage that a fall in the discount rate is represented as a benefit, although the saver in perpetuity suffers a loss if there are taxes on capital or if he is adding to his savings.

What we need is a concept of wealth that avoids these weaknesses. The naive spending-power concept should be modified to allow for the idea that wealth is forward-looking rather than instantaneous and is about a stream of purchasing power in perpetuity rather than the possibility of once-and-for-all consumption through the drawing down of capital. The present-value-of-future-income concept should be modified to recognise the fact that in a taxless world the discount rate is irrelevant to the value of old saving held in perpetuity and that the levying of capital taxes on saving in perpetuity increases the burden (makes the owner worse off) as discount rates fall, whereas the conventional analysis suggests that the owner is better off because his immediate spending power has risen.

A first step to the correct estimation of wealth is (as in the second variant of the present-discounted-value-of-future-income concept) to discount future income by a common market rate, instead of individual rates for each taxpayer. If taxpayer A is taxed at 80 per cent on the income from £ 1 m. and taxpayer B is taxed at 60 per cent on the income from £ 100 th., A is not 10 times as wealthy as B but only 5 times (1,000,000—800,000 = 5 × (100,000—60,000)). But this would still leave intact the anomalous effect of variations in yields. If the yield is 5 per cent instead of 10 per cent, the taxpayer is reckoned to be twice as well off because of the increase in capital values, even though his income stream is the same gross of tax and he may incur additional taxes on his capital.

If the rate of interest rises, new savers gain and negative savers and borrowers lose ; if it falls, new savers lose and negative savers and borrowers gain. Old savers in perpetuity neither gain nor lose. The additional wealth constituted by a fall in the interest rate does not represent additional taxable capacity ; indeed, if net saving is positive (as it is in an expanding economy), new savers lose more than negative savers gain, and savers in aggregate lose (even if there are no taxes on capital). The present-value-of-future-income concept, however, shows this loss as a gain : this concept would therefore still be defective even if there were no taxes on capital.

An alternative concept proposed below agrees with the present-value-of-future-income concept in deducting from wealth the amount attributable to taxes on investment income and its parent capital ; but it is entirely cash-flow-based (income-based or spending-based), as befits a concept that is both valid from year to year and also oriented towards permanent saving (Chapter III). It distinguishes income or expenditure supported by past endeavours from income or expenditure requiring current efforts for its renewal from period to period.

## Stock, yield and flow

The concept of wealth as a cash flow is sharply opposed to traditional ways of thinking in which income, spending and positive and negative new saving are all flows per unit of time whereas wealth is a stock at a moment of time. But there is room for several different concepts, each serving a different purpose. Indeed, if taxation is high or the rate of discount variable, the measures of wealth corresponding to the different concepts may vary by as much as several hundred per cent. Statistics of the distribution of wealth will vary almost beyond recognition according to the conceptual basis on which they are compiled. In particular, the wealth statistics of the Royal Commission on the Distribution of Income and Wealth were compiled on a basis which systematically and grossly exaggerated the inequality of its distribution [2].

The present-discounted-value-of-future-income concept calculates the value of wealth by applying a discount rate to the stream of income which the wealth generates. But this process is open to the grave objection that losses are recorded as gains and gains as losses for savers in perpetuity when the discount rate changes and the burden of capital taxation rises or falls as a result. We are nearer the truth if we omit the discounting process and take net-of-tax investment income as the measure of wealth.

The concept of wealth as a cash flow, like the concept of wealth as the present discounted value of future income, implicitly values wealth as permanent saving, not immediate spending. But it avoids an internal inconsistency in the present-discounted-value concept: if wealth is permanent saving, changes in its value as a result of changes in the discount rate are irrelevant, because this value is never realised.

In a society where for reasons of law or custom all assets were purchased to be held in perpetuity and assets were sold only by the traders who produced them, the distinction between the value of wealth and the value of its yield would diminish or disappear. The value of a herd or a factory would be what it produced each year.

There are three reasons for sales of assets by parties other than their producers. First, the owner may wish to rearrange his portfolio of assets: but any change in the yield will show up in the cash flow and need not be treated separately. Second, the owner may be obliged to sell by taxation; he would hold in perpetuity if he could, and the reduction in his portfolio shows up in the cash flow. Third, the saving may be temporary and the disposal voluntary; here again, the reduction in cash flow represents the reduction in the portfolio.

It is only in the third case that an increase in the value of wealth through a reduction in the discount rate is relevant to the distribution of wealth and may be thought to constitute a proper object for taxation. The cash-flow concept of wealth abstracts from this question, which may be a disadvantage for some purposes. But for long-term and perpetual saving it gives a better representation of reality than the other two concepts. Indeed, since the cash-flow concept measures wealth in terms of the flow in a given period, the distinction between temporary and permanent saving is correctly represented by the difference between the flow in one period and the flow in another: temporary saving drops out of the reckoning as it is drawn down. Temporary saving is potentially permanent saving, and there is no need to distinguish between the two in advance.

### Investment income and earnings

In the cash-flow concept of wealth, income is divided between income from investment and income from earnings. Investment income is regarded as permanent and income from earnings as temporary. Earnings are taken net of income tax and investment income net not only of income tax but also of any wealth or transfer taxes levied on the parent capital [3]. Average and marginal rates are used to show respectively the taxpayer's position and changes in his position.

If earned and investment income are taxed jointly at graduated rates, the results will be affected by whether earnings are taken before investment income or afterwards [4]. Since investment income is regarded as permanent, investment income is taken first and earnings are treated as marginal. This procedure increases both the measure and the inequality of wealth by comparison with the alternative procedure of taking earnings first and treating investment income as marginal. This latter procedure, or a compromise between the two, may also have its uses ; as we shall see, the cash-flow concept of wealth offers a number of different choices, and it is a strength of the concept, not a weakness, that it provides a range of possibilities rather than a unique formula for the measurement of wealth.

## Growth, risk and marketability

Although the cash-flow concept of wealth ignores the general rate of discount and changes in that rate, it need not ignore variations in discount rates between taxpayers.

If taypayer A has assets yielding the market rate of 10 per cent and B has assets yielding 5 per cent because the income is expected to grow, B's position is understated if only current income is taken into account. It is possible to allow for this consideration by doubling the value put on B's income as a measure of his wealth (or less than doubling if tax is graduated over the range concerned). Similarly, if C has assets yielding 20 per cent because they are considered risky, the value of his income can be halved (or reduced by less than a half if tax is graduated over the range concerned).

A discount for lack of marketability is analogous to a discount for risk. If D has shares in a private company which yield 20 per cent because there is no market for them, the argument is similar to that for C in the last paragraph. D cannot rearrange his portofolio of assets except at a substantial loss.

The largest category of unmarketable assets is pension rights. In the United Kingdom, pensions are taxed as earned income, which they are not, instead of investment income, which they are; and the value of pension rights is included as nil in the official wealth statistics on the ground that pension rights are not transferable or marketable. But this restriction merely makes pension rights less valuable, not valueless; the exclusion of pension rights represents a serious distortion in the official statistics. In the cash-flow concept of wealth, pension rights should be included with a substantial double discount, first because they are temporary and second because they are non-transferable. The discounts are inevitably arbitrary; but an arbitrary discount is better than no discount at all and better than excluding the item altogether.

Assets which yield no income stream require a decision. One possibility is to leave them out as being household items, just as it is possible to exclude from income the imputed income from home ownership and the notional income from other

117

services provided autarkically and without payment from within the household. Non-income-yielding assets, however valuable, are the owner's private affair in a way in which income-yielding assets are not. Wealth is then defined as income-yielding wealth, which may be the most appropriate concept for some purposes such as estimating taxable capacity: taxing an asset which yields no income is like taxing an income-yielding asset at more than 100 per cent of its income. But if it is desired to include non-income-yielding assets, a fictitious yield can be imputed to them, the size of the yield depending on the purpose of the calculation; thus, an average market yield might be appropriate if the purpose of the calculation is to measure command over resources.

## Once-for-all spending and sustainable spending

So far, we have been dealing with the income side of the taxpayer's account and wealth has been defined in terms of (permanent) income from investments as opposed to (temporary) income from earnings. But there is a corresponding distinction on the outgo side of the account between sustainable spending (from investment income) and once-for-all spending (from earnings).

This is a different cash-flow concept of wealth from the income-based cash-flow concept. It is wealth defined in terms of spending on goods and services. New saving drops out of the reckoning in any period, since it affects spending on goods and services only in the future.

In the section "Income and outgo" (Chapter IV) we noted that the two sides o the account must balance in any period both for any individual and in aggregate. On the income side, income is divided into income from earnings and income from investments (and mixed income). Part of this income is from current effort (and in this sense once-for-all income) and part is from the ownership of assets (perpetual income). Outgo is the sum of spending and new saving out of earned and investment income; it is also the sum of spending and new saving out of earned and investment income plus spending out of negative saving minus negative saving. If negative saving is brought into the reckoning on the incomings side, however, then on the outgoings side new saving out of earned and investment income is not reduced by the amount of saving drawn down. If net new saving is positive, the account can be made up either gross or net of negative saving. Gross, negative saving is an element of incomings balanced by a corresponding amount of new saving. Net, negative saving disappears from the income side and on the outgo side new saving is reduced correspondingly. Spending is the same in either case.

Total spending can be divided into once-for-all spending and sustainable spending. Sustainable spending is spending the cost of which can be borne by investment income. The balance of spending is once-for-all. If net new saving is negative, once-for-all spending is the sum of earnings and net negative saving. If net new saving and once-for-all spending are positive, new saving is financed entirely out of earnings;

if net new saving is positive and once-for-all spending is zero, new saving absorbs the whole of earnings and the balance is financed from the balance of investment income.

The advantage of this spending cash-flow concept of wealth is that it concentrates entirely on the use of resources and how this use is financed. It avoids the double-counting of net new saving both as an outflow in period 1 and as an inflow in the form of investment income in all subsequent periods. By comparison with the income cash-flow concept of wealth, the spending cash-flow concept increases the importance of wealth relatively to earning as a source of disbursements. It shows how much spending can be supported by property and how much requires to be defrayed by current effort.

The refinements and qualifications on the outgo side, including the possibility of a graduated expenditure tax, are analogous to those already discussed for the income side.

## Conclusion

The naive concept of wealth as instantaneous purchasing power is not consistent with a continuing year-by-year analysis. The purchasing power is not and could not be used in any one year, let alone a succession of years, and yet it is valued year after year in this method as though it could be used without being exhausted. The present-value-of-future-income concept, by contrast, is sustainable from year to year provided that wealth is continually netted down for negative saving. The year-to-year shortcomings of this method are, first, that the discount rate used in the first variant is not a common market rate but a rate varying with each taxpayer's graduated tax rate and, second, that in both variants reductions in the rate of interest which make the taxpayer worse off if taxation is levied on capital and the saving is permanent or long-term are presented as making the taxpayer better off; and *vice versa* when the rate of interest rises. To avoid these inconsistencies, it is necessary to dispense with the rate of interest entirely. This has the advantage of avoiding the bogus conflicts of interest between savers and spenders and also between old savers (existing savers) and the rest of the community when saving is permanent. In so far as saving is temporary, positive savers lose what negative savers gain from a fall in interest rates and *vice versa*. In so far as saving is permanent, the interests of new savers and of spenders are the same and are served by a rise in yields [5]; the interests of old savers are irrelevant.

The conventional income-and-wealth distinction should thus be replaced by an income-and-sustainable-income distinction or more radically by an expenditure-and-sustainable-expenditure distinction. Both the replacements are independent of the average discount rate (which confuses the issue if there are taxes on capital as such by making the saver in perpetuity appear to gain from a fall in interest rates whereas in reality he loses). The expenditure-and-sustainable-expenditure analysis is preferable to the income-and-sustainable-income analysis because it excludes net new saving (which has no additional taxable capacity) and thus avoids an element of double counting; it reduces the problem from three dimensions to two[6]. Sustainable expenditure differs from the naive concept of wealth (1) by recognising that the naive concept of wealth is internally inconsistent because wealth could not all be spent at once; (2) by deducting the implicit tax burden on wealth and the income it generates; (3) by deducting new saving. Allowance for (1), (2) and (3) vastly reduces the measure of wealth in private hands and the inequality of its distribution.

To summarise, there is a valid distinction between stocks and flows. Flows (or incomes or expenditures) are easier to measure reliably. Stocks are more difficult, because they require valuation. But this problem is resolved if stocks are themselves reckoned in terms of income or expenditure flows, irrespective of the average discount rate. This procedure allows for the fact that there may be differences in yields and in tax rates between taxpayers. Each year is treated separately, but the treatment of different years is consistent. Calculation in terms of expenditure rather than income avoids the double counting of the purchase of an asset in one period and the consequent increase in income or expenditure in subsequent periods.

The measured inequality of wealth is substantially reduced, first, by allowing for the tax component in the naive method of measuring wealth (which exaggerates the inequality of wealth even in a taxless world, since wealth cannot all be spent at once) and, second, by reckoning in terms of expenditure rather than income (and thus excluding the element of new saving which in terms of cash flow never represents a claim on real resources). On the other hand, the measured inequality of wealth is increased by taking investment income before earned income when earned and investment income are taxed jointly at graduated rates. And the importance of wealth as a source of finance for expenditure is increased by taking investment income before earned income as the source of disbursements for spending. The rate of discount or interest is irrelevant to the relationship between once-for-all expenditure and expenditure in perpetuity out of existing investment income. If the double-count items of taxation and new saving are removed, there is a large reduction in the inequality of wealth in the sense of sustainable expenditure out of existing resources.

Thus, naive measures of the inequality of wealth are exaggerated (1) by ignoring the impossibility of simultaneous realisation through once-for-all spending and (2) by ignoring the tax component in sustainable spending and (3) by ignoring the distinction between sustainable spending within a given period and increments to sustainable spending in future periods. But it is possible for the distribution of once-for-all spending to be more unequal than that of sustainable spending if the taxation of income from investments is more egalitarian than the taxation of income from earnings.

120

There is not one single concept of wealth but a number of concepts differing widely in meaning and magnitude, both absolutely and as between taxpayers. Each concept can be valid for some purposes though invalid for others. In particular, the naive concept of wealth is an appropriate index of market value and of individual spending power but an inappropriate index of taxable capacity or of collective spending power, whether once-for-all or sustainable.

This appendix has put forward an interrelated family of concepts that remedy the weaknesses in the naive concept and the present-discounted-value-of-future-income concept. Some members of the family are simpler and others more complex. Even the simplest, such as the use of the income figures net of income tax (and still gross of capital taxes) could provide estimates of wealth superior to the traditional figures for purposes of distributive analysis and fiscal policy.

# THE ALGEBRA OF CORPORATE TAXATION

This appendix relates five systems of corporate taxation to each other by means of a common algebraic terminology. (Definitions). The five systems are those mentioned in the text (page 85): (I) classical, (II) two-rate [1], (III) imputation, (IV) avoir fiscal, (V) integrated system.

V is the simplest system: if the shareholder's marginal rate is 75 per cent, all profits are taxed at 75 per cent whether they are distributed or retained, although it is possible to combine this system for distributions with a composite proportional rate for retentions. I is the next simplest system: all profits are subject to the same rate of corporation tax, whether distributed or retained, and dividends are subject to graduated income tax in the shareholders' hands, without relief for corporation tax paid at the level of the company. There is no interplay between tax at the level of the company and tax at the level of the shareholder in I or in either variant of V. But this interplay is a complicating characteristic of systems II—IV. These systems are therefore illustrated with numerical examples, showing the effect of maximising either distributions or retentions.

Systems II—IV can be equivalent, and the examples are taken from the same set of figures, namely those published by the British Government for illustrative purposes before the rate of corporation tax was first fixed after the introduction of the new system in 1972. These rates are: corporation tax (on retained profits) 50 per cent; basic rate of income tax and rate of tax credit 30 per cent. The tax burden on distributed profits is as follows as a proportion of unity: —

| | | |
|---|---|---|
| Definitive corporation tax | .2857 | .2857 |
| Tax at 30 per cent on | .7143 | .2143 |
| Tax at 50 per cent on | 1.0000 | .5000 |

There is thus a distinction between the nominal rates and the real rates. The nominal and real rates on retentions are the same at 50 per cent. But the nominal tax credit of 30 per cent is 21.43 per cent of pre-tax profits; and the nominal difference of 20 per cent is 28.57 per cent of pre-tax profits.

The algebra is given initially in nominal terms (30 per cent and 20 per cent); but the real implications can be recognised from the figures above (.2857, .7143, .2143). Table 3 gives the algebraic translation from the nominal rates to their real equivalents.

## Definitions

$P$ = marginal pre-tax profits = 1
$R$ = marginal retained profits net of tax
$T$ = marginal total tax on corporation and shareholders
$D$ = marginal post-tax dividend in hands of shareholders
$\therefore P = R + T + D = 1$

$d$ = rate of corporation tax on dividends
$r$ = rate of corporation tax on retained profits = rate on all profits when $r = d = c$
   (rate of corporation tax on retained and distributed profits)
$b$ = basic rate of income tax
$m$ = marginal rate of income tax on shareholders
$b_1$ = rate of tax credit
$a$ = avoir fiscal = proportion of pre-tax distributed profit credited to shareholder
$x$ = proportion of corporation tax on distributed profits imputed to avoir fiscal
$\therefore a = xrP$

$D$ = post-tax dividend in hands of shareholders
$D_1$ = cash paid by corporation to individual shareholders net of basic rate of income tax
   deducted at source

$\therefore D/(1 - m) = D_1/(1 - b)$

$D_2 = D_1$ grossed up at basic rate of income tax
$\therefore D = D_2(1 - m)$ and $D_1 = D_2(1 - b)$

$D_3 = D_1$ grossed up at rate by which tax credits are imputed
$\therefore D_1 = D_3(1 - b_1)$

In the examples for Systems II—IV,
$d$ = .20
$r$ = .50
$b = m = b_1 = .30$
$a$ = .2143
$x$ = .4286 = $b_1/(1 - b_1) \times (1 - r)/r$
$D = D_1 = .50$
$D_2 = D_3 = .7143$

## The five systems

### System I

The classical system with basic rate income tax deducted at source
(1)   $R = 1 - r - bD_2 - D_1$
(2)   $D = D_2(1 - m)$

(3) $\quad T = r + bD_2 + (m - b)D_2$; tax on corporation comes before tax on shareholder

(4) $\quad P = 1 = \dfrac{R}{1 - c} + \dfrac{D}{(1 - c)\,(1 - m)}$

Let $r = .40$

(1) Then if $R = 0$, $bD_2 + D_1 = .60$

(4) $\qquad\qquad D = 0$, $R = .60$

## System II

(1) $\quad R = 1 - r(1 - D_2) - dD_2 - bD_2 - D_1$

(2) $\quad D = D_1 - (m - b)D_2$

(3) $\quad T = r(1 - D_2) + dD_2 + bD_2 + (m - b)D_2$

(4) $\quad P = 1 = \dfrac{R}{1 - r} + \dfrac{D(1 - r + d)}{(1 - r)\,(1 - m)}$

If $R = 0$,

(1) $\quad 1 = .50 \times .2857 + .20 \times .7143 + .30 \times .7143 + .50$

(3) $\quad .50 = .50 \times .2857 + .20 \times .7143 + .30 \times .7143$

(4) $\quad 1 = \dfrac{.50(1 - .50 + .20)}{.50 \times .70}$

If $D = 0$,

(1) $\quad .50 = 1 - .50$

(3) $\quad .50 = .50$

(4) $\quad 1 = \dfrac{.50}{1 - .50}$

## System III

(1) $\quad R = 1 - (r - b_1D_3) - b_1D_3 - D_1$

(2) $\quad D = D_1 - (m - b)D_3$

(3) $\quad T = r - bD_3 + bD_3 + (m - b)D_3$

(4) $\quad P = \dfrac{R}{1 - r} + \dfrac{D(1 - b_1)}{(1 - r)\,(1 - m)}$

If $R = 0$,

(1) $\quad 1 = .50 - .30 \times .7143 + .30 \times .7143 + .50$

(3) $\quad .50 = .50 - .30 \times .7143 + .30 \times .7143$

(4) $\quad P = 1 = \dfrac{.50(1 - .30)}{.50 \times .70}$

If $D = 0$,

(1) $\quad .50 = 1 - .50$

(3) $\quad .50 = .50$

(4) $\quad 1 = \dfrac{.50}{1 - .50}$

## System IV

(1) $\quad R = 1 - r - D_1$

(2) $\quad D = (D_1 + a)\,(1 - m) = D_1\left(1 + \dfrac{xc}{1 - c}\right)(1 - m)$

(3)   $T = r + m(D_1 + a) - a$

(4)   $P = \dfrac{R}{1-r} + \dfrac{D}{(1 - r + rx)(1 - m)}$

If  $R = 0$,

(1)     $1 = .50 + .50$
(2)     $.50 = (.50 + .2143).70$
(3)     $.50 = .50 + .30(.50 + .2143) - .2143$
(4)     $1 = \dfrac{.50}{(1 - .50 + .2143).70}$

If  $D = 0$,

(1)     $.50 = 1 - .50$
(3)     $.50 = .50$
(4)     $1 = \dfrac{.50}{1 - .50}$

### System V

(1)   $R = 1 - r - D_1$
(2)   $D = D_1 - m + r$
(3)   $T = r + m - r$
(4)   $P = \dfrac{R}{1-m} + \dfrac{D}{1-m}$

## Rates of exchange between sources and uses of funds

Table 2 shows the rates of exchange between sources and uses of funds for the five systems: for example, what is the cost in net-of-tax dividends of putting another £100 to reserves? In the column headed "II–IV" it is assumed that the rate of corporation tax on retained profits is 50 per cent, that the effective rate of corporation tax on distributed profits is 28.57 per cent and that the shareholder's marginal rate of income tax is 30 per cent.

### TABLE 2
#### Rates of exchange between sources and uses of funds

|   | System I | System II | System III | System IV | II–IV | System V |
|---|---|---|---|---|---|---|
| V | $1 - r$ | $1 - r$ | $1 - r$ | $1 - r$ | .50 | $1 - m$ |
| W | $(1 - r)(1 - b)$ | $\dfrac{(1 - r)(1 - b)}{1 - r + d}$ | $1 - r$ | $1 - r$ | .50 | $1 - r$ |
| X | $(1 - r)(1 - m)$ | $\dfrac{(1 - r)(1 - m)}{1 - r + d}$ | $\dfrac{(1 - r)(1 - m)}{1 - b_1}$ | $(1 - r + rx)(1 - m)$ | .50 | $1 - m$ |
| Y | $1 - b$ | $\dfrac{1 - b}{1 - r + d}$ | $1$ | $1$ | 1.00 | $1 - r$ |
| Z | $1 - m$ | $\dfrac{1 - m}{1 - r + d}$ | $\dfrac{1 - m}{1 - b_1}$ | $\dfrac{(1 - r + rx)(1 - m)}{1 - r}$ | 1.00 | $1$ |

$V = \delta R / \delta P$ = maximum proportion of marginal profit that can be put to reserve
$W = \delta D_1 / \delta P$ = maximum proportion of marginal profit that can be paid in cash by the corporation to the shareholders

$X = \delta D/\delta P$ = maximum proportion of marginal profit that can be left net of tax in the hands of the shareholder

$Y = -\delta D_1/\delta R$ = cost of marginal addition to post-tax reserves in terms of cash payments by corporation forgone by shareholders (= proportion of reduction in post-tax reserves which could be paid out in cash to shareholders)

$Z = -\delta D/\delta R$ = cost of marginal addition to post-tax reserves in terms of net-of-tax dividends left in hands of shareholders (= proportion of reduction in post-tax reserves which could be left net of tax in hands of shareholders)

## Effective rates of corporation tax in terms of nominal rates

Table 3 expresses the effective rates of tax in Systems I—V in terms of the nominal rates above. (See page 122). In the numerical example the nominal rate of 20 per cent tax at corporate level on distributed profits corresponds to an effective rate of 28.57 per cent and the nominal additional rate of 30 per cent on undistributed profits (= tax credit on dividends) corresponds to an effective rate of 21.43 per cent. As a proportion of pre-tax profits, the tax credit in System III is 21.43 per cent, not 30 per cent, and the avoir fiscal in System IV is 21.43 per cent, not 42.86 per cent. Let the effective rate of corporation tax on dividends be $t_1$(= .2857 in the example) and let the rate of tax credit or avoir fiscal or additional tax on retentions be $t_2$ as a proportion of pre-tax profits (= .2143 in the example). Then

$$t_1 = 1 - \frac{1-r}{1-r+d} = \frac{d}{1-r+d}$$

$$t_2 = r - t_1$$

Table 9 shows the nominal rates in the foregoing analysis corresponding to the effective rates $t_1$ and $t_2$. It thus enables the effective rates to be calculated from the nominal rates, which are the rates specified in the legislation.

**TABLE 3**

**Nominal and effective rates of corporate taxation**

| Effective rates | $t = t_1 + t_2$ | $t_1$ | $t_2$ |
|---|---|---|---|
| Common economic terminology | $1 - \delta R/\delta P$ | $1 - 1/(1-b) \times \delta D_1/\delta P$ | $1/(1-b) \times \delta D_1/\delta P - \delta R/\delta P$ |
| Effective rates in terms of nominal rates | | | |
| System I | $r$ | $r$ | $0$ |
| System II | $r$ | $\dfrac{d}{1-r+d}$ | $r - \dfrac{d}{1-r+d}$ |
| System III | $r$ | $\dfrac{r-b_1}{1-b_1}$ | $\dfrac{b_1(1-r)}{1-b_1}$ |
| System IV | $r$ | $r(1-x)$ | $rx$ |
| System V | $m$ | $0$ | $m$ |

126

# THE "REGRESSIVENESS" OF TAXES ON SAVING

I have shown elsewhere that in a country like present-day Britain where taxes on saving rise to prohibitive levels an increase in taxes on saving at the top of the scale increases the inequality of spending (and inequality in total) [1]. The purpose of the present appendix is to generalise this conclusion by showing that the inequality of spending (the difference in standards of living between rich and poor) is increased by *any* proportional tax on saving (and *a fortiori* by *any graduated* tax on saving). Thus all taxes on saving are "regressive" in the sense of increasing the difference between living standards of rich and poor [2].

## The concepts

Net-of-tax *income* is the sum of gross-of-tax *spending* and gross-of-tax *saving*.

The *price elasticity of demand* is the percentange change in quantity (or volume) purchased as the result of a given percentage change in price (whether for fiscal reasons or otherwise). The price elasticity of demand is *unitary* if a small *increase* in price (say 1 per cent) causes the same proportionate *reduction* in quantity purchased, turnover (or the amount spent) remaining the same. Demand is *elastic* if turnover falls when price rises and *inelastic* if turnover rises. Volume purchased falls as price rises unless the response is *perverse*.

The *income elasticity of demand* is the percentage change in quantity purchased as the result of a given percentage change in income (whether for fiscal reasons or otherwise). The income elasticity of demand is *unitary* if a small *increase* in income causes the same proportionate *increase* in quantity purchased and turnover, price remaining the same. Demand is *elastic* (or has a *more than unitary* elasticity) if the quantity purchased rises faster than income and *inelastic* if it rises more slowly. Goods and services for which the demand is income-elastic are *luxuries;* those for which the demand is income-inelastic are *necessaries* (necessities); those for which the income elasticity of demand is negative are *inferior*.

The concepts apply to *aggregate spending* and to *new saving* as to individual goods and services. In the long term (in a consistent system) all saving is new saving, since old saving becomes negligibly unimportant [3]. Thus "saving" may be used for "new saving". The volume of spending is the same as its value (or turnover or the amount spent) so long as the average price level remains the same; the volume of spending falls at a given level of turnover if prices rise. The amount of saving is the sum saved and is thus gross of taxes on saving; the real worth of saving is the net-of-tax investment income purchased and is thus net of taxes on saving; the price of saving is the amount of saving per unit of net-of-tax investment income purchased

## The assumptions

(1) The proportion of net-of-tax income absorbed by gross-of-tax saving rises with income if taxes on spending and saving are zero or proportional. (The income elasticity of demand for saving is more than unitary). This assumption would seem to be accepted universally as a statement of fact, even though it is arguably not a logical necessity. The analysis would require qualification if the rates of tax on spending rose more as income increased than the rates of tax on saving, but this qualification is an unnecessary refinement at present, since few existing tax systems, if any, have a more "progressive" structure of taxes on spending than on saving, and even the advocates of an expenditure tax recommend that this bias against saving should be preserved [4].

(2) The proportion of incremental income that is spent remains positive however high the level of income as long as the relative prices of spending and saving are unchanged. (Spending is not an *inferior good*: the income elasticity of demand for spending is always positive). Again, this is not a contentious assumption; its relaxation would complicate the argument without materially altering the conclusions.

(3) The analysis can be made in terms of a comparison between taxpayers all of whose savings are positive. The argument would be complicated if allowance were made for taxpayers with zero or negative savings; but the conclusions would not be materially altered.

(4) The price elasticity of demand for saving is more than unitary. In other words, the amount of saving rises or falls with the yield. This proposition is realised provided (a) that savers are rational (or more rational than irrational) and (b) that saving is not dominated by the "Sargant effect" [5] (is not intended primarily to produce a given temporary income but serves other purposes such as permanent enrichment or the maximisation of long-term income). In the sections of this appendix before "Second-round effects", the Sargant effect is disregarded as being untypical. This is done solely for simplicity of exposition. Since the Sargant effect, if it exists at all, must diminish as income increases, the argument of this appendix is complicated

but not materially altered if the Sargant effect is taken into account. The Sargant effect must diminish as income increases because more saving is for luxuries and more saving is permanent. (Chapter III, "Temporary and permanent saving").

## The diagram

In the diagram the vertical axis measures proportions of net-of-tax income saved and the horizontal axis measures the size of net-of-tax income (income net of income tax but gross of taxes on outgoings, that is, taxes on spending and saving). The proportion of income above the line AB is the proportion spent when the tax on saving is zero; the proportion below the line AB is the proportion saved. The proportion saved rises with income but never attains 100 per cent. AB and the other lines in the diagram are shown as straight lines for simplicity of exposition. The gradient of AB must eventually fall but may initially rise.

A proportional tax is now levied on saving, taxes on spending remaining the same. Saving is now more expensive relatively to spending and spending is cheaper relatively to saving, the two relative prices being reciprocals of each other.

At point W there is a shift of AC from saving to spending as a result of the tax on saving. The diagram shows three lines starting at C. CD is a constant proportion of AB: along CD saving is reduced by the same proportion at all income levels. Along CE spending is increased by the same proportion at all income levels. Along CF the reduction in saving and increase in spending are equal absolutely at all income levels. The significance of these lines is discussed in the following sections [6].

## The income effect

The horizontal scale of the diagram is income net of income tax but gross of taxes on spending and saving. It is therefore unaffected by changes in taxes on spending and saving. But these changes affect the taxpayer's standard of living, just as changes in the general level of prices affect his standard of living even when nominal rates of tax remain unaltered. The income elasticity of demand is determined by real, not nominal, changes in the taxpayer's situation, including price changes and changes in the taxes on his outgoings (spending and saving).

The imposition of a proportional tax on saving reduces the taxpayer's standard of living and it follows from assumption (1) that at any level of income net of income tax but gross of tax on spending and saving the proportion of income net of income tax that is disbursed on spending rises and the proportion that is disbursed on saving falls. This income effect (the income effect of a tax on saving on the proportion of income saved) is separate from the price effect (the change in the relative prices of saving and spending) and itself increases as a proportion of net-of-tax income as income increases: first, because the proportion of income saved before the imposition of the proportional tax on saving increases as income increases

## DIAGRAM

### The "Regressiveness" of Taxes on Saving

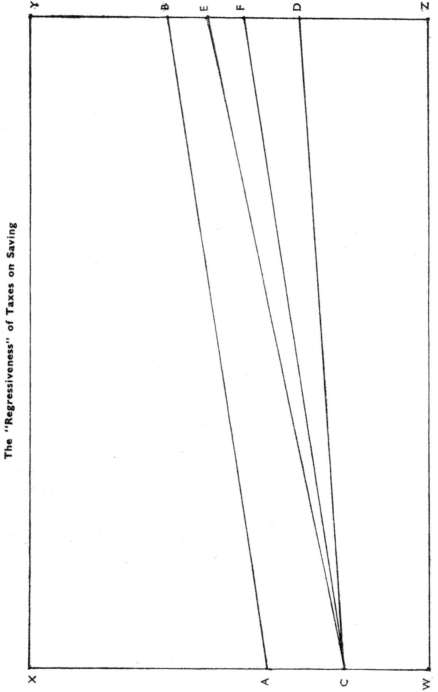

Proportion of net-of-tax income saved (scale from zero to unity)

Size of net-of-tax income

and, second, because the proportional tax on saving consequently reduces larger real incomes proportionately more than smaller real incomes and, third, because the proportion of this reduction in real income accounted for by the reduction of saving increases as income increases.

In the diagram if (at the limit) the income effect is nil when income net of income tax is W, a proportional tax on saving pushes the saving/spending line below AB so that it starts at A and finishes below B; if the income effect at income W is a reduction of saving from A to C, the saving/spending line is reduced below CF. Even if the demand for spending and saving is completely price-inelastic and thus the price effect is zero at all income levels, the imposition of a proportional tax on saving increases the inequality of spending: the inequality of spending is increased along any line starting at C and lying below CE.

## The price effect

Between CD and CE, saving falls less than proportionately and spending rises more than proportionately as income increases: along the line CF, the fall in saving and the rise in spending are a constant proportion of income (net of income tax but gross of taxes on spending and saving).

Along the line CD, the price elasticity of demand for saving remains constant as income increases, while for spending it rises; this is because CD is a constant proportion of AB. Along the line CE, the price elasticity of demand for spending remains constant as income increases, while for saving it falls. These relationships merely reflect the fact that spending is a falling proportion of income and saving a rising proportion as income increases. Along the line CF, the price elasticity of demand for saving falls as income increases while for spending it rises. The line AB represents the balance between the price elasticities and the income elasticities of demand as income increases in the original situation; the line CF represents the balance between the effects of the price elasticities on the proportions of income spent and saved in response to the tax on saving. The decreasing proportion of income spent as income increases means that a given proportionate increase in spending is a falling proportion of income; but a given proportionate reduction in saving is likewise a rising proportion of income and the line CF is a compromise between these two influences.

The line CE represents a logical extreme. The price elasticity of demand for spending must rise as income increases [7] because richer people spend proportionately more on luxuries which are more price-sensitive than necessaries. But the price elasticity of demand for saving also increases as income increases, partly because more saving is for luxuries and partly because more saving is permanent. (Chapter III, "Temporary and permanent saving").

This need not mean that the line starting at C must lie below CD. If the saving of richer taxpayers is a large multiple of their spending, it may be difficult

131

to increase spending sufficiently to yield this result. This may be called the *Croesus problem*. But it is correspondingly easy to reduce saving; and it was shown in the last paragraph but one that the line CF represents the reconciliation of these conflicting pressures: CF gives the neutral solution of the Croesus problem. But CF does not allow for a general increase in price elasticity as income rises. *Since the price elasticity of demand rises with income both for spending and for saving, the new line starting at C must lie below CF on grounds of price elasticity alone.* The last section showed that the income effect works in the same direction and reduces still further the finishing level of the new line starting at C. The new line may lie below CD; the limit is a horizontal line from C, since any lower line would conflict with assumption (1). Since the new line lies below CF, saving switched to spending is a rising proportion of income as income increases; if the new line lies below CD, it is also a rising proportion of saving. As income increases, the amount switched rises more rapidly as a proportion of spending than as a proportion of income and more rapidly as a proportion of income than as a proportion of saving.

### Effects on inequality

The conventional measurement of saving (wealth) is gross of taxes on saving (Appendix I); this implies that for comparability spending should be measured gross of taxes on spending. On this basis, the inequality of income (net of taxes on income) is unaffected by changes in the taxation of spending or saving. If the amount of saving falls in response to a proportional tax on saving, the inequality of spending is increased. The inequality of saving may rise or fall or remain unchanged. The inequality of net income remains unchanged even if the inequalities of spending and saving have both increased because saving is distributed more unequally than spending and the weight of saving (or its ratio to net income) has fallen.

Even if there is no graduated expenditure tax levied on individuals, taxes on expenditure may nevertheless be "progressive" in the sense of charging luxuries more heavily than necessaries. It is legitimate to take this into account only if the graduation of taxes on saving is taken into account likewise. Spending and saving are in competition with each other: their distribution should be reckoned either both gross of tax or both net and not part and part. It is not legitimate to calculate income distributions from an amalgam of spending net of tax and saving gross of tax, as is traditional at the Central Statistical Office[8].

This general consideration is of particular relevance here, since the "implicit progressivity" of taxes on goods and services (luxuries being taxed more heavily than necessaries) could, in principle and perhaps in practice, cause the inequality of the net-of-tax distribution of spending to fall while the inequality of the gross-of-tax distribution rose (just as gross-of-tax income inequality may rise while net-of-tax inequality falls: see under "Second-round effects" below). The argument of this appendix is based on gross outgoings (spending plus saving) which equal income net of income tax; this is the conventional concept. The argument could be adapted to a net-of-tax basis (which is one element in Appendix I), and there is a strong case for reckoning all distributions net of all fiscal charges; if this were done, the initial measures of inequality would be reduced — slightly for spending, moderately for income, drastically for saving and wealth; and the changes in the measures as a result of changes in the tax on saving would alter correspondingly.

Since the inequality of net income is unaltered by the tax on saving if saving and spending are reckoned gross of tax, it may be considered that the tax on saving has had no effect on inequality. But there are two counterarguments. The first is that a tax which certainly increases the inequality of spending and possibly increases the inequality of saving may for these two reasons be regarded as increasing inequality even if the inequality of net income is unaltered. The second is that spending weighs more heavily in the total calculation than saving per unit of income. Spending is about living standards and life styles, which are the very stuff of inequality. Saving is merely about potential spending and purchasing power; its relation to spending is that of shadow to substance. On this argument, any increase in the inequality of spending, combined with an increase in its weight as a proportion of total net income, increases the substantive inequality of net income even though the inequality of net income is unchanged if substance and shadow are weighted equally per unit of income. The conventional treatment, which weights substance and shadow equally, is at variance with the common sense of the matter; this latter implies that in the common sense of the terms a proportional tax on saving *must* increase the inequality of spending and inequality in total and *may* increase the inequality of saving as well [9] Thus, in the common sense of the terms, a proportional tax on saving *must* be "regressive" (proportionately heavier on poor than on rich), in terms of both income and spending and *may* be regressive in terms of saving as well.

### A graduated tax on saving

The conclusion is reinforced if the tax on saving is graduated instead of proportional. The imposition of a graduated instead of a proportional tax on saving increases the inequality of spending faster as income rises; similarly the inequality of saving falls faster (or falls instead of rising). Aggregate spending acquires a heavier weight relatively to aggregate saving; and there is a more rapid rise in overall inequality or inequality not otherwise qualified.

### Second-round effects

So far the analysis has been in terms of a single period. If the distribution of investment income is less equal than that of earned income, the imposition of a proportional (and *a fortiori* a graduated) tax on savings will reduce the inequality of

133

net income in subsequent periods at the cost of a general reduction in prosperity as the result of a tax-induced switch from saving to spending. Gross-of-tax income inequality may rise in the second round if the Sargant effect predominates [10] (though in the absence of this effect income inequality will fall gross of tax as well as net) Thus the inequality of income gross of tax may rise while net of tax it falls; and this illustrates the dangers of the conventional measurement of inequality gross of tax: the politically significant distribution is net, whether the inequality is of income, expenditure or wealth.

The gross-of-tax inequality of wealth may rise or fall as the result of a proportional tax on saving; it is more likely to fall if the tax rates are graduated, since the Sargant effect must diminish as income and wealth increase and permanent saving becomes more important relatively to temporary saving. If the inequality of wealth falls, the fall will be less than the rise in the inequality of spending, both absolutely (because wealth exceeds spending in the period in which the distribution of spending is reckoned) and also proportionately (because the distribution of wealth is more unequal than that of spending).

Since the economic taxable capacity of saving is in general nil (Chapter III), there are in general no gains for non-savers; and non-savers lose as well as savers if any positive economic taxable capacity of temporary saving is exceeded by the negative economic taxable capacity of permanent saving. (Senses four and five of "The taxable capacity of saving", Chapter III). Non-savers are more likely to lose if the taxation of saving is graduated instead of proportional. There is an inescapable conflict between the taxation of saving and prosperity; any reduction in the inequality of wealth achieved by a proportionate (and *a fortiori* a graduated) tax on saving may or may not be considered sufficient justification for the reduction it inflicts on general prosperity and even on the prosperity of non-savers.

If taxes on saving are already high (prohibitive or nearly prohibitive), savers have relatively little to lose from the imposition of additional taxes on saving; the main burden of additional taxes on saving is in these circumstances borne by spenders. These are the circumstances of present-day Britain. Taxes at the top of the scale are prohibitive [11] and even at modest levels of wealth almost prohibitive. The gains from marginal reductions in such taxes, which appear to go to savers, in reality go largely to spenders.

## Conclusion

The inequality (a) of income net of income tax is identically equal to the inequality of outgo gross of taxes on saving and spending. In addition, within any one period there are also the inequality (b) of income gross of income tax and the inequality (c) of outgo net of taxes on saving and spending, the differences between the three inequalities being determined by the pattern of taxation levied within the period; and over a succession of periods there are the changes in the inequalities of gross income (and thus in the other two inequalities) as a result of the pattern of taxation levied in previous periods. Finally, there is the inequality of wealth, gross of tax and net of tax.

A proportional tax on saving must increase the inequality of gross-of-tax spending (in the diagram, any new spending/saving line starting at A must lie below AB and any new spending/saving line starting at C must lie below CE — indeed, below CF). It will also increase the inequality of net-of-tax spending if the taxation of spending is unchanged. These effects are intensified if the taxation of saving is graduated.

It is wrong to reckon the inequality of spending net of tax unless the inequalities of saving (per period) and wealth (cumulatively) are also reckoned net of tax; the adoption of this method is indeed desirable, but it would require a revolution in conventional attitudes to distribution and inequality. (Appendix I). Spending and saving should be treated both gross of tax or both net. The conclusion of our gross-of-tax analysis is unequivocal: the distribution of spending is made more unequal by a proportional tax on saving and even more unequal if the tax on saving is graduated.

Wealth differs from spending in being a stock, not a flow, cumulative, not instantaneous. A proportional tax on saving may either reduce or increase the inequality of wealth, either instantaneously or cumulatively, either gross of tax or net. A graduated tax is more likely to reduce the inequality of wealth gross of tax and still more likely to reduce it net. But even if the inequality of wealth is reduced, the inequality of spending will rise much more in any period, both absolutely (because the amount of wealth is a substantial multiple of the amount of spending) and also proportionately (because the inequality of wealth is necessarily much larger than the inequality of spending). The inequality of the substance rises faster than the inequality of the shadow falls. In aggregate, there is a rise in overall inequality or inequality not otherwise qualified, both year by year and cumulatively.

But what of the three other senses of overall inequality, inequalities (a)—(c) in the first paragraph of this section? They are all hybrids in that they deal simultaneously either with income from earnings and income from investments or with outgo to spending and outgo to saving. Moreover, these three different senses of overall inequality differ among themselves in any one period and differ further over a succession of periods. The reconciliation of these different conceptions of overall inequality would be no easy task both because they are all hybrid and also because they all refer either backwards to past periods or forwards to future periods or both. The simplest conception of overall inequality is the one I put forward in *Redistribution in Reverse*: a reconciliation of the inequality of spending with the inequality of wealth, the two being distinct (and not hybrids) both in dimension) (flow/stock) and in activity (spending/saving). On this basis a proportional (and *a fortiori* a graduated) tax on saving must increase both the inequality of spending and inequality in aggregate and be complemented by a cumulative reduction in the general level of prosperity, not only for savers but for the whole taxpaying community. This conclusion is in line with the argument of Chapter III that saving has in general no positive economic taxable capacity and with the argument of *Redistribution in Reverse* that an increase in graduated taxes on saving to prohibitive levels increases not only the inequality of spending but also inequality overall.

The taxation of saving (or wealth) is thus in conflict both with the reduction of inequality and with the increase of prosperity. *All taxes on saving that diminish the amount of gross-of-tax saving or wealth in private hands are "regressive", not only on spending but in general; and this effect is intensified if the taxes are graduated instead of proportional. If the economic taxable capacity of saving is on balance negative, non-savers as well as savers lose from the reduction of general prosperity.*

# THE EMPIRICAL MATERIAL

### The Camel's Back and subsequent changes

Table 4 gives figures for seven indicators of absolute and relative tax burdens for the years 1972, 1975, 1978 and 1979. 1972 was chosen as the most recent year for which tax yields were discussed in *The Camel's Back;* 1978 as the most recent year on which the OECD had reported comprehensively at the time of writing in *Revenue Statistics of OECD Member Countries* (although the figures for Greece were missing); 1975 as the mid-year between 1972 and 1978; and 1979 as the most recent year for which provisional figures were available at the time of writing. Together, these four years give an indication of the present position and recent trends. Each British indicator is followed by the percentage of the corresponding average for the OECD (including Britain) [1].

Row (1) of Table 4 shows total tax revenue as a percentage of gross domestic product (GDP). The British percentage fell from 37.56 in 1970 to 31.96 in 1973 as a result of the Heath Government's tax-cutting programme, a programme which unfortunately was not extended to cuts in government expenditure. These tax cuts were later reversed, and the percentage in 1979 was nearly as high as in 1972 Meanwhile, the average OECD tax take increased steadily year by year and, for this reason only, Britain's relative position improved.

Row (3) shows total tax revenue net of the "para-fiscal" element represented by "social-security" (or "national-insurance") contributions. The picture is similar, although British social-security contributions rose slightly from 5.29 per cent of GDP in 1972 to 6.05 per cent in 1979: row (3) therefore shows a decline of about 1 percentage point over this period.

Row (5) shows that the percentage of British gross domestic product taken in taxes on income and profits was almost the same in 1979 as in 1972. Meanwhile, the OECD average had risen substantially.

The proportion of British taxation contributed by taxes on goods and services (not shown in Table 4) fell from 28.46 per cent in 1972 to 24.51 per cent in

TABLE 4

Comparative position of United Kingdom 1972—1979

| | 1972 | 1975 | 1978 | Percentages 1979 |
|---|---|---|---|---|
| (1) Tax revenue including social-security contributions as percentage of GDP | 34.06 | 36.23 | 34.45 | 33.79 |
| (2) = (1) as percentage of OECD average | 108.16 | 107.60 | 96.23 | (91.50) |
| (3) Tax revenue excluding social-security contributions as percentage of GDP | 28.76 | 29.93 | 28.25 | 27.74 |
| (4) = (3) as percentage of OECD average | 115.64 | 116.32 | 109.79 | (99.75) |
| (5) Tax revenue from income and profits as percentage of GDP | 13.30 | 16.10 | 13.91 | 13.55 |
| (6) = (5) as percentage of OECD average | 113.19 | 121.79 | 96.26 | (93.84) |
| (7) Tax revenue from property as percentage of GDP | 5.01 | 4.58 | 4.13 | 4.31 |
| (8) = (7) as percentage of OECD average | 239.71 | 241.05 | 224.46 | (237.47) |
| (9) Tax revenue from specific goods and services as percentage of GDP | 6.75 | 5.34 | 5.35 | 4.57 |
| (10) = (9) as percentage of OECD average | 125.23 | 108.98 | 114.07 | (99.78) |
| (11) Tax revenue including social-security contributions but excluding revenue from goods and services as percentage of GDP | 24.37 | 27.03 | 25.31 | 25.51 |
| (12) = (11) as percentage of OECD average | 115.94 | 114.20 | 99.06 | (97.89) |
| (13) Tax revenue excluding social-security contributions and taxes on general consumption as percentage of GDP | 26.58 | 26.75 | 25.13 | 24.63 |
| (14) = (13) as percentage of OECD average | 130.94 | 126.36 | 113.05 | (108.60) |

Source: Revenue Statistics of OECD Member Countries 1965—1979, Tables, 3, 4, 8, 22, 24, 28, 30

Notes: (1) Tax revenue excluding social-security contributions as a percentage of GDP is the sum of (5), (7), taxes on goods and services, employers' payroll or manpower taxes, and "other" taxes. Taxes on goods and services took 9.14 per cent of British GDP in 1978; payroll or manpower taxes took 0.99 per cent; "other" taxes took 0.07 per cent.

(2) The OECD have substantially revised the 1972 figures that were used in The Camel's Back; Table 4 shows the revised figures. The revisions are partly due to changes of basis.

(3) The figures for 1978 exclude Greece. The figures for 1979 exclude Greece and Australia, and some of the figures for 1979 exclude Japan, Luxembourg and Turkey. The averages for 1972 and 1975 are thus based on 23 countries; the averages for 1978 on 22 countries; and the averages for 1979 on 18—21 countries. Since Greece, Japan and Turkey are low-tax countries the figures for 1978 and 1979 underestimate the relative burden of British taxation, especially for 1979. Also the 1979 figures of gross domestic product are provisional. For these reasons the percentages of the OECD averages in 1979 are bracketed as provisional. (Iceland is omitted from all tables in this book: although Iceland is an OECD and Scandinavian country, no figures for Iceland have ever been published in Revenue Statistics of OECD Member Countries).

1979. This represents a substantial shift from indirect to direct taxation and is a trend opposed to the long-standing policy of the Conservative Party to shift the balance of taxation from direct to indirect.

Taxes on property have been heavier in Britain than in any other OECD country in each of the years 1972—1979. (Row (7)). Taxes on property comprise local rates, taxes on financial transactions and estate duty/capital transfer tax, which is heavier in Britain than its equivalents elsewhere. Table 11 of the Inland Revenue Green Paper *Taxation of Capital on Death: A possible Inheritance Tax in place of Estate Duty* (Cmnd. 4930, 1972), which is reproduced as Table 5 of *The Camel's Back*, shows that this was so in 1969. The more extensive information in Table 0.4 of *The Taxation of Net Wealth, Capital Transfers and Capital Gains of Individuals* (OECD, 1979) shows that in 1976 death and gift duties were a higher proportion of GDP at market prices than in Britain only in Australia, New Zealand and the United States of the twenty-one member countries for which figures are given: and these taxes have been almost entirely abolished in Australia since 1976.

Row (9) shows excise duties, which took a declining proportion of British GDP over the period 1972—1979, although this decline may since have been reversed. Britain has traditionally been a country with high specific duties by OECD standards, and increases in the rates of duty since 1979 may well have restored that position.

Row (11) provides a measure of the *tax burden on international competitiveness* (the tax burden on exporting and competing with imports). Over the period 1972—1979 this burden increased a little absolutely but declined more substantially by comparison with the OECD average, in consequence of the substantial rises abroad. Since 1979, the high exchange rate of sterling by comparison with its relative purchasing power has been a much more noticeable, and probably a much more serious, barrier to international competitiveness than the structure of the tax system.

Row (13) provides a measure of *tax awareness* or *fiscal pain*. The rationale is that broadly-based and moderately-rated taxes like social-security contributions and general consumption taxes are less sharply perceived and less acutely felt than taxes on income and capital and high-rate excise duties. By libertarian standards, the taxes that are most bitterly resented are the best taxes, since they maximise the incentive to bring taxes down. Consistently with this argument, however, taxes that are the most resented do the most damage until such time as the pressure to reduce them becomes effective. By the criterion of fiscal painfulness in row (13), row (14) shows that the British tax system is more painful than the OECD average, though this difference has been diminishing since 1972. Chapter IX ("Quantity and quality") mentions the possibility of different methods of weighting tax yields to calculate the *qualitative burden* [2].

To sum up, the British tax take fell from 1972 to 1973 but more than recaptured its former level in 1974; since then it has stayed at about 35 per cent of GDP and has been gradually overtaken by the OECD average. The relative improvement in the British position during recent years has therefore been due to the absolute deterioration elsewhere in the OECD. And the British tax system still has a heavy qualitative burden in the sense of heavy taxes on sensitive items like property as well as high rates at the top of the scale.

*Short Measure from Whitehall*

Since 1969 the Central Statistical Office have published in Economic Trends each December or thereabouts an article entitled *International Comparisons of Taxes and Social Security Contributions*. This is the main official publication in Britain on the subject of international tax comparisons; it has been accepted uncritically in many quarters, and it has had an important influence on opinion.

In *Short Measure from Whitehall: How CSO Statistics Understate the British Tax Burden* (Centre for Policy Studies, 1977) I explained why the British tax burden was higher than appeared from the CSO articles. The principal reasons were (a) the samples of countries in the Economic Trends comparison were small and unrepresentative; (b) the Economic Trends figures omitted taxes on capital which were higher in Britain than in any other country of the OECD (row (8) in Table 4 above); (c) the Economic Trends figures omitted taxes on expenditure from the measure of gross national product, which understated the burden of British taxation by comparison with that of other industrialised countries.

The CSO addressed itself to these criticisms in the next article in the series, which took in the year 1975 and was published in Economic Trends of December 1977. This article is much longer and more thorough than its predecessors and represents a substantial improvement in the CSO's treatment of the subject. In consequence, as we shall see, the reader is given a different (and more accurate) assessment of how heavily the United Kingdom is taxed by comparison with other countries.

(a) *Size of sample.* This is the most important point, as well as being the least technical. The December 1977 article compares nineteen OECD countries, whereas previous articles compared only thirteen. Since on the CSO's own "national accounts" basis of computation all six of the additional countries (Australia, Finland, Greece, Ireland, Spain, Switzerland) were taxed less heavily in 1975 than the United Kingdom, the United Kingdom moved from ninth out of thirteen to ninth out of nineteen. This alone transforms the situation. But the CSO could have gone further. Of the four remaining OECD countries for which figures were available, only one was a high-tax country (Luxembourg); the other three were low-tax countries (New Zealand, Portugal, Turkey). If these four countries had been added, the United Kingdom would have moved to tenth place out of twenty-three in 1975.

In the article for 1974 published in Economic Trends November 1976, the CSO showed the United Kingdom as coming seventh out of seven in a comparison based on the new System of National Accounts (SNA) and fourth out of five in a different comparison based on the old SNA: in all, tenth out of eleven countries, the eleventh being Japan. (Table 1(a), page 109 of the Economic Trends article). Tenth out of eleven is very different from tenth out of twenty-three.

The size of the sample has been a major determinant of official interpretation. The Economic Progress Report for September 1977, prepared by the Information Division of the Treasury, says: "Our tax burden was lighter than that of many developed industrial nations in 1974 (the latest figures available),with the notable exception of Japan". The December 1977 Economic Trends article says: "Other high percentage countries in 1975 — in excess of 40 per cent — were Austria, Belgium, Germany (FR), France, Finland and the United Kingdom". This move from low-tax status in 1974 to high-tax status in 1975 was not due to an increase in United Kingdom taxation; taxation increased little more between the two years in the United Kingdom than in the rest of the Economic Trends sample. The change of status was due to the increase in the number of countries brought into the reckoning.

(b) *Taxes on capital.* If taxes on capital are omitted, a country that raised all its tax revenue from taxes on capital would be shown as having no tax burden at all. This alone shows the absurdity of leaving out taxes on capital; the reasons for including them are further discussed in *The Camel's Back*, page 36 and *Is Capital Taxation Fair?*, Chapter IV.

The December 1977 Economic Trends article includes taxes on capital, which were excluded by earlier articles in the series. On the former SNA taxes on capital as a percentage of gross national product at factor cost in 1975 were half as high again in the United Kingdom as in any of the other countries cited, which accords with the official figures for death duties quoted in *The Camel's Back*, Table 5. But on the new SNA taxes on capital in the United Kingdom were only one third as high as on the former SNA in 1970 and less than half as high in 1975, which illustrates how apparently technical changes of national accounting can transform tax comparisons. Even at this lower level, taxes on capital in the United Kingdom were heavier than the average of the other countries cited. Thus the inclusion of taxes on capital increased the measure of the tax burden in the United Kingdom by comparison with elsewhere.

(c) *Measurement of gross national product (GNP) or gross domestic product (GDP).* GNP exceeds GDP by the amount of net property income from abroad. Both GNP and GDP may be measured either at market prices (including taxes on expenditure net of subsidies) or at factor cost (excluding taxes on expenditure net of subsidies). Thus GNP and GDP are larger at market prices than at factor cost; the measure of the tax burden is *absolutely larger* at factor cost than at market prices but *relatively smaller* for a country such as the United Kingdom which takes a relatively small proportion of its GNP or GDP in taxes on expenditure. By contrast with (a) and (b) above, the CSO have not tried to meet the criticism that market prices give the truer measure and that factor cost therefore understates the British tax burden.

The CSO rightly argued in December 1977 that a change from factor cost to market prices has no dramatic consequences for the ranking of countries. Moreover, within the OECD as a whole the relative tax burden of the United Kingdom is little increased. But within the EC it is increased more substantially, since the burden of taxes on expenditure is further below the average of the EC than it is below the average of the OECD.

The difference of basis is less important in practice than in theory. Theoretically, the market-price basis has a decisive advantage. First, the factor-cost basis can lead to the paradoxical result of taxation absorbing more than 100 per cent of GNP or GDP. Second, market prices are real whereas factor costs are constructs. Third, the distinction between "direct" and "indirect" taxes is not sufficiently sharp to warrant such a difference of treatment: some taxes, like selective employment tax, are on the margin between the two. Fourth, and more radically, no such difference of treatment between one tax and another is justified: either all taxes should be included in GNP or GDP or all should be excluded (in which case the popular concept of tax take requires revision, since tax take will frequently exceed 100 per cent of GNP or GDP). This leads to the fifty point. The CSO argue for factor cost on the ground that the measure of the tax burden is unaffected by switches within a given total between "direct" and "indirect" taxation. But this advantage is illusory. If there is a switch to "indirect" taxation, prices rise and with them the measures of GNP and GDP at market prices. The market-price basis of measurement correctly records a reduction in the tax take: tax revenue is the same in monetary terms, while GNP or GDP in monetary terms has risen in correspondence with the fall in the value of money. Finally, the factor-cost basis appears to imply the contentious proposition that "indirect" taxes are passed forwards whereas "direct" taxes are not.

The innovations introduced in December 1977 have been maintained in subsequent articles in the series in Economic Trends. In December 1980, the basic comparisons covered 17 countries out of the OECD's 23 member countries reporting tax statistics (Table 4). Since three of the missing countries were high-tax countries (Denmark, Finland, Luxembourg) and three were low-tax countries (New Zealand, Portugal, Turkey), the position of the United Kingdom was little affected. (Revenue Statistics of OECD Member Countries 1965—1979, Table 1, page 42). But elsewhere in the article (Table B, page 102), the CSO cited OECD figures for 1979 covering the 18 countries for which figures were available but omitting Luxembourg (high-tax) and Australia, Greece, Japan, Turkey (low-tax). This omission moved Britain from eleventh out of 23 to tenth out of 18 and thus from the high-tax half to the low-tax half of the league, which illustrates how sensitive rankings can be to changes in the sample.

Taxes on capital are still included in the Economic Trends articles on the basis of the new SNA (which classifies capital gains taxes as taxes on income). However, the CSO, unlike the OECD, omit local rates (recurrent capital taxes on immovables), which in 1976 were a larger proportion of GDP in Britain than in any of the other 20 OECD countries for which figures were available. *(The Taxation of Net Wealth, Capital Transfers and Capital Gains of Individuals,* OECD, 1979, Table 0.4, page 23). This omission understates the total burden of taxation in Britain.

There is also a small continuing understatement due to the calculation of GNP at factor cost instead of market prices. Taxes on goods and services were 9.14 per cent of GDP in Britain in 1978 as compared with 10.25 per cent in the OECD as a whole; this suggests that the factor-cost method of calculating GDP in the Economic Trends articles understates the relative burden of taxation in Britain by about 1 per cent (or about one third of one percentage point). The understatement is twice as large (about 2 per cent) relatively to the rest of the EC.

In sum, the CSO articles continue to understate the British tax burden (regularly under (b) and (c) and occasionally under (a) above), though much less than they did before 1977. But the pattern of taxation may be as important as its weight; and Britain has for many years supported an exceptionally heavy *qualitative burden*.

## The qualitative burden

*Quantity and quality*

Overall measures of tax take, as in row (1) of Table 4, are calculated by adding together the yields of all the various taxes. But taxes are not equal in this sense for all purposes. Row (13) of Table 4 gives a measure of fiscal pain or awareness calculated by deducting the yields of social-security contributions and taxes on general consumption from the figures of tax yield in aggregate. By this comparison, Britain still has a relatively painful tax system, though less so than at the beginning of the seventies [2].

The concept of a qualitative burden is apparently accepted by a Labour Administration. The Treasury's Economic Progress Report for September 1977 says: "Together with the high marginal tax rates imposed on any extra income earned all this means that our tax burden feels more painful even though it may not be so in actual fact". Similarly, the CSO article from Economic Trends December 1980 cited above under "*Short Measure from Whitehall*" speaks of "an alternative approach which may better reflect the impact of taxes and contributions as perceived by the taxpayer".

*Tax yields and tax rates*

Still more sensitive measures of the qualitative burden can be provided by calculations based on tax rates. Tax rates, not tax yields, are what governments or parliaments determine by law and what particular taxpayers are charged.

Although investment incentives and other erosions of the tax base reduce the damage done by high rates of tax, the structure before allowance for these reliefs serves as a standard of reference, both economically and politically, because it represents the charge on taxpayers exposed to the full weight of the system.

143

Incentives and avoidance are directly related to marginal rates of tax and only indirectly to curves of maximum yield constructed from real or imaginary revenue aggregates.

Marginal rates of tax are also preferable to tax yields as the basis of calculating tax "progressivity", whether for single taxes or for the whole tax system. I have explained elsewhere both the advantages of using tax rates for this purpose [3] and the disadvantages of using tax yields [4].

Table 5 gives the maximum percentage rates of tax levied at the start of 1981 in Scandinavia and the European Community on earned income, investment income, transfers to lineal descendants, capital gains, wealth and expenditure on goods and services. The latter figure is a weighted average [5] of the tax rates levied on various goods and services; it is given for 1979, the last year for which figures were available at the time of writing, and Greece, for which no 1979 tax revenue figures were available, is omitted from the table. The four bracketed figures to the right of columns (3) and (5) are tax rates adjusted for comparability with the other columns. The German and Luxembourg wealth taxes have been translated into the equivalent rate of transfer tax on the assumption that saving is maximised over a generation of twenty-five years [6]. Inheritance tax is then netted down by this amount; in other words, wealth tax is treated as a charge for purposes of transfer tax [7].

Table 5 shows the differences between the United Kingdom tax system and the other systems in a sharper focus than the comparison of yields in Table 4.

**TABLE 5**

Maximum percentage rates of tax in Scandinavia and the European Community 1981

Percentages

| | (1) Earned income | (2) Investment income * | (3) Transfers to lineal descendants | (4) Capital gains | (5) Wealth * | (6) Expenditure on goods and services 1979 |
|---|---|---|---|---|---|---|
| Scandinavia | | | | | | |
| Denmark | 66.67 | 70.00 | 32.00 | — | (2.200) | 30.63 |
| Finland | 66.00 | 80.00 | 11.00 | — | (1.700) | 25.31 |
| Norway | 69.00 | 90.00 | 35.00 | — | (2.600) | (33.66) |
| Sweden | 83.00 | 85.00 | 65.00 | — | (2.500) | 23.98 |
| EC | | | | | | |
| Belgium | 67.50 | 67.50 | 25.00 | — | — | 18.29 |
| Denmark | 66.67 | 70.00 | 32.00 | — | (2.200) | 30.63 |
| France | 54.00 | 60.00 | 20.00 | — | — | 20.72 |
| Germany | 56.00 | 56.00 | 35.00(30.88) | — | 0.500(11.78) | 18.36 |
| Ireland | 60.00 | 60.00 | 50.00 | — | — | (21.40) |
| Italy | 72.00 | 72.00 | 31.00 | — | — | 13.36 |
| Luxembourg | 57.00 | 57.00 | 5.00(4.41) | — | 0.500(11.78) | (14.64) |
| Netherlands | 72.00 | 80.00 | 17.00 | — | (0.800) | 20.00 |
| United Kingdom | 60.00 | 75.00 | 75.00 | 30.00 | — | 13.44 |
| 11-country average | 65.74 | 70.68 | 29.64 | 0.00 | 0.091 | 21.85 |

* where the figure in (5) is in brackets, the figure in (2) is the "ceiling" or overall limitation for income tax and wealth tax (in the Scandinavian countries and the Netherlands), subject to qualifications and exceptions varying from country to country.

144

*Sources:* (1) and (5): *Supplementary Service to European Taxation B* (International Bureau of Fiscal Documentation, Amsterdam), March 1981.

(2) and (4): *The Taxation of Private Investment Income* (*Guides to European Taxation,* Volume III, IBFD, Amsterdam), Section A for each country, November 1980.

(3) *The Taxation of Net Wealth, Capital Transfers and Capital Gains of Individuals* (Organisation for Economic Co-operation and Development, Paris, 1979),

(6) Taxation: *Revenue Statistics of OECD Member Countries 1965—1979* (OECD, 1979), pages 138—139, item 5000. Expenditure: for Norway, 1979 private consumption in current prices, *Monthly Bulletin of Statistics*, Oslo, 3/1981, page 7; for Ireland and Luxembourg, 1978 private final consumption expenditure in current prices (*UN Monthly Bulletin of Statistics February 1981*, pages 191 and following), updated by the 1979/1978 change in consumption by households (*Eurostatistics Data for Short-term Economic Analysis 4/1981*, page 2); for other countries, 1979 private final consumption expenditure from the *UN Monthly Bulletin of Statistics*, as for Ireland and Luxembourg.

*Notes:* (a) Greece is omitted, since no tax figures for column (6) are available from *OECD Revenue Statistics 1965—1979.*

(b) For (1) — (5) the figures represent the position at the beginning of 1981; for (6) they represent the average for 1979: (6), which is for calendar 1979, is the ratio of revenue from taxes on goods and services to private final consumption expenditure and is thus always some two years behind (1) — (5), which are merely rates of tax. The bracketed figures in column (6) indicate that the expenditure figures for 1979 are estimates, as is explained under *Sources*. The figures in column (6) are relatively stable from year to year, so that Table 5 is not likely to be subject to much revision when the 1981 tax rates for column (6) become available towards the end of 1982.

(c) For the figures in brackets in columns (3) and (5), see the text.

(d) Belgium (1) and (2) exclude optional municipal surcharge. Denmark (1) is collective limitation of State income tax, national pension contribution, local income tax and county municipality income tax. Finland (1) includes 15 per cent local income tax (the rate charged in Helsinki, which is near the average for the country). France (1) is 60 per cent minus 6 per cent (= 10% × 60%) *frais professionnels*. Germany (1) and (2) exclude church taxes. Italy (1) and (2) exclude local taxes. Norway (1) includes 21 per cent local income tax; (5) includes 1 per cent municipal wealth tax. Sweden (1) includes 25 per cent local tax. Capital gains tax is put at nil where there is no general tax on capital gains: for example, in Denmark, where the *saerlig indkomstskat* is levied only on certain extraordinary gains; in Sweden, where movables other than shares held for five years or longer are exempt; in France and Ireland, where there are provisions for the exemption of long-term gains.

The UK tax on expenditure on goods and services is well below the 11-country average (though not far below the OECD average) and the maximum tax on earned income is about a tenth lower. On the other hand, the UK tax system is exceptionally burdensome on saving (investment income and its parent capital). The maximum tax on investment income is several points higher than the 11-country average, even though the latter includes five wealth tax "ceilings" (overall limitations for wealth tax and income tax as a proportion of income). Only two countries, Germany and Luxembourg, have a wealth tax without such a ceiling, and then at a rate of 0.5 per cent, so that the average rate of wealth tax for the 11 countries is less than a tenth of one per cent. By contrast, the United Kingdom is the only country to levy a general capital gains tax, and that at 30 per cent without allowance for inflation. And, most important of all, the maximum U.K. rate of tax on family transfers is more than two and a half times the 11-country average.

*Tax height*

The *height* of the tax system is a concept used in *The Measurement of Fiscal Policy* (Chapter VII A) as an indicator of the collective or aggregate burden of tax at the top of the scale. The tax rates in Table 5 are added together, expenditure being taken twice (once for expenditure out of earnings and once for expenditure out of investment income or capital) [8]. Table 6 shows the height of tax in this sense at gross or tax-inclusive tax rates for the countries of Scandinavia and the EC in 1981. Column (1) shows collective height absolutely, column (2) shows it as a proportion of the theoretical maximum and column (3) ranks the twelve countries from highest to lowest.

Even after the tax cuts of the June 1979 Budget, the height of the tax system in the United Kingdom was second only to that of Sweden among the twelve countries for which figures are given in Table 6. Tax height in the United Kingdom in 1981 was 9 per cent above the average for Scandinavia, which is rightly regarded as the highest-tax area among the major groups of countries. It was 26 per cent above the 11-country average (the rest of the European Community together with Scandinavia) and 35 per cent above the rest of the European Community.

*Tax basis*

For taxpayers who have and make no savings the tax burden is the combined weight of tax on earning and on spending; for example, in the United Kingdom it is as much as 60.00% + 13.44% of (1—60.00%) or 65.38% altogether. (Lower rates of tax are treated as concessionary: *The Measurement of Fiscal Policy*, Chapters III and IV and Appendix VII D). If the tax burden on saving were the same as this tax burden on earning and spending, the weight of the combined taxes on saving would also be 65.38% [9].

The tax on earnings, however, is not only a tax on spending but also a tax on saving, since some earnings are saved. In a comparison between the taxation of spending and the taxation of saving, the tax on earnings therefore falls out of the reckoning. Thus, if there were no taxes on transfers, capital gains or wealth, the tax burden on spending would be the same as the tax burden on saving if the tax on spending equalled the tax on investment income. In fact, the tax on investment income is much higher than the tax on spending in all the nine countries of the Community for which figures are given in Table 5, even though all nine countries have at least one other tax on saving. There is thus a large bias against saving and in favour of spending.

A measure of this bias is explained in *The Measurement of Fiscal Policy*, Chapters VII B, VIII E and VIII F. The tax on expenditure is subtracted from the sum of the taxes on capital (investment income, transfers, capital gains, wealth). This measures the *basis* of the tax system (its *pattern* or *bias against saving*), when account is taken of the height of tax on spending. The logic of deducting the tax on spending from the tax on investment income as an element in the computation of the discrimination between spending and saving is the same as the logic of deducting the tax on earnings from the tax on investment income to give the investment income surcharge or earned-income relief or any other form of discrimination in favour of earnings and against income from investments. By comparison with Table 6, the tax on earned income (which falls partly on spending and partly on saving and is included once in Table 6) is deducted once and the tax on expenditure, which is included twice in Table 6, is deducted three times. The bias against saving represented by tax basis is the tax burden on capital (and thus on industry) after allowance has been made for the level of taxation in general.

## TABLE 6

Tax height 1981

|  | (1)<br>Collective height<br>of gross tax rates | (2)<br>Percentages<br>of the maximum | (3)<br>Ranks |
|---|---|---|---|
| **Scandinavia** | | | |
| Denmark | 229.93 | 32.86 | 4 |
| Finland | 207.62 | 29.67 | 7 |
| Norway | 261.32 | 37.34 | 3 |
| Sweden | 280.96 | 40.15 | 1 |
| **EC** | | | |
| Belgium | 196.58 | 28.09 | 9 |
| Denmark | 229.93 | 32.86 | 4 |
| France | 175.44 | 25.07 | 11 |
| Germany | 191.38 | 27.35 | 10 |
| Ireland | 212.80 | 30.41 | 5 |
| Italy | 201.72 | 28.83 | 8 |
| Luxembourg | 159.47 | 22.79 | 12 |
| Netherlands | 209.00 | 29.87 | 6 |
| United Kingdom | 266.88 | 38.14 | 2 |
| Scandinavian average | 244.96 | 35.00 | |
| EC average (excluding UK) | 197.04 | 28.16 | |
| 11-country average (excluding UK) | 211.47 | 30.22 | |

*Source:* Table 5.

*Notes:* (1) Bracketed figures have been used for Germany and Luxembourg in columns (3) and (5) of Table 5. For the Scandinavian countries and The Netherlands, the wealth tax figures in column (5) of Table 5 are subsumed under the investment-income tax figures in column (2).

(2) In column (1) of Table 6 the tax on expenditure in column (6) of Table 5 is added to the tax rates in columns (1) — (5), despite its being some eighteen months earlier because column (6) is relatively stable from year to year. Similarly for the subtraction of column (6) of Table 5 from columns (2) — (5) in Table 7 below.

Table 7 gives the figures of tax basis for the countries of Scandinavia and the EC in 1981, *basis* being the bias against saving in the sense explained in the last paragraph. Column (3) shows tax basis absolutely and column (4) shows it as a proportion of the theoretical maximum.

Table 7 shows that in 1981 the sum of the taxes on saving (column (1)), was higher in the United Kingdom than in any country in Scandinavia or the EC: 20 per cent higher than in the nearest competitor (Sweden), 54 per cent above the Scandinavian average and 90 per cent above the rest of the EC. For the column (3) figures of tax basis (the tax burden on capital, and thus on industry, after allowance has been made for the level of taxation in general) the contrast is even more striking: 1981 tax basis in the United Kingdom was 32 per cent above the nearest competitor (Sweden), 88 per cent above the Scandinavian average and 122 per cent above the average for the rest of the EC.

## TABLE 7

Tax basis 1981

|  | (1) Taxes on investment income and its parent capital | (2) Tax on spending | (3) =(1)−(2) | (4) Percentages of the maximum | (5) Ranks from (3) |
|---|---|---|---|---|---|
| Scandinavia |  |  |  |  |  |
| Denmark | 102.00 | 30.63 | 71.37 | 34.27 | 9 |
| Finland | 91.00 | 25.31 | 65.69 | 33.14 | 10 |
| Norway | 125.00 | (33.66) | (91.34) | 38.27 | 3 |
| Sweden | 150.00 | 23.98 | 126.02 | 45.20 | 2 |
| EC |  |  |  |  |  |
| Belgium | 92.50 | 18.29 | 74.21 | 34.84 | 8 |
| Denmark | 102.00 | 30.63 | 71.37 | 34.27 | 9 |
| France | 80.00 | 20.72 | 59.28 | 31.86 | 11 |
| Germany | 98.66 | 18.36 | 80.30 | 36.06 | 6 |
| Ireland | 110.00 | (21.40) | (88.60) | 37.72 | 5 |
| Italy | 103.00 | 13.36 | 89.64 | 37.93 | 4 |
| Luxembourg | 73.19 | (14.64) | (58.55) | 31.71 | 12 |
| Netherlands | 97.00 | 20.00 | 77.00 | 35.40 | 7 |
| United Kingdom | 180.00 | 13.44 | 166.56 | 53.31 | 1 |
| Scandinavian average | 117.00 | 28.39 | 88.61 | 37.72 |  |
| EC average (excluding UK) | 94.54 | 19.67 | 74.87 | 34.97 |  |
| 11-country average (excluding UK) | 102.03 | 21.85 | 80.18 | 36.04 |  |

*Sources:* (1) Table, 5, sum of columns (2) — (5).
  (2) Table 5, column (6).
  (4) = ((3) + 100) ÷ 5

*Notes:* (1) In *The Measurement of Fiscal Policy* (Table 10, page 77), column (3) is called the gross-rate capital tax coefficient and column (4) is called the coefficient of basis.
  (2) See Table 6, note (2).

The bias of the United Kingdom tax system against capital and thus industry is a phenomenon of long standing. The United Kingdom figure for column (1) of Table 7 in 1937—38 (since when tax rates have risen both in the United Kingdom and elsewhere in Europe) was 102.59, almost the same as the 11-country average in 1981 [10].

## Numerical and conceptual neutrality

Table 7 is based on the concept of *numerical* neutrality between saving and spending, and of the deviations from this neutrality. This concept understates the total tax burden on saving, since saving is not immune from taxes on spending. The value of saving is its purchasing power, and taxes on spending reduce real purchasing power as much as they reduce the real value of spending itself. True or *conceptual* neutrality between spending and saving is realised when there are no taxes on investment income, transfers, capital gains or wealth and when saving is taxed only through taxes on spending [11]. This is the system least burdensome on industry. A separate tax on earnings is for the same reason unnecessary, since all earnings are either spent or saved and earnings saved are taxed by means of the tax on spending. The tax system that is the least burdensome on industry is also the system that is truly neutral between spending and saving, where there are no taxes on income or capital and all taxation is levied on spending.

## Aggregate tax burden on saving

Whether taxes on spending are or are not included in the total burden of taxes on saving, the tax burden on saving in perpetuity may be calculated by a method representing in the simplest possible form the aggregate burden on saving as such: on the assumption that the tax system remains unaltered, the saver is given the opportunity of prepaying at any rate from zero to 100 per cent on investment income the sum of all taxes on investment income and its parent capital for saving in perpetuity. Thus if income tax is 50 per cent and there are no taxes on capital, the saver in perpetuity can pay half of his saving to the fisc in order to purchase tax exemption for the investment income for ever. As a proportion of the initial yield, the burden of an annual wealth tax would be heavier on an asset whose yield was expected to rise. As a proportion of the initial yield, the burden of transfer taxes could be determined actuarially or by bargaining between the taxpayer and the fisc. For saving in perpetuity, capital gains tax falls out of the reckoning. The advantage of this method is that it brings together all taxes on saving as a proportion of the yield in perpetuity. The taxation of spending as a proportion of spending can be compared directly with the taxation of saving as a proportion of the yield from saving [12]. Taxes on saving are calculated either inclusive or exclusive of taxes on spending itself, in accordance with the distinction between conceptual and numerical neutrality. In the inclusive method the taxes on spending and on saving can be taken in either order. For example, if the tax on spending is 30 per cent gross and the tax on investment income is 50 per cent, the combined tax charge of 65 per cent is either 30 + 50 (1—.3) or 50 + 30 (1 —.5). In both the inclusive and the exclusive methods comparability breaks down only if the taxation of saving is prohibitive.

*Fiscal prohibition of saving*

In the United Kingdom, the aggregate tax burden on saving as defined in the last section rises to more than the whole of the yield, so that the tax system imposes a prohibition on saving at the top of the scale [13].

A measure of this effect is shown in Table 8. Column (1) gives 100 grossed up at the maximum rate of transfer tax. Column (2) gives the yield required to obtain column (1) from 100 after 25 years. Column (3) gives column (2) grossed up at the maximum rate of income tax. Column (3) is thus the minimum or break-even yield required for the preservation of capital when both inflation and consumption out

**TABLE 8**

Minimum gross yield required for the preservation of capital, 1981

| | (1) | (2) | (3) |
|---|---|---|---|
| Scandinavia | | | |
| Denmark | 147.06 | 1.5546 | 5.1820 |
| Finland | 112.36 | .4727 | 2.3635 |
| Norway | 153.85 | 1.7382 | 17.3820 |
| Sweden | 285.71 | 4.2886 | 28.5907 |
| EC | | | |
| Belgium | 133.33 | 1.1573 | 3.5609 |
| Denmark | 147.06 | 1.5546 | 5.1820 |
| France | 125.00 | .8976 | 2.2440 |
| Germany | 174.40 | 2.2497 | 5.1130 |
| Ireland | 200.00 | 2.8114 | 7.0285 |
| Italy | 144.93 | 1.4954 | 5.3407 |
| Luxembourg | 119.32 | .7090 | 1.6488 |
| Netherlands | 120.48 | .7480 | 3.7400 |
| United Kingdom | 400.00 | 5.7018 | 22.8072 |
| Scandinavian average | | | 13.3795 |
| EC average (excluding UK) | | | 4.2322 |
| 11-country average (excluding UK) | | | 7.4722 |

*Sources:* (1) = 100 grossed up at the maximum rate of transfer tax (column (3) of Table 5)
$(2) = \left(25 \sqrt{(1) \div 100} - 1\right) \times 100$ = yield required to obtain (1) from 100 after 25 years.
(3) = (2) grossed up at the maximum rate of income tax (column (2) of Table 5).

*Note:* Where Table 5 has a figure in brackets in column (3), the rate of transfer tax used for grossing up in column (1) of Table 8 is the sum of the bracketed figures in columns (3) and (5) of Table 5: Germany 30.88 + 11.78 = 42.66; Luxembourg 4.41 + 11.78 = 16.19.

of investment income are nil; if inflation or consumption is positive, the yield required to preserve the real value of capital is correspondingly higher. The yield required is also higher if allowance is made for capital gains tax, which is relevant only to the United Kingdom. (Table 5).

Table 8 shows the break-even yield for the United Kingdom, at 22.8 per cent, as intermediate between Sweden (28.6 per cent) and Norway (17.4 per cent). These yields are far above what is regularly attainable in conditions of stable money, and these countries' tax rates are thus far above the levels at which they become prohibitive. All the other break-even yields are much lower. The United Kingdom yield is 70 per cent above the Scandinavian average, over three times as high as the 11-country average and over five times as high as the average for the rest of the EC. Since the break-even yield in the United Kingdom at the top of the scale is so far above what is commercially attainable, it follows that the UK tax system imposes a fiscal prohibition on saving not only at the top of the scale but also on taxpayers of relatively modest means. The point of fiscal prohibition (or the *range* of fiscal prohibition corresponding to the *range* of commercially attainable yields) is not much over £ 100,000 at full rates of capital transfer tax even if prices are stable (and is lower if prices are rising): at full rates of capital transfer tax, estates of as little as some £ 100,000 can be preserved only if they are subsidised out of trading income or other earnings.

# MAXIMUM TAX YIELD

## Introduction

This appendix discusses the question whether and in what sense a rate of tax may be "too high" by the criterion of yielding less tax revenue than if it were lower.

By contrast with the conventional approach to the matter, the question is asked, not about the aggregate tax take, but about the rate structures of single taxes when the rest of the tax system is taken as given. It concerns the qualitative rather than the quantitative tax burden.

The point of maximum revenue yield for each tax is determined not only by purely economic influences but also by moral and political considerations.

## Improving on conventional agnosticism

As the rate of any tax rises, the effective price increase which the rise represents has two effects: it makes the good or service subject to the tax *dearer* (the *price* or *substitution* effect) and it makes the taxpayer *poorer* (the *income* effect). The argument applies to any tax (on income, expenditure, capital or any other base) and to taxpayers either singly or collectively. The income effect of a rise in the tax on any commodity is a reduction in the consumption of one or more other commodities; *commodity* in this sense is anything from a single good or service (including leisure) at one extreme to the aggregates of earning, spending or saving at the other.

These two effects may work in opposite directions. As the tax on work rises, for example, untaxed leisure becomes more attractive (price effect); but the taxpayer may nevertheless work as hard or harder in order to attain or maintain a given standard of living. Hence the traditional scepticism about incentives. It is also traditional to impose the entire burden of proof on the taxpayer arguing for tax reductions — an impossible burden, since no conclusion on these matters can be demonstrated with certainty.

This attitude is unnecessarily sceptical and negative. If the analysis of the problem is refined and the burden of proof is shared between the taxpayer and the authorities, it is possible to establish, within limits, the relative and even absolute probabilities of different results.

A recent attempt to improve on traditional scepticism was made by Beenstock [1] who concluded from a number of surveys and econometric studies of United Kingdom data that "the marginal cost of £1 of revenue in terms of disincentive effects is approximately £3": at the margin and in aggregate, the loss of gross domestic product from additional taxation is three times as large as the gain of the fisc (and the loss of the taxpayers is therefore four times as large).

A recent example of the conventional attitude is provided by Hemming and Kay [2] (who dismiss Beenstock's time-series analysis on grounds which, if valid, would also invalidate all other use of time series to estimate elasticities). The question they are discussing is the "maximum average tax rate" for the United Kingdom, in the sense of the *tax take* or ratio of total tax revenue to gross domestic product (currently about 35 per cent in the United Kingdom), *not* the maximum rate above which a graduated tax on income becomes counterproductive even for the revenue. "The Brown, Levin and Ulph results", they say, "suggest values of this maximum average tax rate of around 80 and 82 per cent . . . The majority of estimates imply maximum average tax rates higher than those suggested by the Brown, Levin, Ulph work and several suggest rates above 90 per cent ... It is possible that this process could go on indefinitely: as taxes rise higher and higher, the amount of work increases more and more as taxpayers struggle desperately to obtain sufficient income to live on. The limits of tax revenue are then set only by the limits of human endurance ... It is when people prefer to give up their leisure than their consumption when the tax burden increases that tax revenue may go on increasing indefinitely. For the majority of the studies cited, this is in fact the case. In fact there are only three which suggest there are reasonable limits to the proportion of national income which can be absorbed in tax ... We conclude that the evidence runs strongly against the argument that tax rates in Britain, or any other country, are at levels such that the maximum available tax revenue is close to being obtained ... It follows that any view that cuts in taxation might ultimately prove self-financing through the beneficial effects of taxation on incentives is chimerical."

Econometric studies have their uses; but their value depends on the reasonableness of the assumptions on which they are based. There is something seriously wrong with any studies suggesting that a government can capture over four-fifths or even nine-tenths of aggregate value added. It is not merely that Hemming and Kay seem never to have heard of bloody revolution, let alone the black economy; even under conditions of slavery a ratio of 80 per cent or more can have few historical precedents, if any, and is probably unattainable on any substantial scale.

The present appendix tries to improve on the conventional approach by using plausible assumptions and a different analytical framework to yield credible conclusions.

There is one sense in which the argument of Hemming and Kay is valid, though it is hardly what they intended. As time passes, any given rate of tax becomes more familiar and thus more acceptable passively, partly because avenues of escape multiply, through shifts of activity and other forms of avoidance and evasion [3]. The rate of tax that yields the maximum revenue increases over time through increasing familiarity (even though it runs into barriers of economic and political resistance, and even though the maximum is reduced over time through the erosion of the tax base by increasing evasion and avoidance). Thus, the maximum-yield tax rate is in part a function, not only of the absolute level of the tax structure, but also of its recent history. But the process can also work in reverse. Taxpayers can become familiar with lower rates of tax as well as with higher. If a government is trying to implement a tax-cutting programme (as in Britain in the early nineteen-eighties), then the maximum-yield tax rate falls in so far as the government is successful. It is ironical that in these circumstances the arguments of the Inland Revenue work against what they imagine to be their own best interest. The Inland Revenue house doctrine (with which I agree) is that the habit of tax avoidance becomes so ingrained that it would be undone only gradually, if at all, as tax rates fell [4]. But this implies (in my opinion rightly) that upward and downward movements are not symmetrical and that escape through avoidance and evasion has more effect in limiting the rise in the maximum-yield tax rate when the tax structure rises than it has in limiting the fall in the rate when the tax structure falls.

### The Camel's Back Appendix

It is a matter of common sense that the fisc may be too greedy for its own good, that it is possible to kill the goose that lays the golden eggs [5]. The likelihood of this outcome increases as the rate of tax rises. Moreover, a higher rate of tax is a larger proportion of the market price than a lower rate of tax, so that an increase in a lower rate of tax has less effect on market prices than the same proportionate increase in a higher rate of tax [6].

Using these simple insights, the Appendix to *The Camel's Back* provided an analysis of the *relative* probabilities that tax revenue would be increased as a result of increases in various rates of tax. The probabilities were calculated relatively to the probability of an increase in tax revenue as a result of an increase in a tax rate of 50 per cent gross. The chance of an increase in tax revenue as a result of an increase in the rate of tax was conservatively estimated at 50 times as large for a 50 per cent rate as for a 98 per cent rate. The estimate was conservative because the analysis explicitly understated the relative disadvantage of high rates of tax as a result of its being based on the hypothesis of constant turnover (unitary price elasticity of demand). This hypothesis is unduly favourable to high rates of tax because turnover must eventually fall as tax rates rise.

*Curve of revenue yield*

*The Camel's Back* Appendix also provided an analysis (page 59) of the relationship between the change in tax revenue and the change in turnover as the price and price elasticity of demand increase. The analysis is equally appropriate to goods, services, work and saving.

As tax rises from zero until it becomes prohibitive, three points are passed on the way. At unitary price elasticity of demand, turnover is unchanged (although price is rising and volume is falling). At the zero-sum point the proportionate rise in the price equals the proportionate rise in the revenue yield. At the point of maximum revenue yield the rise in the revenue yield has fallen to zero. The point of unitary price elasticity may be as low as a nil rate of tax. The point of maximum revenue yield must come after the other two; if the point of unitary price elasticity is below a tax rate of 50 per cent gross it comes before the zero-sum point, and if it is above a tax rate of 50 per cent gross it comes after. In the present analysis we can ignore the zero-sum point and concentrate exclusively on the points of unitary price elasticity and maximum revenue yield.

The point of unitary price elasticity, where demand becomes elastic instead of inelastic relatively to price, is of cardinal importance to the analysis. As the tax rate rises, the income effect first increases more rapidly, and is more powerful, than the price effect and then increases less rapidly and is less powerful. At the point of unitary price elasticity, or maximum turnover, the rising force of the price effect for the first time fully offsets the declining force of the income effect. The point of unitary price elasticity (neglected in traditional analysis) thus provides a point of equipoise and a point of reference between the conflicting influences of price and income effects.

*Laffer curve*

The curve of revenue yield starts at zero when tax is zero, rises to a maximum and falls to zero when the rate of tax becomes prohibitive at 100 per cent (gross) or less. Thus every level of revenue below the maximum is yielded by two different rates of tax, one above and one below the rate that maximises revenue. If the actual rate is above the rate that maximises revenue, revenue is increased by a cut in the rate.

This bell-shaped curve is now sometimes called the Laffer curve after the American economist Arthur Laffer. Laffer gave his name to a concept that had been nameless before, although he did not invent it and the relationships it represents had long been understood by those interested in public finance. The concept of the Laffer curve applies to single taxes and taxation in total.

The analysis of the curve of revenue yield in the present appendix is consistent with the simplistic concept of the Laffer curve; but it uses the concepts of price and income elasticity to extract more from the argument than Laffer's truism can provide of itself.

*Shifts of activity*

The taxpayer may avoid tax by moving part of his activities to less highly taxed transactions or reducing his activity in the cash economy by shifting to the household economy (including leisure) which is not taxed at all. Conversely, if tax is cut the taxpayer may move in the opposite direction, because the incentive to avoid tax is diminished or removed. Tax reduction can thus increase tax revenue in three different ways.

First, if the rate of tax is reduced towards the revenue-maximising rate, tax revenue is increased even at a constant level of activity provided that taxpayers are shifting from less heavily taxed transactions. For example, revenue is increased if the tax on whisky is reduced towards the point of maximum revenue yield and consumers switch to whisky from wine.

Second, tax revenue may also be increased by a reduction in the tax rate towards the point of maximum revenue yield leading to an increase in activity: for example, an increase in whisky consumption, not at the expense of wine, but as a result of an increase in activity in consequence of the lowering of the tax on whisky.

Third, below the point of maximum revenue yield tax cuts may still increase tax revenue if the revenue from other taxes rises by more than the fall in revenue from the tax that has been cut. This is possible either as a result of an increase in activity or even without an increase in activity as a result of a shift into more highly taxed transactions. Below the point of maximum revenue yield, an increase in tax revenue at a constant level of activity implies a move out of less highly taxed commodities if the rate of the tax being cut is above the point of unitary price elasticity and into more highly taxed commodities if the rate of the tax being cut is below this point.

The argument is general and applies to taxes on work or saving as it does to taxes on commodities like whisky.

## The present appendix

The present appendix offers an analysis complementary to *The Camel's Back* appendix and providing an *absolute as well as a relative measure* of the likelihood that an increase in tax rates will reduce tax revenue. The move from relative to absolute probability requires one or more additional assumptions. The present appendix is intended to be intelligible independently; but interested readers are referred to *The Camel's Back* Appendix for additional background and explanation [7].

"All but the completely unworldly", says Lord Robbins, "would agree that a marginal rate of 100 per cent would have some adverse effects on the disposition to work or save of most ordinary people. Why then assume that the rates which actually prevail in the United Kingdom in the present day should not operate in the same way? Is it really to be supposed that the disincentive is absent until one reaches 99.9 per cent and then suddenly becomes complete?" [8]

The present appendix examines the arithmetical implications of this argument. The key concept is the *distribution of fiscal veto* (or *fiscal annihilation* or *prohibition*), which is the aggregate of *fiscal discouragement*. At a tax rate of zero there is no fiscal involvement. At a rate of 100 per cent gross (infinity net) there is a fiscal veto: rational economic activity must cease at this rate of tax (and may cease earlier). For example, if earnings from work are taxed at 100 per cent gross, then rational economic work is at an end; people may go on working as a hobby or as a form of public service, but these are other dimensions and the work is not done from economic motives. The fiscal veto must be total at 100 per cent gross; it may be total at less, even much less: a tax well below 50 per cent gross may be enough to kill a particular activity. What is not in dispute is that between a tax rate of zero and a tax rate of 100 per cent (or less) tax destroys the whole of the economic activity that would exist if tax were nil. What is disputable is just where on the scale tax takes its toll.

Room must be found somewhere for fiscal discouragement and its aggregate, fiscal veto (the adverse effect on incentives amounting ultimately to prohibition). For example, if a tax rate of 98 per cent gross does no damage, all the damage is done by the last 2 percentage points. Although this is not conceptually impossible, it is difficult to believe. It is easier to believe that the damage is spread out more evenly. To put the same point differently, fiscal discouragement and fiscal veto differ in degree, not in kind; the recognition of fiscal veto (which is undeniable) implies the recognition of fiscal discouragement (which is often denied), since veto is the arithmetical sum of discouragement. Our task is to consider how fiscal veto can be most credibly decomposed into discouragement or discouragement aggregated into veto.

## The two key variables

The two key variables required for our analysis are (1) the rate of tax at which the point of unitary price elasticity is reached and (2) the distribution of fiscal discouragement between this tax rate and 100 per cent gross, at which point (if not earlier) it must sum to fiscal veto. Fiscal veto or annihilation is a *cumulative* concept; fiscal discouragement is *marginal*.

At the point of unitary price elasticity turnover is unaffected by a small change in the rate of tax. If the tax is on whisky, the same amount gross of tax is spent on whisky by consumers. If the tax is on work, the same amount gross of tax is earned from labour by workers. Up to this point demand is price-inelastic: the consumer spends more on whisky as the tax rises, although he buys less; the worker puts in more effort or more hours, although they yield less net income. Up to this point the fisc is sitting pretty: as the tax rate rises, any distortion of economic activity is to the benefit of the fisc. More work is done and more is spent on whisky; the taxpayer just receives less in exchange. Thus, over the range from a tax rate of zero to the point of unitary price elasticity, turnover increases. It is only at the point of unitary price elasticity that this process comes to an end.

The position on the tax scale of the point of unitary price elasticity will vary rom one activity to another and from one taxpayer to another. It will not be the same for A's whisky as for B's whisky or for A's work as for B's work. As between taxpayers, these conflicts are reconciled by weighted averages yielding a unique figure. As between activities, similar weighted averages are indeed possible, giving a unique figure for the whole tax system; but it is more useful to reckon separate taxes, as they are levied, separately.

From the point of unitary price elasticity to the point of fiscal annihilation, turnover declines. The worker's gross-of-tax earnings fall, the consumer spends less on whisky. At this point the distortions imposed by the tax system start to come into the open. The whisky drinker is no longer paying the tax by cutting down on other expenditures: he starts to spend less on whisky. The worker is no longer paying the tax by working longer hours: he starts to work less. The unitary price elasticity of demand is a *marginal* concept: it is the point on the tax scale where these things begin to happen. But there may be a substantial aggregate effect of raising the tax from zero to the point of unitary price elasticity of demand. This aggregate is a *total* concept: it represents the cumulative diversion of individual preference from leisure to work.

These diversions are distortions that reduce efficiency and welfare. They are ignored here in the interest of simplicity. Any tax creates a distortion by comparison with the situation if the tax were zero. Any cumulative distortion in turnover at the point of unitary price elasticity must be reversed by the time the tax rate has reached the point of fiscal annihilation. As the tax is raised from unitary price elasticity to fiscal annihilation, it gradually destroys not only the turnover at the point of zero tax but also the additional turnover at the point of unitary price elasticity. An increase in the tax rate to the point of fiscal veto is in this sense more destructive if the starting point is unitary price elasticity than it is if the starting point is a tax rate of zero. By ignoring the cumulative increase in turnover between zero tax and unitary price elasticity we understate the damage done to the interest of the fisc by raising the rate from unitary price elasticity to fiscal annihilation. The cumulative increase in turnover at the point of unitary price elasticity is most easily ignored by assuming it to be negligibly small, which is the procedure followed here. If it is not negligibly small but substantial (as is implied by those who belittle fiscal discouragement on the ground that tax makes people work harder), it can be taken into account at the cost of adding a further stage to the argument; and the damage done to the fisc by raising the rate of tax from unitary price elasticity to fiscal annihilation is correspondingly larger.

Thus the assumption of the present appendix is that the increase in turnover between zero tax and unitary price elasticity is negligibly small. Turnover at unitary price elasticity is the same as at zero tax. Between unitary price elasticity and fiscal annihilation, which may be at 100 per cent gross or below, this turnover is gradually destroyed. This process of destruction must work itself out completely within the range: in so far as it operates less at one point, it operates more at another. The distribution of the fiscal veto provides a common conceptual framework for those who believe most strongly that taxes damage incentives and for those who are most sceptical about these effects. Each party can be asked to say how he believes fiscal discouragement to be distributed. The sceptic may say that there is no effect until the tax rate is 98 per cent gross or 99 per cent or 99.5 per cent or 99.9 per cent ...; but he is then obliged to explain why fiscal discouragement should be so heavily concentrated at one end of the scale instead of being spread more evenly. And every assumption about the distribution of the fiscal veto indicates the point of maximum revenue yield, beyond which increases in tax rates reduce the yield of tax.

The position on the tax scale of the point of fiscal annihilation constitutes another key variable. More damage is done by a tax rate of 79 per cent gross if fiscal annihilation is reached at 80 per cent than if it is reached at 100 per cent. But the possibility that fiscal veto is reached before 100 per cent is left till later ("Understatement?"). Since fiscal veto may be attained at rates much below 100 per cent, the understatement may be considerable. Allowance can be made for this additional dimension of fiscal destruction at the cost of adding a further stage to the argument.

### The range of assumptions

There is a wide range of possible assumptions about the position of unitary price elasticity and the distribution of fiscal veto. But some of these assumptions are more plausible than others. And the internal logic of the argument imposes further constraints on the possible patterns of fiscal discouragement.

Two possible positions of unitary price elasticity are important conceptually. One is at zero tax; zero tax and unitary price elasticity then coincide, and there is no band over which tax acts as an incentive to turnover (turnover rising as tax increases). The other is at a gross tax rate of 50 per cent; unitary price elasticity then coincides with the zero-sum point at which the proportionate rise in price equals the proportionate rise in revenue yield. The coincidence of unitary price elasticity and zero tax is both a logical extreme and a practical possibility; the other logical extreme (a 100 per cent tax rate) is not a practical possibility, and anything over 50 per cent may be considered high. For example, unitary price elasticity at 50 per cent would mean that a rise in an income tax rate at that level would have no effect on the willingness to work overtime. Nevertheless, Tables 9—11 illustrate unitary price elasticity at 80 per cent as well as zero and 50 per cent [9].

Given unitary price elasticity and an assumed fiscal veto at 100 per cent, there are also logical extremes for the pattern of fiscal discouragement. One extreme is an even distribution over the range. For example, if turnover is 100 and unitary price elasticity is at zero tax, turnover falls by one unit for each percentage point that the rate of tax rises. The trouble with this assumption is that it conflicts with the principle that high taxes are more damaging to incentives than low taxes. The other extreme is that fiscal discouragement is concentrated in the last percentage point (when tax rises from 99 per cent to 100 per cent) and is negligible over the rest of the range; this possibility is of no practical interest. Thus something intermediate is required.

The problem is structurally the same as the problem of distributing depreciation allowances over the life of an asset, except that there departures from a linear pattern generally *accelerate* allowances (so that the pattern is *degressive* over time) whereas here departures from a linear pattern are required to *postpone* fiscal discouragement (so that the pattern is *progressive* as tax rates rise).

Given the starting point and the finishing point and the number of terms, a series is defined if it is an arithmetical progression (increasing by equal absolute amounts) or a geometrical progression (increasing by equal proportions). There are also a number of other possibilities in which the absolute or proportionate increases themselves rise or fall instead of remaining the same. There is no need to consider this range of possibilities in detail, since it raises no questions of principle that are not covered by the simplest option, an arithmetical progression (sum of the tax rates) [10]. If unitary price elasticity is at a tax rate of 50 per cent gross, then fiscal discouragement has to be distributed over the ranges 50—51 per cent, 51—52 per cent ... 98—99 per cent, 99—100 per cent. These ranges give the arithmetical progression 51, 52 ... 98, 99, 100. Subtracting 50 from every term, we have 1,2...48, 49, 50 for each successive rise in the rate of tax. Turnover is 1275 when tax is 50 per cent, 1274 when tax is 51 per cent ...99 when tax is 98 per cent, 50 when tax is 99 per cent and zero when tax is 100 per cent. Tables 9—11 are constructed on this basis [11].

**The tables**

Tables 9—11 all follow the same lines. Column (1) gives the gross rate of tax. Column (2) gives the price calculated from column (1). The price is 1 plus the net rate of tax. Thus, if the gross rate of tax is .80 (or 80 per cent), the net rate is 4.00 (or 400 per cent), since $4 = .8 \div (1 - .8)$. The price is 5 $(= 1 + 4)$. For example, if a bottle of whisky costs £5, of which £4 is tax, the gross rate of tax is .80 $(= 4 \div 5)$, the net rate is 4 and the price is 5. The price is also the percentage increase in the price when the gross rate of tax rises from 1 percentage point lower. For example, if the gross rate of tax is .79, the price is 4.7619; if the gross rate of tax is. 80, the price is 5; and 5 is 5 per cent more than 4.7619. Column (2) is also the reciprocal of the tax-exclusive element of the price. For example, if the tax rate is 80 per cent, the tax-exclusive element of the price is .20$(=1-.80)$, and the reciprocal of .20 is 5, which is the price. Column.(3) is turnover calculated on the principles already explained. Column (4) is quantity (or volume) calculated as turnover divided by price. Column (5) is tax yield calculated either as quantity multiplied by the tax element in price (quantity multiplied by the excess of column (2) over unity) or

160

as the excess of column (3) over column (4), that is, as the excess of turnover over quantity. Column (6) gives the percentage increase or decrease in column (5), just as column (2) gives the percentage increase in itself.

Table 9 shows the relationships when unitary price elasticity is attained at a tax rate of 50 per cent gross. In column (2), which is independent of the unitary price elasticity, price rises from 2 at a tax rate of 50 per cent gross to 100 at a tax rate of 99 per cent gross. The volume of business in column (4) declines by larger absolute amounts (though by smaller proportionate amounts) at intermediate tax rates than at the highest; this relationship is a necessary consequence of specifying fiscal annihilation in terms of a decline in turnover calculated as a sum-of-the-tax-rates arithmetical progression. Column (6) shows that the tax yield reaches a maximum somewhere between gross tax rates of 66 and 67 per cent.

## TABLE 9

Maximum tax yield (unitary price elasticity at a tax rate of 50 per cent gross)

| (1) | (2) | (3) | (4) | (5) | (6) |
|------|--------|------|-------|-------|--------|
| .50 | 2.0000 | 1275 | 637.5 | 637.5 | (2.03) |
| .51 | 2.0408 | 1274 | 624.3 | 649.7 | 1.91 |
| .52 | 2.0833 | 1272 | 610.6 | 661.4 | 1.80 |
| .53 | 2.1277 | 1269 | 596.4 | 672.6 | 1.69 |
| .54 | 2.1739 | 1265 | 581.9 | 683.1 | 1.56 |
| .55 | 2.2222 | 1260 | 567.0 | 693.0 | 1.45 |
| .56 | 2.2727 | 1254 | 551.8 | 702.2 | 1.33 |
| .57 | 2.3256 | 1247 | 536.2 | 710.8 | 1.22 |
| .58 | 2.3810 | 1239 | 520.4 | 718.6 | 1.10 |
| .59 | 2.4390 | 1230 | 504.3 | 725.7 | .99 |
| .60 | 2.5000 | 1220 | 488.0 | 732.0 | .87 |
| .61 | 2.5641 | 1209 | 471.5 | 737.5 | .75 |
| .62 | 2.6316 | 1197 | 454.9 | 742.1 | .62 |
| .63 | 2.7027 | 1184 | 438.1 | 746.0 | .53 |
| .64 | 2.7778 | 1170 | 421.2 | 748.8 | .38 |
| .65 | 2.8571 | 1155 | 404.3 | 750.7 | .25 |
| .66 | 2.9412 | 1139 | 387.3 | 751.7 | .13 |
| .67 | 3.0303 | 1122 | 370.3 | 751.7 | .00 |
| .68 | 3.1250 | 1104 | 353.3 | 750.7 | −.13 |
| .69 | 3.2258 | 1085 | 336.3 | 748.7 | −.27 |
| .70 | 3.3333 | 1065 | 319.5 | 745.5 | −.43 |
| .71 | 3.4483 | 1044 | 302.8 | 741.2 | −.58 |
| .72 | 3.5714 | 1022 | 286.2 | 735.8 | −.73 |
| .73 | 3.7037 | 999 | 269.7 | 729.3 | −.88 |
| .74 | 3.8462 | 975 | 253.5 | 721.5 | −1.07 |
| .75 | 4.0000 | 950 | 237.5 | 712.5 | −1.25 |
| .76 | 4.1667 | 924 | 221.8 | 702.2 | −1.45 |
| .77 | 4.3478 | 897 | 206.3 | 690.7 | −1.64 |
| .78 | 4.5455 | 869 | 191.2 | 677.8 | −1.87 |
| .79 | 4.7619 | 840 | 176.4 | 663.6 | −2.10 |

| (1) | (2) | (3) | (4) | (5) | (6) |
|---|---|---|---|---|---|
| .80 | 5.0000 | 810 | 162.0 | 648.0 | −2.35 |
| .81 | 5.2632 | 779 | 148.0 | 631.0 | −2.62 |
| .82 | 5.5556 | 747 | 134.5 | 612.5 | −2.93 |
| .83 | 5.8824 | 714 | 121.4 | 592.6 | −3.25 |
| .84 | 6.2500 | 680 | 108.8 | 571.2 | −3.61 |
| .85 | 6.6667 | 645 | 96.7 | 548.3 | −4.01 |
| .86 | 7.1429 | 609 | 85.3 | 523.7 | −4.49 |
| .87 | 7.6923 | 572 | 74.4 | 497.6 | −4.98 |
| .88 | 8.3333 | 534 | 64.1 | 469.9 | −5.57 |
| .89 | 9.0909 | 495 | 54.4 | 440.6 | −6.24 |
| .90 | 10.0000 | 455 | 45.5 | 409.5 | −7.06 |
| .91 | 11.1111 | 414 | 37.3 | 376.7 | −8.01 |
| .92 | 12.5000 | 372 | 29.8 | 342.2 | −9.16 |
| .93 | 14.2857 | 329 | 23.0 | 306.0 | −10.58 |
| .94 | 16.6667 | 285 | 17.1 | 267.9 | −12.45 |
| .95 | 20.0000 | 240 | 12.0 | 228.0 | −14.89 |
| .96 | 25.0000 | 194 | 7.8 | 186.2 | −18.33 |
| .97 | 33.3333 | 147 | 4.4 | 142.6 | −23.42 |
| .98 | 50.0000 | 99 | 2.0 | 97.0 | −31.98 |
| .99 | 100.0000 | 50 | .5 | 49.5 | −48.97 |
| 1.00 | ∞ | 0 | 0 | 0 | −100.00 |

(1) Gross rate of tax
(2) Price = 1 + net rate of tax
    = the percentage increase in (2)
    = the reciprocal of the tax-exclusive element of the price
(3) Turnover, which is assumed to decline in an arithmetical progression from unitary price elasticity to fiscal annihilation
(4) Quantity or volume = (3) ÷ (2)
(5) Tax revenue or yield of tax = (3) − (4) = (4) × ((2) − 1)
(6) Percentage change in (5), comparable with (2), which is the percentage change in itself.

This is a notable result. None of the assumptions used is implausible and in general they have been biased by understating the damage done by high rates of taxation to the economy and even to the fisc itself. Yet on the assumptions used, the fisc itself loses money by trying to charge tax at 67 per cent or more. Since United Kingdom taxes on capital transfers and investment income both rise to 75 per cent, Table 9 illustrates how far the United Kingdom fisc may at present be too greedy even for its own good, let alone the good of the economy; the rates of tax that maximise the private interest of the fisc are significantly higher than those that maximise the interest of the economy (that is, society as a whole, or the combined interest of the fisc and the taxpayer) [12]. Moreover, these taxes are levied *cumulatively* on the same act of saving so that the maximum rate of tax on saving is certainly well over 75 per cent and probably well over 100 per cent. (Table 8). It is the *cumulative* rate of taxation on saving that should be reduced to the level of maximum revenue yield, not merely the rates of the individual taxes.

In Table 10 the point of unitary price elasticity is put at the high tax rate of 80 per cent gross, which is about the order of magnitude of the taxes levied in the United Kingdom on spirits and tobacco, the most highly taxed of all goods and services. It is possible, though perhaps unlikely, that an increase in a tax rate of 80 per cent gross (400 per cent net) will have no effect on the amount that consumers are willing to spend on their whisky. It is possible, though perhaps even more unlikely, that an increase in a tax rate of 80 per cent gross will have no effect on the willingness to work (in other words, that the amount of overtime worked will be the same at an 80 per cent tax rate as at a rate of 81 per cent). Possible, though unlikely. 80 per cent has been chosen as a plausible maximum for the unitary price elasticity of any tax whatsoever.

In Table 10, maximum tax yield is reached at about 82 per cent. This is proportionately much nearer to the lower limit of the range than when unitary price elasticity is reached at 50 per cent and maximum tax yield at between 66 and 67 per cent. This contrast merely points the obvious moral that as the fisc pushes its luck harder and harder, it is less and less likely to succeed. It is a bonus for the fisc if unitary price elasticity is at a relatively high tax rate; 50 per cent gross may be regarded as high, even though higher rates are conceivable. But if unitary price elasticity is at a high tax rate, the point of maximum tax yield follows correspondingly sooner. The higher (and the more implausible) the unitary price elasticity of

## TABLE 10

Maximum tax yield (unitary price elasticity at a tax rate of 80 per cent gross)

| (1) | (2) | (3) | (4) | (5) | (6) |
|------|----------|-----|-------|--------|---------|
| .80 | 5.0000 | 210 | 42.00 | 168.00 | |
| .81 | 5.2632 | 209 | 39.71 | 169.29 | .76 |
| .82 | 5.5556 | 207 | 37.26 | 169.74 | .27 |
| .83 | 5.8824 | 204 | 34.68 | 169.32 | − .25 |
| .84 | 6.2500 | 200 | 32.00 | 168.00 | − .88 |
| .85 | 6.6667 | 195 | 29.25 | 165.75 | −1.34 |
| .86 | 7.1429 | 189 | 26.46 | 162.54 | −1.94 |
| .87 | 7.6923 | 182 | 23.66 | 158.34 | −2.58 |
| .88 | 8.3333 | 174 | 20.88 | 153.12 | −3.30 |
| .89 | 9.0909 | 165 | 18.15 | 146.85 | −4.10 |
| .90 | 10.0000 | 155 | 15.50 | 139.50 | −5.00 |
| .91 | 11.1111 | 144 | 12.96 | 131.04 | −6.06 |
| .92 | 12.5000 | 132 | 10.56 | 121.44 | −7.33 |
| .93 | 14.2857 | 119 | 8.33 | 110.67 | −8.87 |
| .94 | 16.6667 | 105 | 6.30 | 98.70 | −10.82 |
| .95 | 20.0000 | 90 | 4.50 | 85.50 | −13.37 |
| .96 | 25.0000 | 74 | 2.96 | 71.04 | −16.91 |
| .97 | 33.3333 | 57 | 1.71 | 55.29 | −22.17 |
| .98 | 50.0000 | 39 | .78 | 38.22 | −30.87 |
| .99 | 100.0000 | 20 | .20 | 19.80 | −48.19 |
| 1.00 | ∞ | 0 | 0 | 0 | −100.00 |

Meaning of columns as in Table 9.

demand, the less the difference between unitary price elasticity and maximum revenue yield. At a tax rate of 80 per cent, there is little difference between the two.
If a tax rate of 80 per cent is regarded as an empirical maximum for unitary
price elasticity and if fiscal discouragement is calculated by the sum-of-the-tax-rates
method, a tax rate of 83 per cent or more reduces the yield of tax revenue as well
as inflicting still greater losses on the economy. Since 80 per cent is a high rate
of tax for unitary price elasticity, 83 per cent is in this sense a maximum rate for
the maximum yield of tax revenue. But a more credible maximum rate for the
interest of the fisc is, not 83 per cent, but 67 per cent, when the unitary price
elasticity is put, not at a tax rate of 80 per cent but at the more plausible level
of 50 per cent (which may still be regarded as high).

   This conclusion is confirmed by Table 11, which shows the relationships on
the assumption that unitary price elasticity is reached at a tax rate of zero. The
meaning of columns (1)—(5) is as in Tables 9 and 10. But, in order to economise
on space, Table 11 gives only every tenth tax rate (10 per cent, 20 per cent ...
90 per cent). In consequence column (6) is omitted, since in the other tables this
gives the increase or decrease of revenue yield by reason of tax rate changes of
1 per cent, not 10 per cent. Table 11 shows that the maximum revenue yield is
attained at about 60 per cent gross if unitary price elasticity is reached at a tax
rate of zero; the exact figure is between 57 and 58 per cent. If unitary price elasticity coincides with a tax rate of 50 per cent, Table 9 shows that the maximum
revenue yield is attained between 66 and 67 per cent. If unitary price elasticity
coincides with a tax rate of 80 per cent, Table 10 shows that the maximum

**TABLE 11**

Maximum tax yield (unitary price elasticity at a tax rate of zero)

| (1) | (2) | (3) | (4) | (5) |
|------|---------|------|--------|--------|
| .10 | 1.1111 | 4995 | 4495.6 | 499.4 |
| .20 | 1.2500 | 4840 | 3872.0 | 968.0 |
| .30 | 1.4286 | 4585 | 3209.4 | 1375.6 |
| .40 | 1.6667 | 4230 | 2538.0 | 1692.0 |
| .50 | 2.0000 | 3775 | 1887.5 | 1887.5 |
| .55 | 2.2222 | 3510 | 1579.5 | 1930.5 |
| .56 | 2.2727 | 3454 | 1519.8 | 1934.2 |
| .57 | 2.3256 | 3397 | 1460.7 | 1936.3 |
| .58 | 2.3810 | 3339 | 1402.4 | 1936.6 |
| .59 | 2.4390 | 3280 | 1344.8 | 1935.2 |
| .60 | 2.5000 | 3220 | 1288.0 | 1932.0 |
| .70 | 3.3333 | 2565 | 769.5 | 1795.5 |
| .80 | 5.0000 | 1810 | 362.0 | 1448.0 |
| .90 | 10.0000 | 955 | 95.5 | 859.5 |
| 1.00 | ∞ | 0 | 0 | 0 |

Meaning of columns as in Tables 9 and 10.

revenue yield is attained at about 82 per cent. Thus the tax rate giving the maximum revenue yield is not very sensitive to changes in the tax rate at which the price elasticity of demand is unitary.

## Overstatement?

Is it possible that the argument overstates the damage done by high rates of tax and thus gives too low a figure for the rate of tax that yields the maximum revenue?

The first variable on which the answer depends is the tax rate corresponding to unitary price elasticity. Although this rate will vary from tax to tax and from taxpayer to taxpayer, the argument has covered all practical possibilities. Tables 9—11 show tax rates at unitary price elasticity ranging from zero through 50 per cent to 80 per cent. 80 per cent was chosen as being at or above the top of the range and appropriate, if at all, only for a limited number of addictive commodities like spirits and tobacco which serve to identify a ceiling for taxes on all goods and services.

The second variable is the distribution of fiscal discouragement, which is assumed to take the form of an arithmetical progression. This is more arguable: and the point of maximum revenue would be higher, for example, if the progression were geometrical rather than arithmetical. However, the opposite is also possible: the point of maximum revenue falls if fiscal discouragement is spread more evenly than by an arithmetical progression. The increasing concentration of discouragement serves to offset the effect on the maximum-revenue tax rate of reducing the tax rate corresponding to unitary price elasticity; and the concentration of fiscal discouragement cannot be much further increased at the top of the scale without coming into conflict with Lord Robbins's argument.

## Understatement?

It is much more likely that the damage done by high tax rates has been understated by the argument so far and that too high a figure has been given for the rate of tax that yields the maximum revenue.

The argument so far has been based on the assumption that fiscal prohibition is reached at a tax rate of 100 per cent. But this is a logical extreme; in practice, a much lower figure will generally be prohibitive. If the rate of prohibition is below 100 per cent, the maximum-revenue rate is reduced correspondingly.

It is also not unlikely that fiscal discouragement is distributed between the tax rates more equally than by an arithmetical progression.

## A central position

The situation described in Table 11 occupies a central position in the argument, since the choice of the lowest possible tax rate (zero) for the point of unitary price elasticity serves to offset the choice of the highest possible tax rate (100 per cent) for the point of prohibition. Moreover, the distribution of fiscal discouragement by the sum-of-the-tax-rates method is the simplest form of unequal distribution, since it is linear and uniquely determined. However, the 58 per cent point of maximum revenue yield given by Table 11 is more likely to be too high than too low, not only because its distribution of fiscal discouragement may be too unequal, but also because the point of maximum revenue yield is overestimated by putting fiscal prohibition at 100 per cent more than it is underestimated by putting unitary price elasticity at zero.

*Whether for a single tax or for taxation in aggregate, 58 per cent is more likely to be too high than too low as an estimate of the point of maximum revenue yield.* Increasingly implausible assumptions are required to raise the maximum-revenue rate above this level.

### The burden of proof

No quantitative conclusion on these matters can be demonstrated as certain [13]. It cannot be proved either that taxes have an adverse effect on incentives or that they have not. All conclusions depend on a balance of probabilities. There is no justification for the assumption sometimes underlying discussions on these questions that the whole burden of proof lies on the taxpayer arguing for tax reductions. No useful conclusion can be reached on the basis of this assumption. The most useful procedure is to share the burden of proof equally between fisc and taxpayer. This avoids exaggerating the importance of taxes that are actually collected by comparison with taxes that could be collected if the system were less oppressive.

### Differences between taxes

The argument does not apply equally to all taxes. It applies in so far as the taxpayer can escape, whether legally or illegally, tax levied on a taxable object representing the transfer of money or money's worth with or without consideration. It thus applies only obliquely to a poll tax, where the taxable object coincides with the taxable subject: even though a poll tax can be evaded by concealment and avoided by emigration, it is not imposed on a transfer of money or money's worth.

The argument applies only in so far as the taxpayer can escape and it does not therefore apply to taxes levied retrospectively. Taxes are leved retrospectively on work if the rate of tax is determined after the work is done (as for corporation tax and income tax on the self-employed in the United Kingdom) [14]; but the most important example of retrospective taxation is the taxation of savings — investment income tax, investment income surcharge, capital gains tax and capital transfer tax, all of which in any year fall primarily on savings made before the year began. However, the argument applies to new saving in so far as the saver regards the existing tax system as representative of the burdens that he will have to bear in future; and it applies even to old saving in so far as tax can be escaped by spending, evasion or emigration [15]. The tax on saving is the aggregate of income and capital taxes as a proportion of the yield [16]. Theory and practice alike indicate that saving (like working) is generally less addictive than smoking and drinking and that its maximum-revenue tax rate is thus substantially lower than theirs (which may be as high as 80 per cent): the argument holds good for saving generally, since it applies not only to new saving without qualification but also more and more, as time passes, to the drawing down of old saving. As was noted earlier (pages 150—1), the combination of taxes on saving in the United Kingdom rises to levels that are prohibitive in the sense of amounting to more than 100 per cent of the yield: this fiscal prohibition applies not only instantaneously to new saving but more and more, as time passes, to old saving as well.

Among taxes on saving, taxes on gifts are especially susceptible to avoidance by postponement or emigration. In the OECD countries for which figures are available, revenue from taxes on gifts is generally well below a tenth of the revenue from taxes on transfers at death [17]. And some of the countries with relatively mild taxation of gifts bring in relatively more revenue from this source. The point of maximum revenue yield is especially low for the taxation of gifts [18]. And the point of maximum revenue yield is reduced, for all taxes on saving and all taxpayers liable to their charge, when allowance is made for the effect of inflation on the value of the capital.

The responsiveness of demand to taxation is higher for luxuries than for necessaries (in technical terms, their price elasticity of demand is higher). Saving is a "luxury" or "superior good" in the technical sense that it rises more rapidly than income as income rises (in technical terms, its income elasticity of demand is more than one). "Luxuries", including saving, have lower points of maximum turnover and maximum revenue yield than necessaries: for example, the tax rates at the points of maximum turnover and maximum revenue are lower for saving than for necessaries like food and fuel.

These various arguments indicate that the present aggregate rate of tax on saving is far above the rate that maximises revenue in the long term or even in the medium term; it increases short-term revenue, if at all, only at the cost of a drastic erosion of the continuing capital base.

### Interplay between taxes

Is has been argued in the foregoing section and elsewhere in this appendix that the economic effect of the various taxes on investment income and its parent capital is cumulative, each tax being a separate charge on the same act of saving.

Similarly, for the large proportion of the population who spend what they earn and have little or no interest in other than seasonal saving, general taxes on earned income and general taxes on spending are cumulative in their effect. In Britain, the tax on earnings is general and value added tax (covering about half consumers' expenditure) is sufficiently widespread to be largely unavoidable. Thus the effective rate of tax on earned income is not merely the basic rate of 30 per cent (which has also been the starting rate since 1980—81) but also national insurance contributions and taxes on expenditure. If taxes on expenditure are calculated as an aveirage in the manner of Table 5 column (6) and added to income tax and national-nsurance contributions, the effective marginal rate of tax at the income-tax threshold is of the order of 50 per cent as compared with a maximum-yield rate of some 58 per cent [19]. ("A central position", above).

Similar arguments apply to working for saving, saving for spending and saving for saving [20].

When account is taken of the cumulative burden of tax on the movement of funds from their source to their destination, the effective rate increases and may increase substantially (even though the apparent burden may be diminished by optical illusion, some taxes being more acutely perceived than others: see "The qualitative burden" in Chapter IX). It is the cumulative burden rather than its component parts that should be compared with a maximum-yield rate of some 58 per cent [21].

## Interplay between transactions

The market economy based on Adam Smith's division of labour is highly vulnerable to fiscal attack: it is analogous to a chain of house sales and purchases which may be entirely frustrated if at any single link in the chain the vendor or purchaser does not complete. The market economy is likewise often based on half-a-dozen or more interconnected transactions: if any one link fails because the taxpayer concerned is unwilling to pay the tax bill involved, the whole taxpaying chain breaks down.

The irony is that in this situation the fisc is much more exposed to the risk of loss than the taxpayers. The taxpayers are economic agents and have alternatives to their former taxpaying activities that may be little less attractive to them than the former activities themselves. The fisc, by contrast, is not an economic agent but an arm of the State levying tribute by force: if a taxpaying activity is frustrated by taxation, the loss of the taxpayers is partial and may be slight whereas the loss of the fisc is total. And the loss of each taxpayer is limited to the transactions which affect him directly, whereas the loss of the fisc extends to every transaction in the chain.

This represents an additional dimension for the argument of the present appendix. The potential loss of the fisc from an increase in tax rates is not merely the revenue collected from that tax before the increase but a multiple, even a large multiple, of that tax. There is no reason to believe that such a result is improbable or exceptional. The danger of loss to the fisc is a function of single and cumulative tax rates, and the fisc is increasingly exposed to risk as tax rates rise [22].

A further dimension of the argument is that the taxpayer is not merely *homo economicus* but a political being as well. Resentment and other political motives are additional to the economic motives for tax avoidance and may be effective even when the economic motives are not. This holds good in particular for taxes that are heavy, discriminatory, retrospective or politically motivated — such as many taxes on saving [23].

Even if there is no change in substantial activity, the gain or loss of the fisc from tax changes ought to take into account the interest of the fisc in the economy as represented by the proportion of national income taken in taxation. For example, if a third of the national income goes in taxation, then approximately one-third of the apparent initial cost of a small marginal tax reduction returns to the fisc in the form of additional revenue from other taxes. Similarly for a tax increase: after allowance for losses elsewhere in the tax system, only two thirds of the apparent yield of a tax increase remains in the hands of the fisc.

## Conclusion

The argument of this appendix can give only an indication, not a proof, of the damage done by high tax rates even to the interest of the fisc itself. It provides a common logical framework for differing opinions about incentives and offers a method of quantifying the various possible assumptions.

A central position is that unitary price elasticity is as low as possible at a tax rate of zero and that fiscal prohibition is as high as possible at a tax rate of 100 per cent. On these assumptions, the maximum-yield tax rate is 58 per cent (Table 11). Attempts to charge tax at higher rates than this reduce rather than increase the revenue of the fisc. This conclusion is reinforced if account is taken of differences between taxes, of the interplay between taxes and of the interplay between transactions.

The tax cuts from which the revenue gains most or loses least are cuts in the highest rates of graduated or "progressive" taxes.

# LIST OF TABLES

# NOTES

## CHAPTER I

1. (Page **15**). Barry Bracewell-Milnes: *The Camel's Back: An International Comparison of Tax Burdens* (Centre for Policy Studies, London, 1976). The present book is referred to on page 57 of *The Camel's Back;* but the title *Industry under Attack* has been changed to *The Taxation of Industry.*

2. (Page **15**). Barry Bracewell-Milnes: *A Liberal Tax Policy: Tax Neutrality and Freedom of Choice* (British Tax Review 2/1976).

3. (Page **15**). D. R. Myddelton: *The Power to Destroy: A Study of the British Tax System* (Johnson, London, 1969).

4. (Page **16**). This is a quite different sense of "tax efficiency" from the more recent sense in which transactions are tax-efficient if they reduce or minimise the associated burden of taxation.

5. (Page **16**). Barry Bracewell-Milnes: *The Economics of Tax Reduction* in *Taxation: A Radical Approach* (Institute of Economic Affairs, London, Readings in Political Economy No. 4, 1970), page 78.

## CHAPTER II

1. (Page **18**). F. A. Hayek: *A Tiger by the Tail: The Keynesian Legacy of Inflation* (A 40-years' running commentary on Keynesianism by Hayek, compiled and introduced by Sudha R. Shenoy; Hobart Paper-

back, Institute of Economic Affairs, London, 1972).

2. (Page **18**). Colin Robinson and Eileen Marshall: *What Future for British Coal?* (Institute of Economic Affairs, London, Hobart Paper 89, 1981). Tastes vary, and the judgments of this paragraph may be more representative of the readers of this book than of the population in general. However that may be, individual preferences are most economically expressed by a market system without subsidies in any direction; thus, even if some people prefer dirty jobs, that is no reason for according them fiscal preferences.

3. (Page 18). The creation of wealth through services is the theme of Russell Lewis: *The New Service Society* (Longmans, London, 1973).

4. (Page 22). This concept of wealth is the present discounted value of the income *for ever*. It thus implicitly assumes that saving is *permanent*. For temporary and permanent saving, see *A Liberal Tax Policy* (Chapter I, note 2 above), pages 115—117 and also my *Is Capital Taxation Fair? The Tradition and the Truth* (Institute of Directors, London, 1974), page 61. This concept of wealth is spelt out in the evidence of the Unquoted Companies' Group to the

Select Committee on a Wealth Tax (Session 1974—1975, Volume III, pages 874—875).

5. (Page 23). Institute of Directors evidence to the Royal Commission on the Distribution of Income and Wealth (Selected Evidence Submitted to the Royal Commission for Report No. 1: Initial Report on the Standing Reference, 1976), page 127, paragraphs H and I.

6. (Page 24). *Is Capital Taxation Fair ?* (Chapter II, note 4), pages 91—93. Also Barry Bracewell-Milnes: *The Measurement of Fiscal Policy: An Analysis of Tax Systems in Terms of the Political Distinction between "Right" and "Left"* (Confederation of British Industry, London, 1971), Appendix VII C (iii). (This book is obtainable from the author at 26 Lancaster Court, Banstead, Surrey SM7 1RR, United Kingdom).

7. (Page 24). Liability to taxes not only on the first transfer but also on all subsequent transfers can be discharged in advance at their present discounted values. *Is Capital Taxation Fair ?* (Chapter II, note 4), page 92.

8. (Page 24). *The Measurement of Fiscal Policy* (Chapter II, note 6), Appendix VII D.

9. (Page 26). A more detailed critique of Kaldor's income-stream method is given in *The Measurement of Fiscal Policy* (Chapter II, note 6), Appendix VII C (iii) (b).

10. (Page 26). The vulnerability of commitment to taxation is discussed in my *Tax Avoidance and Evasion: The Individual and Society* (Panopticum Press, Upminster, 1979), pages 94—101.

11. (Page 28). The argument that taxes on spending fall also on saving is discussed in *The Measurement of Fiscal Policy* (Chapter II, note 6), pages 39, 47 and 65, and *Is Capital Taxation Fair?* (Chapter II, note 4), pages 59 and 89.

12. (Page 29). *Tax Avoidance and Evasion.* See Chapter II, note 10.

13. (Page 29). The richer individual enjoys an "economic rent" on the gross-of-tax return from his saving, a "saver's surplus" analogous with the "consumer's surplus" which is a synonym for economic rent.

14. (Page 30). This is one of the four methods of wealth creation summarised at the start of Chapter III.

15. (Page 34). Pliny the Elder: *Naturalis Historia*, XIII 88.

16. (Page 35). Further records have been set and broken since this passage was drafted. On 29 May 1980, John Grisanti, a restaurateur from Memphis, Tennessee, paid a world record price of $31,000 for a single bottle of 1822 Chateau Lafite at an auction in San Francisco ; the previous record was $28,000, also for a bottle of Chateau Lafite.

17. (Page 37). Matthew XIX 16—24 ; Luke VI 24. Henry Simons: *Personal Income Taxation* (The University of Chicago Press, 1938), page 19: "Prevailing opinion to the contrary notwithstanding, it is only an inadequate degree of progression which has no effect upon production and economic progress". ("Progression" here means the graduation of taxes).

18. (Page 38). For example, Ludwig von Mises: *Human Action: A Treatise on Economics* (Hodge, London, and Yale University Press, New Haven, 1949) ; Friedrich Hayek: *Individualism and Economic Order* (Routledge and Kegan Paul, London, 1949) ; Carl Snyder: *Capitalism the Creator: The Economic Foundations of Modern Industrial Society* (New York, 1940) ; Murray Rothbard: *Man, Economy and State: A Treatise on Economic Principles* (Van Nostrand, Princeton, 1962). For the exposition of socialism, see for example Oskar Lange and Fred M. Taylor: *On the Economic Theory of Socialism* (ed. B. E. Lippincott, University of Minneapolis Press, 1938) ; M. D. Dickinson: *Economics of Socialism* (Oxford University Press, 1939) ; A. P. Lerner: *The Economics of Control: Principles of Welfare Economics* (Macmillan, New York, 1944). A comparison of capitalism and socialism is provided by George Halm in *Economic Systems: A Comparative Analysis* (Rinehart, New York, 1952).

19. (Page 38). *Is Capital Taxation Fair ?* (Chapter II, note 4), page 40.

20. (Page 39). This subject is further discussed in Chapter III, "Wealth and investment: four methods of wealth creation".

21. (Page 39). This remains true even of discoveries due to luck, serendipity or providence and of artistic achievements due to inspiration rather than effort. Unexpected successes ("undeserved" in the sense of being a disproportionate reward for endeavour) are merely the counterpart of unexpected failures.

22. (Page 40). Barry Bracewell-Milnes: *Industry for the People: Investment Financing through Partially Guaranteed Securities* (Selsdon Policy Series No. 4, Selsdon Group, 170 Sloane Street, London SW1), Summary (iv), page vi.


CHAPTER III

1. (Page 42). Volatility is not central to the argument; but in practice the second-hand market is often less volatile than the market for new "productive" assets such as newly-mined metals and other real commodities.

2. (Page 43). A. P. Lerner: *The Economics of Control* (Chapter II, note 18), page 90: "Every speculator who buys cheap and sells dear improves the allocation of resources between the different products. He provides the rest of society with something that is valued more highly in place of something that is valued less highly."

3. (Page 43). *Is Capital Taxation Fair?* (Chapter II, note 4). Chapter II.

4. (Page 44). Barry Bracewell-Milnes: *Saving and Switching* (Sussex Tapes, 85 Linden Gardens, London W2; 1971). *Is Capital Taxation Fair?* (Chapter II, note 4), page 51.

5. (Page 46). This contention is supported by the neglect of ownership in E. J. Mishan: *A Survey of Welfare Economics, 1939—59* (The Economic Journal, June 1960).

6. (Page 46). The theme of this paragraph is spelt out in my submission to the Select Committee on a Wealth Tax, published as Appendix 64 in the Appendices to Minutes of Evidence (Session 1974—75, Volume IV), especially paragraphs 11—16.

7. (Page 46). See Chapter I, note 3.

8. (Page 47). *The Camel's Back* (Chapter I, note 1), Section H and the Appendix; Appendix V of the present book.

9. (Page 48). *Is Capital Taxation Fair?* (Chapter II, note 4), pages 91—93, 114—115.

10. (Page 48). Matthew XXV 14—30.

11. (Page 48). Barry Bracewell-Milnes: *Freedom under Siege: Capital Taxation and Political Conformity* (The Society for Individual Freedom, 55 Park Lane, London W1; 1975), especially paragraph 30.

12. (Page 48). The traditional Western doctrine is represented by the quotation from Murray Rothbard in note 15 below.

13. (Page 49). *A Liberal Tax Policy* (Chapter I, note 2), pages 115—117.

14. (Page 51). See the next section, "The taxable capacity of saving", pages 151—152.

15. (Page 51). For example, Henry Simons in *Personal Income Taxation* (Chapter II, note 17), page 97: "In a world where capital accumulation proceeds as it does now, there is something sadly inadequate about the idea of saving as postponed consumption". Murray Rothbard in *Power and Market: Government and the Economy* (Institute for Humane Studies Inc., Menlo Park, California, 1970), page 75: "There is nothing after all, especially sacred about savings; they are simply the road to future consumption". The reconciliation between these two concepts is provided by the distinction between temporary and permanent saving (Chapter II, note 4). Permanent saving is permanent, not through the saver's intention to make it so or to treat it as such, but simply by virtue of never being drawn down.

16. (Page 51). See Chapter III, note 15. It is ironical that the attitudes of both Simons and Rothbard to this matter are unfavourable to their own fiscal policies, each being more favourable to the fiscal policy of the other.

17. (Page 52). The theme of this paragraph is the subject of *Saving and Switching* (Chapter III, note 4).

18. (Page 54). Brian Reading's *A Survey of Britain's Savings Institutions* (The Economist,

29 November 1975) carried this headline (page 23): "All the financial institutions have failed in their first duty — to protect the savers' interests".

## CHAPTER IV

1. (Page 55). Henry Simons: *Personal Income Taxation* (Chapter II, note 17), page 24: "Both progress and justice are costly luxuries — costly, above all, in terms of each other".

2. (Page 55). *Is Capital Taxation Fair?* (Chapter II, note 4), pages 1—4.

3. (Page 55). The meaning of "a logical concept of fairness" is explained in *Is Capital Taxation Fair?* (Chapter II, note 4), Chapter IV.

4. (Page 56). Robert Nozick: *Anarchy, State and Utopia* (Basil Blackwell, Oxford, 1974), especially Part II.

5. (Page 57). *The Measurement of Fiscal Policy* (Chapter II, note 6), Chapter II, Chapter VI C, Appendix I.

6. (Page 57). *Is Capital Taxation Fair?* (Chapter II, note 4), fallacies 1—6 in Chapter II.

7. (Page 58). See Chapter III, note 6.

8. (Page 59). Barry Bracewell-Milnes: *Redistribution in Reverse: More Equal Shares of Wealth Mean Less Equal Shares of Spending* (Aims of Industry, London, 1974).

9. (Page 59). *Incomings* are income plus negative saving. *Outgoings* are spending plus new saving without deduction of negative saving. Net saving is positive in an expanding economy and negative in a declining economy. In an expanding economy, positive new saving may be taken gross or net of negative (new) saving (the drawing down of old savings). In a declining economy, negative saving may be taken gross or net of positive new saving. In an expanding economy, negative saving is the excess of incomings over income or of outgoings over outgo. In a declining economy incomings and outgoings exceed spending by the amount of new (positive) saving

and spending exceeds income by the amount of net negative saving. The analysis applies to individuals as well as to the economy. In any period any individual may have both positive and negative savings. For the individual or for the economy, negative saving is the drawing down of temporary saving.

On the outgoings side, new saving is capitalised positive marginal future income; on the incomings side, negative saving or the drawing down of capital is capitalised negative marginal future income. Capital drawn down or new saving forgone is available for spending. New saving is logically antecedent to the drawing down of capital; otherwise positive and negative saving are symmetrical.

See Appendix I, page 118.

10. (Page 59). *Is Capital Taxation Fair?* (Chapter II, note 4), pages 91—93.

11. (Page 60). *Is Capital Taxation Fair?* (Chapter II, note 4), pages 81—83.

12. (Page 60). *Is Capital Taxation Fair?* (Chapter II, note 4), pages 61—67.

13. (Page 61). Both should be either tax-inclusive (gross) or tax-exclusive (net). Gross and net tax rates are explained in *The Measurement of Fiscal Policy* (Chapter II, note 6), page 13 and in *The Structure and Reform of Direct Taxation* (Report of a Committee chaired by Professor J. E. Meade, George Allen and Unwin, London, for The Institute for Fiscal Studies, 1978), pages 28—29.

14. (Page 61). See Chapter II, note 11. I owe this point to Peter Wann.

15. (Page 61). *Is Capital Taxation Fair?* (Chapter II, note 4), page 77.

16. (Page 64). Directors are in effect employees except to the extent of their shareholdings.

17. (Page 65). The Meade Report (Chapter IV, note 13) recognises that a switch from income taxation to expenditure taxation makes saving cheaper and spending dearer; but it does not do justice to the complementary argument that the addition to an expenditure tax of a tax on wealth or capital

transfers runs counter to the logic of an expenditure tax by making saving dearer and spending cheaper. Taxes on wealth and capital transfers are not less at variance with the logic of an expenditure tax than is a tax on income. *Is Capital Taxation Fair?* (Chapter II, note 4), pages 61—67, 91—93 and my *The Meade Report and the Taxation of Capital* (British Tax Review 1/1979).

18. (Page 65). George Polanyi and John B. Wood: *How Much Inequality?* (Research Monograph 31, Institute of Economic Affairs, London, 1974).

19. (Page 65). Chapter III, "The taxable capacity of saving", fourth sense.

20. (Page 67). *A Liberal Tax Policy* (Chapter I, note 2).

21. (Page 67). P.-J. Proudhon: *Théorie de l'Impôt: Question mise au concours par le Conseil d'Etat du Canton de Vaud*, en 1860 (Oeuvres complètes, tome 15, Paris 1868), pages 170—171.

22. (Page 67). For a graduated tax on earnings as a surrogate for a graduated tax on spending, see *Is Capital Taxation Fair?* (Chapter II, note 4), pages 110—111.

23. (Page 67). In a system without saving, incentive arguments apply equivalently to earning and to spending; and high taxes on earnings and on spending create the same risk of counterproductiveness (a lower revenue yield than if tax rates were lower · Appendix V). High effective marginal rates of tax may be no less counterproductive at the bottom of the scale (through the poverty trap) than at the top (through tax graduation).

24. (Page 68). Since the richer taxpayer's spending or earnings are taxed at higher rates, the opportunity cost of his *leisure* falls relatively to that of the poorer taxpayer. But if saving is permitted, the graduated taxation of earnings or income instead of spending reduces the opportunity cost to the richer taxpayer not only of his leisure but also of his *spending* relatively to the corresponding cost to the poorer taxpayer.

25. (Page 68). See Chapter II, note 11.

26. (Page 68). Saving is overtaxed relativel₁ to spending ( and the costless creation of wealth through ownership is impeded) if there is *any* tax on earnings or saving; and saving is overtaxed (and spending undertaxed) more for the rich than the poor if the earnings tax is graduated, still more so if the tax on savings is graduated, and more so again if there is more than one graduated tax on saving (as in present-day Britain).

27. (Page 68). Or even zero or negative. *Is Capital Taxation Fair?* (Chapter II, note 4), page 64.

28. (Page 68). *The Measurement of Fiscal Policy* (Chapter II, note 6), first footnote on page 44; *Freedom under Siege* (Chapter III, note 11), paragraphs 56—63.

29. (Page 68). The taxation of saving is *confiscatory* if the various taxes on investment income and its parent capital absorb more than 100 per cent of the current yield. See Chapter IX and Appendix IV, "Fiscal prohibition of saving".

30. (Page 68). For the meaning and measurement of the sharpness of graduation, see *The Measurement of Fiscal Policy* (Chapter II, note 6), Chapters III and IV.

31. (Page 69). *The Measurement of Fiscal Policy* (Chapter II, note 6), Chapter VIII.

32. (Page 69). *Is Capital Taxation Fair?* (Chapter II, note 4), Chapter III.

33. (Page 69). See Appendix III. Also *Redistribution in Reverse* (Chapter IV, note 8).

34. (Page 69). See Chapter III, note 6.

35. (Page 71). See Chapter IV, note 33.

36. (Page 71). See Chapter IV, note 33. *The Measurement of Fiscal Policy* (Chapter II, note 6), Chapter VI C.

37. (Page 71). See Chapter IV, note 33.

CHAPTER V

1. (Page 72). R. H. Tawney: *Equality* (George Allen and Unwin, London, 1931).

2. (Page 74). See Chapter IV, note 15.

3. (Page 75). As exemplified by Jude Wanniski: *The Way the World Works* (Simon and Schuster, New York, 1979).

4. (Page 75). The moral and political costs of taxation are discussed in *Tax Avoidance and Evasion* (Chapter II, note 10), especially Chapter VI. Some, but not all, of these moral costs have a material equivalent: "though vexation is not strictly speaking, expense, it is certainly equivalent to the expense at which every man would be willing to redeem himself from it". (Adam Smith: *The Wealth of Nations*, V II II). The moral and political arguments against taxation are equally relevant to para-fiscal charges: "social-security contributions" are recognised by the OECD and others as being in all essentials a form of taxation. It is arguable that "social-security contributions" are worse than taxes because they pretend to be something different. (Arthur Seldon: *The Great Pensions 'Swindle'* (Tom Stacey Books, 1970)).

5. (Page 75). "The fiscal prohibition of saving", Chapter IX and Appendix IV.

6. (Page 76). Barry Bracewell-Milnes: *Intension, Inflation and Growth: How Variations in the Tax Base Affect the Graduation of Tax Schedules* (Institut International de Finances Publiques, Proceedings of 1973 Barcelona Congress), Section IX.

7. (Page 76). Chapter IX and Appendix IV, "Fiscal prohibition of saving". *The Measurement of Fiscal Policy* (Chapter II, note 6), Appendix VII C (iii); *Is Capital Taxation Fair?* (Chapter II, note 4), page 64.

8. (Page 77). *Inflation Accounting* (Report of the Inflation Accounting Committee, Cmnd 6225, Her Majesty's Stationery Office, London, 1975).

## CHAPTER VI

1. (Page 78). Investment in second-hand industrial assets may be almost equivalent to investment in first-hand industrial assets for the investor; but for the economy in general it resembles investment in second-hand non-productive assets because it uses no real resources and it increases the value of the existing stock.

2. (Page 79). Vito Tanzi: *International Tax Burdens* in *Taxation: A Radical Approach* (Chapter I, note 5). *The Camel's Back* (Chapter I, note 1), Section F.

3. (Page 79). See Chapter IV, "Impact and incidence".

4. (Page 82). The most substantial work on the development of property rights to have appeared so far is Eirik G. Furubotn and Svetozar Pejovich: *The Economics of Property Rights* (Ballinger Publishing Company, Cambridge, Mass., 1974).

## CHAPTER VII

1. (Page 83). *Revenue Statistics of OECD Member Countries* (OECD, Paris, annually). *International Comparisons of Taxes and Social Security Contributions* by the Central Statistical Office is published annually in Economic Trends. (Appendix IV under *Short Measure from Whitehall*). The United Kingdom figures are also given in the CSO's annual "blue book" *National Income and Expenditure*.

2. (Page 84). If earned income and investment income are taxed jointly at graduated rates, the relative tax yields of the two depend on which is taken first (in other words, on which is regarded as marginal to the other). In Appendix I ("Investment income and earnings") it is argued that investment income should be taken first and earnings should be treated as marginal, because earnings require a renewal of input in each period, which investment income does not.

3. (Page 84). Fiscal *prohibition* (Appendix IV "Fiscal prohibition of saving") is a distinct question from fiscal *deterrence* (Appendix V) though they share a common boundary.

4. (Page 84). Barry Bracewell-Milnes and J. C. L. Huiskamp: *Investment Incentives: A Comparative Analysis of the Systems in the EEC, the USA and Sweden* (Kluwer, Deventer, 1977), Chapter VIII, "Repayment of tax never paid".

5. (Page 84). In Hong Kong, perhaps the best contemporary example of a capitalist economy, figures for 1977/78, the last year available at the time of writing, indicate that distribution and finance were the

princ al taxpayers, together contributing 58 p cent of revenue from profits tax on corporations. Manufacturing contributed only 19 per cent: this despite the importance of Hong Kong manufactures in the world econo my — for example, Hong Kong is the most important exporter of toys and is re arded as a major competitive threat to many Western economies in a number of d fferent product lines.

6. (Page 86). In an article entitled *United Kingdom Corporation Tax Structure* (European Taxation, May 1974), I analysed the principal systems of corporation tax in terms of the effective rates of tax at the level of the corporation, first, on all profits ($t_1$ in Appendix II) and, second, additionally on undistributed profits ($t_2$ in Appendix II). *Tax Credits under the Proposed EEC Directive on Company Taxation* (Intertax 8/1976) applied this analysis to the nine corporation tax systems of the Member States of the European Community, showing the effective rates on distributions and retentions in comparable terms irrespective of nominal differences between the systems. The May 1974 article extended the algebraic analysis to cover British fiscal discrimination against corporate income from abroad.

The Meade Report (Chapter IV, note 17) contains on pages 265—268 a succinct algebraic analysis of five different corporation tax systems in terms of nominal rates, together with a key for the translation of these nominal rates into effective rates. Appendix II was written in the summer of 1976 on the basis of an exchange of letters between Professor Meade and me, in which I provided the analysis in terms of effective rates and he provided the analysis in terms of nominal rates. Professor Meade very generously put his algebra at my disposal, although of course I remain solely responsible for any defects in Appendix II. Despite a certain overlap with the Meade report, it has seemed worthwhile still to publish Appendix II for the following reasons. (a) Appendix II sets out the algebra in parallel with a common arithmetical example for ease of exposition. (b) Appendix II (like the

May 1974 article) integrates the analysis with the treatment of variations in the shareholder's marginal rate of income tax. (c) Appendix II includes a linked analysis of rates of exchange between sources and uses of funds. For these reasons, the meaning of certain symbols differs between the Meade report and Appendix II.

7. (Page 86). Table 1 updates and expands Table 7 of *Investment Incentives* (Chapter VII, note 4).

8. (Page 89). Barry Bracewell-Milnes: *Overseas Development and British Taxation* in *Private Foreign Investment and the Developing World* (Praeger Publishers, New York, 1971), especially page 108.

9. (Page 89). If the foreign income is taken first (that is, imputed to the first tranche of total income), then the exemption of foreign income may be valueless, foreign income being completely covered by the initial tax-free slice of the graduated scale. If the foreign income is taken last, the principle of *réserve de progressivité* is ineffective. Thus in practice some form of averaging is used.

10. (Page 90). *Overseas Development and British Taxation* (Chapter VII, note 8), especially Appendix A.

11. (Page 90). *United Kingdom Corporation Tax Structure* (Chapter VII, note 6), Appendix III.

12. (Page 90). For the position before the 1981 Budget, see David Ross: *North Sea Oil* (British Tax Review 2/1976). Lindsay Duncan: *The Taxation of Oil Profits from the UK Sector of the North Sea* (Intertax 2/1978). Lindsay Duncan: *UK: Further Proposals to Increase the Taxation on North Sea Oil* (Intertax 3/1981).

13. (Page 90). See Chapter VII, note 4.

14. (Page 90). *Tax Credits under the Proposed EEC Directive on Company Taxation* (Chapter VII, note 6).

15. (Page 91). *Investment Incentives* (Chapter VII, note 4), pages 95—96, 134. *Tax Avoidance and Evasion*, (Chapter II, note 10), pages 14—18. "Tax expenditures" do more than general tax cuts to restore incentives

in so far as they have more effect than general cuts on marginal rates of tax: incentives are determined at the margin.

CHAPTER VIII

1. (Page 93). *The Power to Destroy* (Chapter I, note 3) quotes Chief Justice John Marshall : "The power to tax is the power to destroy". (Page 15).

2. (Page 94). *Industry for the People* (Chapter II, note 22).

3. (Page 95). See Appendix V.

4. (Page 95). *Is Capital Taxation Fair ?* (Chapter II, note 4), page 51.

5. (Page 95). A brief assessment of the C.B.I. price initiative is given in Barry Bracewell-Milnes : *Pay and Price Control Guide* (Butterworths, London, 1973), paragraph 10.

6. (Page 96). Chapter III, "The taxable capacity of saving", fourth sense.

7. (Page 96). See Chapter II, note 4.

8. (Page 96). Appendix III generalises the argument of *Redistribution in Reverse* (Chapter IV, note 8).

9. (Page 97). Chapter III, "The taxable capacity of saving", senses four and five.

10. (Page 97). The subject of this section is treated more fully in my *The Poor Pay Most: The Paradox of "Progressive" Taxation* (Bow Group, London, 1979). The incidence of "progressive" taxation on the man in the middle rather than the rich is discussed in *Is Capital Taxation Fair ?* (Chapter II, note 4), page 35. In *The Future of Personal Taxation* (Bulletin for International Fiscal Documentation 5/1978) I examined the effective cheapening of rich taxpayers' spending by taxes on their saving. In *The Meade Report and the Taxation of Capital* (Chapter IV, note 17) I criticised the Meade Committee for missing this central relationship and consequently proposing taxes on capital that were at variance with their rationale of taxes on expenditure.

11. (Page 98). *Théorie de l'Impôt* (Chapter IV, note 21), page 84.

12. (Page 98). *Public Finance and Changes in the Value of Money* (Economic Journal, December 1945), pages 374, 376.

13. (Page 98). It is worth emphasising that the percentages of tax take in Chapter IX are not on the same basis as Colin Clark' 25 per cent and doubly understate the excess of collective financing over his critica limit. First, the figures in Chapter IX are for taxation, and the government expenditure figures exceed the taxation figures by the amount of government borrowing. Second, the figures in Chapter IX are percentages of gross domestic product (GDP), which exceeds national income by the differ- ence between capital consumption and net investment income from abroad. Gross domestic product was 116.5 per cent of national income in the United Kingdom in 1980.

14. (Page 98). This is the criterion called *basis* in Chapter IX and Appendix IV (Table 7).

CHAPTER IX

1. (Page 99). Published by the Centre for Policy Studies respectively in 1976 and 1977. For *The Measurement of Fiscal Policy* see Chapter II, note 6.

2. (Page 102). *Investment Incentives* (Chapter VII, note 4), "Investment and consumption" (page 87), "Tax expenditures" (page 95),- "Disadvantages of the conventional approach" (page 126). It is arguable that for foreigners (non-residents and/or non-domiciliaries) these offsets to industrial over- taxation make the United Kingdom a tax haven (Lance Blackstone and David Franks : *The U.K. as a Tax Haven* (Economist Intelligence Unit, 1981)). But for residents and domiciliaries any such effects are exceptional and temporary.

3. (Page 103). Cicero : *Paradoxa Stoicorum* VI, 3, 49.

4. (Page 104). *The Economics of Tax Reduction* (Chapter I, note 5), page 69.

5. (Page 104). See Chapter I, note 5.

6. (Page 104). Select Committee on a Wealth Tax, Report Volume II (Minutes of Evidence)

(11 November 1975), pages 149—165, especially pages 155—165. The draft report proposed by one group of MP$_8$ says: "We thank all those who appeared before us, especially because, while they inevitably had their own sectional interests at heart (from the Jockey Club, which sought relief for bloodstock, to the Inland Revenue, which argued the case for exempting occupational pension rights), this in no way detracted from the value of the evidence given". (Volume I, page XCVIII).

7. (Page 104). British underachievement is a phenomenon of long standing. For example, Edward F. Denison: *Why Growth Rates Differ: Postwar Experience in Nine Western Countries* (Brookings Institution, Washington, 1967); Angus Maddison: *Explaining Economic Growth* (Banca Nazionale del Lavoro, September 1972); John H. Dunning: *Profitability and Performance of the World's Largest Industrial Companies* (Economists Advisory Group, 1975).

## CHAPTER X

1. (Page 107). Amartya K. Sen: *On Economic Inequality* (Oxford University Press, 1973).

2. (Page 107). *The Measurement of Fiscal Policy* (Chapter II, note 6), Appendix I F.

3. (Page 107). See Appendix III for the conflict between the taxation of saving and the equality of spending. The difficulties inherent in the concept of the "progressiveness" of the whole tax system are discussed in *The Measurement of Fiscal Policy* (Chapter II, note 6), Chapter VI B.

4. (Page 107). *Is Capital Taxation Fair?* (Chapter II, note 4), Chapter IV.

5. (Page 107). *Freedom under Siege* (Chapter III, note 11).

6. (Page 107). See the passage from Henry Simons quoted in Chapter II, note 17.

7. (Page 108). The case for levying tax only on consumption is explained on grounds of freedom of choice rather than creation of wealth in my *A Liberal Tax Policy* (Chapter I, note 2). The argument from neutrality, that saving is fully and properly charged through the taxation of spending, is explained in

*The Measurement of Fiscal Policy* (Chapter II, note 6), pages 39, 47, 65, and *Is Capital Taxation Fair?*, pages 59 and 89. (Chapter II, note 11, above). The interrelationships between the taxes on spending, earning and saving that underlie the "implications for policy" in this section are analysed under "Income and outgo" in Chapter IV, above.

8. (Page 109). I have argued elsewhere that the tax on capital transfers should be not just reduced or reformed but abolished. *A Tax for the Axe: The Case for Abolishing Tax on Capital Transfers* (CUT, The Taxpayers' Union, 1979). The damage done by taxes on capital to the principle of an expenditure tax is the theme of my article *The Meade Report and the Taxation of Capital* (Chapter IV, note 17).

9. (Page 109). *Is Capital Taxation Fair?* (Chapter II, note 4), pages 49—52.

10. (Page 109). *Tax Avoidance and Evasion* (Chapter II, note 10), Chapter V and *passim*.

## APPENDIX I

1. (Page 114). Both the concepts of wealth discussed in the present section are exposed to this criticism. The present discounted value of future income rises when the discount rate falls even though the net-of-tax income itself falls at any constant rate of discount.

2. (Page 115). Institute of Directors evidence to the Royal Commission on the Distribution of Income and Wealth (Chapter II, note 5).

3. (Page 116). *The Measurement of Fiscal Policy* (Chapter II, note 6), Appendix VII C (iii). *Is Capital Taxation Fair?* (Chapter II, note 4), pages 91—93.

4. (Page 117). See Chapter VII, note 2. The combination of graduated tax schedules is discussed in *The Measurement of Fiscal Policy* (Chapter II, note 6), Chapter VII C (v).

5. (Page 119). Chapter III, "The taxable capacity of saving", fourth sense.

6. (Page 120). *The Measurement of Fiscal Policy* (Chapter II, note 6), Chapter VII. *Is Capital Taxation Fair?* (Chapter II, note 4), pages 82—83.

## APPENDIX II

1. (Page 122). The system shown is the former West German system in which distributed profits are taken to mean the cash dividend after deduction of the corporation tax on the dividend; this system raises the effective rate of corporation tax on dividends by subjecting the nominal rate of corporation tax on dividends to a further tax charge as undistributed profits.

## APPENDIX III

1. (Page 127). *Redistribution in Reverse* (Chapter IV, note 8).

2. (Page 127). The argument that the addition of a proportional expenditure tax to a graduated income tax makes the tax system as a whole less "progressive" or more "regressive" is criticised in *The Measurement of Fiscal Policy* (Chapter II, note 6), Chapter VI B.

3. (Page 128). *Is Capital Taxation Fair?* (Chapter II, note 4), pages 49—52.

4. (Page 128). *The Meade Report and the Taxation of Capital* (Chapter IV, note 17)•

5. (Page 128). The "Sargant effect" is an increase in the amount saved in consequence of a reduction in the yield, whether for tax reasons (the net-of-tax yield) or otherwise (the gross-of-tax yield). William Lucas Sargant: *Recent Political Economy* (Norgate and Williams, London, 1867), Chapter IV.

6. (Page 129). If the Sargant effect at lower levels of income were taken into account, it would be represented by a position of C above A instead of below.

7. (Page 131). *The Measurement of Fiscal Policy* (Chapter II, note 6), page 50, paragraph 16.

8. (Page 132). *The Measurement of Fiscal Policy* (Chapter II, note 6), Chapter VI A.

9. (Page 133). A proportional tax on saving may reduce the saving of the poor absolutely less than that of the rich but proportionately more.

10. (Page 134). See assumption (4) above.

11. (Page 134), "Fiscal prohibition of saving", Chapter IX and Appendix IV.

## APPENDIX IV

1. (Page 137). The 1972 figures differ from those in *The Camel's Back* partly because of revisions and partly because the OECD revenue statistics are now based on gross domestic product (GDP), not gross national product (GNP). GNP exceeds GDP by the amount of net investment income from abroad. The OECD made this change in order to bring themselves into line with the other international organisations (European Community, International Monetary Fund, United Nations), which were already using GDP. The result of the change is to increase the measure of the burden on countries with positive net investment income from abroad (net investors) and to reduce it for those whose net investment income is negative. The OECD countries are divided half-and-half between these two categories. The changes in the measured tax burden are of the order of 1 per cent (and thus less than 1 percentage point). The measured tax burden rises by about 1 per cent in Britain as a result of the change. In general, the change from GNP to GDP makes little difference to the results; but it can be significant in comparisons between countries important as outward investors (such as the United States) and countries important as inward investors (such as Canada).

2. (Pages 139, 143). An alternative measure of tax awareness or fiscal pain, which shows the relative burden in the United Kingdom as even heavier than on the basis of Table 11 in *The Camel's Back* or Table 4 above, was explained in my article *The Weight of Tax in OECD Countries* (Maandblad Belastingbeschouwingen, Jubilee number 1978), of which copies are available on request. Measures of tax awareness weight taxes differently per unit of revenue yield, and a number of different sets of weights can be used for this purpose.

3. (Page 144). *The Measurement of Fiscal Policy* (Chapter II, note 6); especially Chapters III and VI.

4. (Page 144). *The Measurement of Fiscal Policy* (Chapter II, note 6) ; also *Measurement of Progressivity: A Comment* (Economic Journal, September 1979).

5. (Page 144). These averages are given as gross rates of tax (tax-inclusive), for comparability with columns (1) — (5), although value added tax and other taxes on goods and services are more often expressed net (tax-exclusive).

6. (Page 144). The formula is $d = 1 - (1-c)^{25}$, where $c$ is the rate of wealth tax and $d$ the equivalent rate of transfer tax. *(The Measurement of Fiscal Policy* (Chapter II, note 6), page 63).

7. (Page 144) *The Measurement of Fiscal Policy* (Chapter II, note 6), Appendix VIII (8).

8. (Page 146). For the rationale of *tax height*, see *The Measurement of Fiscal Policy* (Chapter II, note 6), Chapters VII A, VIIIE, VIIIF. The method of Table 6 differs in one respect from the method in *The Measurement of Fiscal Policy*, where taxes on transfers in and on transfers out are counted as two separate taxes. The rationale of that procedure is that transfers in and transfers out are separate transactions, which should be counted separately for two reasons : first, because the transferor may be resident or domiciled and the transferee non-resident or non-domiciled or *vice versa;* second, because taxes on transfers in and on transfers out may be differently graduated. However, in Table 6 all the transfer taxes are *either* on transfers out *or* on transfers in and not on both ; it is therefore more economical to amalgamate taxes on transfers out and on transfers in as a single tax and thus to divide the total by 7 instead of 8, which is the procedure followed in column (2). This procedure can also be followed even if there are separate taxes on transfers out and transfers in. If the former is not an allowable charge against the latter, the taxes are simply added ; if it is allowable, the combined rates of tax are as follows where $a$ and $b$ are the gross rates of tax on transfers out and transfers in respectively : —

gross : $a + (1-a)b$, which $= a + b - ab$

net: $a/(1-a) + b/((1-a)(1-b))$, which $= (a + b - ab)/((1-a)(1-b))$.

9. (Page 146). This is the numerical concept of neutrality ; the difference between numerical and conceptual neutrality is discussed in the next section of this appendix.

10. (Page 149). *The Measurement of Fiscal Policy* (Chapter II, note 6), page 84.

11. (Page 149). See Chapter II, note 11. For *numerical* and *conceptual neutrality* see *Investment Incentives* (Chapter VII, note 4), Glossary. For the distinction between the *definition of neutrality* and the measurement of *deviations from neutrality*, see *The Measurement of Fiscal Policy* (Chapter II, note 6), Chapter VII B. The distinction between numerical and conceptual neutrality disappears if the tax on spending is nil. If the tax on spending is positive, the sum of the taxes on saving is more than the deviation from conceptual neutrality. Numerical neutrality implies that taxes on spending reduce the tax bias against saving and leave the tax burden on saving unaltered. Conceptual neutrality implies that taxes on spending leave the tax bias against saving unaltered and increase the tax burden on saving.

12. (Page 149). *Is Capital Taxation Fair ?* (Chapter II, note 4), page 77.

13. (Page 150). The weaknesses in Kaldor's treatment of the concepts of the *futility* and the *impossibility* of saving are discussed in *The Measurement of Fiscal Policy* (Chapter II, note 6), Appendix VII C (iii) (b). See Chapter II, note 9.

APPENDIX V

1. (Page 153). Michael Beenstock : *Taxation and Incentives in the UK* (Lloyds Bank Review, October 1979).

2. (Page 153). R. Hemming and J. A. Kay : *The Laffer Curve* (Fiscal Studies, March 1980).

3. (Page 154). It may also become less acceptable actively, because of increasing resistance at the political level ; but that

is another story, and one that is not inconsistent with the argument.

4. (Page 154). See for example the evidence of the Chairman of the Board of Inland Revenue to the House of Commons Select Committee on Expenditure on 30 June 1975.

5. (Page 154). As a simple example, the Scotch Whisky Association have argued that the 10 per cent increase in the tax on whisky in the 1977 Budget reduced the yield of the tax. In the first eight months of fiscal 1977—78 the tax yielded £292 million, compared with £ 320 million in the first eight months of the previous year when the tax rate was lower.

6. (Page 154). The tax rates in this appendix are measured gross, that is, as a proportion of turnover including the tax; net rates exclude the tax itself from the tax base.

7. (Page 156). *The Camel's Back* Appendix says that the point of unitary price elasticity comes before the zero-sum point. This is correct only if the point of unitary price elasticity is reached at a tax rate of below 50 per cent gross. It is possible, though perhaps unlikely, that the point of unitary price elasticity will not be reached until a higher rate of tax, as in the example in Table 10. *The Camel's Back* Appendix also mentions the point of equiproportionate loss, where the proportionate fall in revenue yield equals the proportionate rise in price. This point is not needed for the analysis of the present appendix. It is not found in all revenue-yield curves, since the fall in revenue yield may never overtake the rise in price (Tables 9, 10). It is to be found in revenue yield curves where the prohibitive effect is not spread out by an arithmetical progression as in the present appendix but concentrated on the higher gross rates of tax by a geometrical progression. In terms of net rates, the point of equiproportionate loss is much nearer to the point of maximum revenue yield than it is in terms of gross rates.

8. (Page 156). *Political Economy Past and Present* (Macmillan, 1976), page 116.

9. (Page 159). The figures in Tables 9—11 and the conclusions drawn from them are appropriate to the aggregates of spending, earnings and saving and to most of their components but not necessarily to all of them if they are taxed at discriminatory rates. Particular goods and services may sustain a heavy burden of taxation if they are addictive, for example, or if they represent a small proportion of consumer spending; tobacco is an example of the former, salt of the latter.

10. (Page 160). This option has been chosen here on grounds of mathematical simplicity. By comparison with a geometrical progression, it overstates the damage done by lower rates of tax and understates the damage done by higher rates.

11. (Page 160). The arithmetically-progressive decline between unitary price elasticity and fiscal annihilation must be in terms of turnover. If it were in terms of volume, it would lead to absurd results, as can be calculated from Table 9: turnover would increase in an arithmetic progression.

12. (Page 162). *The Camel's Back* (Chapter I, note 1), page 56.

13. (Page 166). See Chapter I, note 5).

14. (Page 166). Taxes are also levied retrospectively in so far as they are levied on addiction — specifically, on addiction to drink and tobacco. In the United Kingdom at present duties on tobacco are more retrospective in this sense than duties on drink: many more young people are probably dissuaded by the cost of smoking than by the cost of drinking (even spirits).

15. (Page 167). For the distinction between the taxation of old saving and the taxation of new saving, see "Revolution and a going system", pages 47—52 of *Is Capital Taxation Fair?* (Chapter II, note 4).

16. (Page 167). *Is Capital Taxation Fair?* (Chapter II, note 4), page 77; also Chapter IX of this book, page 102.

17. (Page 167). *The Taxation of Net Wealth, Capital Transfers and Capital Gains of Individuals* (OECD, 1979), Table O.4, page 23.

18. (Page 167). Barry Bracewell-Milnes: *Lifetime Cumulation of Transfers* (British Tax Review 6/1979).

19. (Page 168). The average rate of expenditure tax must be calculated gross, not net, and must be applied to income net of taxes on income and payroll (national insurance). For example, if the net rate of expenditure tax is 25 per cent the gross rate is 20 per cent ($= .25 \div (1 + .25)$); and if taxes on income and payroll amount to 40 per cent of gross income, this 20 per cent is levied on the remaining 60 per cent. The total burden of tax on earning for spending is thus 52 per cent ($= 40 + .6 \times 20$).

20. (Page 168). The logical structure of these relationships is discussed in *Is Capital Taxation Fair?* (Chapter II, note 4), Chapter IV.

21. (Page 168). A different sense of interplay between taxes, resulting from shifts in activity, is discussed in *The Economics of Tax Reduction* (See Chapter I, note 5, above).

22. (Page 168). This conclusion is established in my *Tax Avoidance and Evasion* (Chapter II, note 10), especially Appendix III. Conditions under which the fisc is more likely or less likely to gain revenue from tax avoidance are discussed in my *The Economics of International Tax Avoidance: Political Power versus Economic Law* (Kluwer, Deventer, 1980), Chapter VIII. The interrelationships of the gains and losses from avoidance of the fisc, the avoiding taxpayer and the rest of the taxpaying community are the subject of my *The Limits of Tax Avoidance: How Avoidance Can Benefit Society* (European Taxation 1/1980). In *The Public Interest in Tax Avoidance* (The Journal of Economic Affairs, January 1981) I argued that formal tax avoidance must be in the public interest if the government is unsuccessfully attempting to reduce its own expenditure (as in Britain in the early nineteen-eighties).

23. (Page 169). Political motives for tax avoidance are discussed in *Tax Avoidance and Evasion* (Chapter II, note 10), pages 82—84.

OTHER BOOKS
BY THE SAME AUTHOR
INCLUDE

*The Measurement of Fiscal Policy: An Analysis of Tax Systems in Terms of the Political Distinction between "Right" and "Left"*. Confederation of British Industry, London, 1971. Obtainable from the author at 26 Lancaster Court, Banstead, Surrey SM7 1RR, United Kingdom.

*Is Capital Taxation Fair ? The Tradition and the Truth*. Institute of Directors, London, 1974.

*Economic Integration in East and West*. Croom Helm, London, 1976.

*The Camel's Back: An International Comparison of Tax Burdens*. Centre for Policy Studies, London, 1976.

*Investment Incentives: A Comparative Analysis of the Systems in the EEC, the USA and Sweden*. (With J. C. L. Huiskamp). Kluwer, Deventer, 1977.

*International Tax Avoidance*. Volume A: General report. Volume B: Country reports. (Principal author, with M. A. Wisselink). Kluwer, Deventer, 1978—79.

*Tax Avoidance and Evasion: The Individual and Society*. Panopticum Press, Upminster, 1979.

*The Economics of International Tax Avoidance: Political Power versus Economic Law*. Kluwer, Deventer, 1980.

PRINTED IN ROMANIA